Desire Jesus

One Year Edition

A 365 day devotional to help encourage, refresh, and strengthen your daily walk with Christ

by
John Stange

~ Ivystream Press ~
Philadelphia, Pennsylvania

To contact the author or learn about his other books and resources, please visit ***DesireJesus.com*** *or* ***JohnStange.com***

1

Getting Started

Following Jesus is the greatest privilege of our lives. He has made it possible for us to grow closer to Him and stronger in our faith as a result. Jesus came to this earth and took on flesh, lived the perfect life, died death in our place to pay for our sin, and rose from the grave. In doing so, He secured victory over sin, Satan, and death and He shares His victory with all who trust in Him.

Jesus lives in perfect unity with the Father and the Holy Spirit - one God in three Persons. Jesus is the Lord, Messiah, Savior, and ultimate hope for humanity. We were created to worship Him, walk with Him, and bring Him glory forever. He loves us and He assures His followers that He will be with us always.

All Scripture is pointing our hearts toward Jesus and in the pages of this devotional series, we'll be looking at various Scriptures from both the Old and New Testaments and learning more about what it means to apply those Scriptures to our lives as an expression of our faith in Jesus.

Our prayer is that Jesus will use the content of this devotional to encourage, refresh, and strengthen you in your daily walk with Him.

January 1

> *"Let us then with confidence draw near to the throne of grace, that we may receive mercy and find grace to help in time of need."*
> *-Hebrews 4:16*

Confidence is something that many of us wish we had more of. By nature, we wrestle with personal insecurities and a profound fear of rejection. We want to be accepted, welcomed, embraced and loved, but in many contexts of daily life, we aren't fully confident we'll be received that way.

Thankfully, confidence is something we can have in Christ Jesus. Because of who Jesus is and what He has done for us, we can be confident that through faith in Him, we can come before the throne of God. We can draw near to the Father, knowing for certain that those who have faith in His Son, Jesus Christ are welcomed into His presence.

His love for us isn't a trivial thing. He invites us to live today fully convinced that He is delighted to hold us near to Him. From His hand, we receive grace and mercy. From His hand we find the kind of help we truly need in the midst of the challenges we will face today and every day to come. Through faith in Jesus, we can be confident that the Father is pleased to welcome us into His family and that His strength can be relied upon when our personal strength is insufficient for the challenges that come before us.

January 2

"Therefore, if anyone is in Christ, he is a new creation. The old has passed away; behold, the new has come."
-2 Corinthians 5:17

When Jesus saves us, He isn't interested in merely making us slightly better versions of who we used to be. His presence in our lives isn't about sanding smooth our rough spots and shining us up a little.

In Christ, we are a new creation. Brand new. We aren't who we used to be. Now, we have been made who He has always desired us to be and our day-to -day life is lived for His glory and empowered with His strength.

When Jesus found us, we were dead. Now, through faith in Him, we're alive. We were God's enemies. Now, through Christ, we're His friends. We once had a hopeless future. Now, we have a glorious future that is secured for us by Jesus.

As brand new creations in Christ, why do we allow ourselves to dwell on the past? Why do we let it torture us? Why do we let it produce shame and grief in our hearts when we don't need to any longer?

His word assures us that the old has passed away and the new has come. In Christ, we are no longer who we once were. We have been blessed with the gift of His righteousness and new life that continues forever.

January 3

> *"For the grace of God has appeared, bringing salvation for all people, training us to renounce ungodliness and worldly passions, and to live self-controlled, upright, and godly lives in the present age,"*
> ***-Titus 2:11-12***

In this world, we're surrounded by many different influences. Some influences are good and helpful. Others aren't helpful at all and have the capacity to drag us off course or lead us in an ungodly direction.

Jesus Christ came into this world to save sinners. He didn't come to leave us in the condition we were in when He found us. By His grace, we are being trained to see the priorities and passions of this world from a new perspective. He encourages us to renounce those priorities and passions and live a new kind of life that reflects that fact that His Spirit lives within us and His priorities become our priorities.

As we renounce the ungodliness and passions of this world, we're encouraged to live godly lives that reflect the fact that Jesus is our Lord. Our lives are to demonstrate the fruit of the Spirit who empowers us to live with self-control and godliness. We can't do this in our own strength, but He readily and joyfully supplies all we need to accomplish this so that our lives will continually testify to His power and presence.

9

January 4

*"He has told you, O man, what is good;
and what does the Lord require of you
but to do justice, and to love
kindness, and to walk humbly with your
God?"*
-Micah 6:8

What does the Lord want our lives to look like? In this world, many people choose to strut around and puff themselves up. They look out for their own interests. They love themselves more than they love others and certainly more than they love God. Is that God's desire for us too? Absolutely not.

For the follower of Christ, it is our mission to serve as a mirror that reflects the heart and character of Christ. When people observe the fruit coming from our lives, they should be able to gain a glimpse of the presence of Christ within us.

When Jesus was on this earth, did He strut around? Did He puff Himself up? Did He belittle others to make Himself look better? No. He joyfully and lovingly served people and He invites us to follow His example while being strengthened with His power.

For Christ's glory, we live justly. For Christ's glory, we love kindness and mercy. For Christ's glory, we walk humbly as people who know and deeply love our gracious God.

January 5

"Wash yourselves; make yourselves clean;remove the evil of your deeds from before my eyes; cease to do evil, learn to do good; seek justice, correct oppression;bring justice to the fatherless, plead the widow's cause."
-Isaiah 1:16-17

The life the Lord has called us to live is one that reflects His gracious, merciful, compassionate and loving heart. He has called us to think with the mind of Christ and to live in such a way that our actions line up with the faith He has prompted in our hearts.

But we struggle to do this. The things of this world tempt us. Even when we know we shouldn't be allured by the temptations that surround us, we sometimes give in and even worse, we may at times begin to adopt the dominant patterns of unholy thinking that cloud the discernment of this world.

Yet Christ offers to cleanse us and as people who have been cleansed by Him, we're encouraged not to muddy ourselves up with worldly thinking and living. He implores us to use our days in such a way that His loving heart is on display through us as we seek the well-being of others around us. Widows, orphans, the oppressed. Christ invites us to seek their good and shower them with His mercy as it flows through us.

January 6

"Therefore, preparing your minds for action, and being sober-minded, set your hope fully on the grace that will be brought to you at the revelation of Jesus Christ."
-1 Peter 1:13

Behavior follows belief. What we truly believe eventually starts to show up in the way we conduct our day-to-day lives.

There is a battle taking place over the influence of our minds. Satan would love to be the dominant influencer, but the fruit of believing his falsehoods is death, disease, depression and despair.

Through faith in Jesus, we are given a new mind. We have been blessed with what Scripture refers to as the "mind of Christ." That being the case, we're encouraged to prepare our minds to actively follow through on that which Christ holds before us.

We're to be serious or sober minded. We are never to yield control of our minds over to forces, people or substances that would cloud our judgment or influence us to ignore the voice of Christ.

Ultimately, our minds are to be anchored in the hope of what Christ has promised He will absolutely accomplish for His glory and our greater good. His promises are true and He never disappoints.

January 7

"Therefore be imitators of God, as beloved children. And walk in love, as Christ loved us and gave himself up for us, a fragrant offering and sacrifice to God."
-Ephesians 5:1-2

It is often said that "imitation is the sincerest form of flattery." Sometimes in life, our friends imitate us. Comedians often imitate the words and actions of famous political leaders. Children imitate the words and actions of their parents, for good and for bad.

The Scriptures encourage us to be "imitators of God." We're invited to follow His lead, copy His manner of speaking, implement His pattern of treating others with compassion and adopt His manner of thinking.

During Christ's earthly ministry, He showed us what it means to walk in love. Jesus loved us and gave Himself up for us on the cross as a sacrifice that was made to atone for the sin we had committed. Now, as people who are the beneficiaries of Christ's grace and mercy, we're called to live our earthly lives in such a way that we demonstrate His presence within us.

We do this all knowing that we are God's beloved children. He loves us deeply and He delights to see that His children are mindful to imitate the very traits we see present in Him. We prioritize the needs of others. We love because He first loved us. We show mercy because we are the recipients of His mercy.

January 8

"Seek good, and not evil,
that you may live;
and so the Lord, the God of hosts, will be
with you, as you have said.
Hate evil, and love good,
and establish justice in the gate;
it may be that the Lord, the God of hosts,
will be gracious to the remnant of
Joseph."
-Amos 5:14-15

In this world, our hearts are always seeking something. We seek what we believe will bring us peace, rest and comfort. We long for these things. We value these desires and over time, our lives are poured out in their pursuit.

At different seasons of our lives, we have mistakenly pursued false sources of peace and comfort. We have sought what we believed would bring our hearts rest, only to be disappointed and let down by false promises.

Thankfully, Christ does not disappoint His family. In Him we find ultimate rest, peace and comfort and He calls us to continue to seek what is in line with His heart so that we will not be let down or crushed by the false assurances of this world.

Jesus is who we need. Jesus is the one who satisfies the longings of our hearts.

January 9

"Do not lay up for yourselves treasures on earth, where moth and rust destroy and where thieves break in and steal, but lay up for yourselves treasures in heaven, where neither moth nor rust destroys and where thieves do not break in and steal. For where your treasure is, there your heart will be also."
-Matthew 6:19-21

We are surrounded by the things we treasure. Technology, houses, food and financial provisions. These things are valuable and useful. They are entrusted to us as a stewardship from the Lord, but they make terrible gods.

Many people in this world place their trust in and express their deepest love toward very temporary things. They covet them. They make sacrifices for them. Sometimes they may even steal to acquire more of their earthly idols. At times, even the people they love can become idols of their hearts.

We wrestle with this struggle as well, but Jesus shows us a different way to believe and live. The affections of our hearts will naturally drift toward what we treasure. We can treasure earthly and temporary things or we can treasure Jesus and His kingdom. Jesus invites us to treasure Him and to store up heavenly treasure, knowing that it holds value for eternity, not just a few short earthly decades.

January 10

"but as he who called you is holy, you also be holy in all your conduct, since it is written, "You shall be holy, for I am holy."
-1 Peter 1:15-16

Our lives are not accidents. By God's design, we were created to live when we live and even where we live. And just as our physical life is not an accident, neither is our spiritual life.

If we have come to know Jesus as our God, Lord, Savior and Messiah by faith, the desire to trust in Him did not find its source in us. That is a desire that is fostered by the Holy Spirit who actively convicts this world of sin, righteousness and judgment and who removes the spiritual blinders that we on our eyes and veiling our hearts.

We have responded to God's invitation to receive His gift of salvation because He has called us unto Himself. And when He called us to believe in His Son, Jesus, He didn't call us to remain unchanged. We are a new creations in Christ. The old has gone. The new has come. His calling on our lives is that as new creations, we would utilize His power at work within us daily to live a holy life in the midst of this fallen world.

As the fruit of our redemption, our conduct in this world should continually reflect our Lord's holiness.

January 11

"Out of my distress I called on the Lord;
the Lord answered me and set me free.
The Lord is on my side; I will not fear.
What can man do to me?"
-Psalm 118:5-6

What makes your heart afraid? Is it the fear of the unknown? Is it fear of some unpleasant experience from your past reoccurring in the present? Are you fearing the possibility of betrayal from those you trust? Do you worry about experiencing unforeseen tragedy in your life?

Worry and fear are common to all of us, but they don't bring any benefit to our lives. They rob us of joy and they cause our minds to drift to "what-if" scenarios that often, aren't even likely to take place.

But even if we do experience adversity, is there anything the Lord will allow us to face that won't be for His glory and our benefit? Is there any trial that His strength won't be sufficient for us to rely on? Is Jesus with us always, as He promised, or isn't He?

In our moments of distress, the Lord invites us to call on Him. He doesn't abandon His children and there is nothing that circumstances or other people can ever do to us that won't ultimately be used by Him for our good.

January 12

> *"for in Christ Jesus you are all sons of God, through faith. For as many of you as were baptized into Christ have put on Christ. There is neither Jew nor Greek, there is neither slave nor free, there is no male and female, for you are all one in Christ Jesus."*
> ***-Galatians 3:26-28***

Who do you compare yourself to? Quite frequently, we make comparisons in two directions. We compare ourselves to those we think we're doing better than and we compare ourselves to those we think are doing better than us.

But is that healthy? Is that how things really work in Christ's family? Are some of us loved by Him while others are simply tolerated? That's not the case at all.

In Christ, we all have the inheritance rights of His kingdom just like sons did in ancient cultures. We are one in Christ and who we used to be, particularly when it comes to the labels that are most often used in this world to compare, contrast and categorize people, is not how our value is determined in God's kingdom.

Our new identity isn't locked into worldly labels. It's anchored in Christ. In Christ we're forever loved, blessed, adopted, made holy and righteous because of what He accomplished on our behalf. He invites us to trust in Him, not the labels we used to find value in.

January 13

"that is, in Christ God was reconciling the world to himself, not counting their trespasses against them, and entrusting to us the message of reconciliation. Therefore, we are ambassadors for Christ, God making his appeal through us. We implore you on behalf of Christ, be reconciled to God."
-2 Corinthians 5:19-20

Reconciliation is an interesting concept. It literally means to take something that is far away and bring it near. By nature, we were born at a distance from God. Our hearts were set against Him as His enemies, but in Christ, we were reconciled to God. We have been brought near to Him by grace, through faith.

This produces a sense of peace in our lives and a healthy form of confidence, knowing that we have been forgiven by our Creator and are continually welcomed into His presence.

This also produces a desire to share this blessing with others. Christ calls us to be His "ambassadors." We represent Him to others. We give others a glimpse of His loving heart by displaying the fruit of the Spirit in how we treat everyone He places in our path.

God is making His appeal to others through us today.

January 14

If anyone says, "I love God," and hates his brother, he is a liar; for he who does not love his brother whom he has seen cannot love God whom he has not seen. And this commandment we have from him: whoever loves God must also love his brother.
-1 John 4:20-21

Why is love such an important concept to God. Why does He bring it up so many times in the Scriptures?

God is perfect and every attribute of His character that we see on display can likewise be called a "perfection" of God. God is perfect mercy. God is perfect grace. God is perfect justice and He is also perfect love.

In Christ, we are a new creation. Christ lives within us and His love compels and controls us. If we are controlled by the love of Christ and utter the sentiment, "I love God", but don't actively show His love to others, we clearly don't understand very much about how God's love works.

God's love isn't a vain sentiment. It isn't about blessing those we like and avoiding those we don't. If we love God, He commands us to practice His love toward others who have likewise been made in His image. His love is giving, forgiving, long-suffering and sacrificial. Who is He calling us to love today?

January 15

So Jesus said to the Jews who had believed him, "If you abide in my word, you are truly my disciples, and you will know the truth, and the truth will set you free."
-John 8:31-32

It's one thing to know about someone and another thing to know that someone personally. There are many people in this world who know plenty about Jesus. They know when He was physically born. They know where He lived. They may even be able to quote some of the things He said, but that's not the same as having a relationship with Him.

Jesus uses the word "disciples" to speak of those who know Him well and He encourages all people to come and become His disciples. He calls us to embrace the truth of who He is and what He teaches. He invites us to approach each day with the knowledge that we will be facing every experience of that day with the confidence that He is beside us and within us.

Jesus also tells us that those who truly know Him will abide in His word. When we love Him and are confident of His love for us, it isn't a chore to obey His teaching and live in accordance with His instruction, it's a pleasure to do so because we are thankful that He has freed us from the slavery to false beliefs that we once embraced as true. In Christ we have been set free to walk in grace and truth.

January 16

"But I say, walk by the Spirit, and you will not gratify the desires of the flesh."
-Galatians 5:16

Most physicians tell us that walking is one of the most effective forms of exercise for the human body. It's also a great mood enhancer and it forces our bodies to breathe in more oxygen.

Our bodies, or better said, our old sinful nature, crave unhealthy things as well. We're tempted by the lusts of the flesh, the lusts of the eyes and the boastful pride of life. At times, we may even allow ourselves to believe these sources of temptation will satisfy the cravings of our hearts, but in time, we come to realize that the temptations of this world make empty promises that leave us worse off than we were before giving in to them.

But in Christ, we have a better option. He invites us to walk, or live, by His Spirit. When we're walking by the Spirit, we're welcoming His presence and influence. We're honoring His holiness and valuing what He's revealed in the Scriptures and listening to His prodding within our conscience.

If we're keeping in step with the Spirit, our minds will focus on better things as well and we won't dwell on how to gratify the desires of our old nature. In Christ, we start to see things as they really are and through Him, we're empowered to walk in righteousness.

January 17

"Do all things without grumbling or disputing, that you may be blameless and innocent, children of God without blemish in the midst of a crooked and twisted generation, among whom you shine as lights in the world, holding fast to the word of life, so that in the day of Christ I may be proud that I did not run in vain or labor in vain."
-Philippians 2:14-16

The average lifespan on this earth is somewhere in the vicinity of 27,000 days. What are we doing with the time the Lord has entrusted to us?

Many people, sadly, spend the bulk of their lives complaining and cutting others down. They find fault in others as a way of trying to make themselves feel better. Their fault-finding and grumbling, however, is actually a symptom that reveals their level of dissatisfaction with themselves.

As people who have been made new by Christ, should our lives be characterized by grumbling or complaining? Does that give Him the glory He deserves? Has He called us to continually argue or does He have a higher aim for our lives?

Christ is making His appeal to this world through us. Will He be seen in the words of our mouths and the attitude of our hearts today?

January 18

"No temptation has overtaken you that is not common to man. God is faithful, and he will not let you be tempted beyond your ability, but with the temptation he will also provide the way of escape, that you may be able to endure it."
-1 Corinthians 10:13

Temptation is a trap. It always looks good to us initially, but it carries with it a dark secret. It fills your mind with promises of how wonderful it will be, but conveniently leaves out the pain of the consequences that come with giving into it. It's trying to ruin you, your health, your reputation and your testimony for Christ.

Temptation is something that's all around us every day. It's also within us. Often, we like to blame Satan for our temptations, and he's certainly one source of them, but we're also tempted by the things of this world, other people, and our own evil desires.

During the course of His earthly ministry, Jesus was also tempted, but at no point did He give in to temptation. Now, through faith in Him, we're promised His power and protection when temptation comes our way. We're also told that He will provide a way of escape for us right when we need it.

What temptations are you wrestling with today? Don't linger where you're tempted. Walk away. Take the escape route Christ has opened up for you.

24

January 19

> *"So whatever you wish that others would do to you, do also to them, for this is the Law and the Prophets."*
> *-Matthew 7:12*

Does the joy of others bring us joy? Does their pain cause us pain? It's a wise idea for us to ask ourselves these questions when we're seeking to grow in Christ-likeness because our joy and pain matter to Christ. He is our Savior and the merciful, sympathetic High Priest of our faith according to Scripture and He cares about what happens in our lives.

Many people look at the Bible and consider it a large book, so large in fact that they may never consider actually reading it. Jesus referred to what we call the Old Testament as "the Law and the Prophets." He told those He was speaking to that the Scriptures could be summarized as teaching us to love God with all our hearts and love others as we love ourselves.

Practically speaking, that means if our hearts are motivated by Christ's love, that love will present itself in how we treat those He loves. If we love Jesus, we will love His people. We will treat others as we wish to be treated. We will treat others as we're glad the Lord treats us.

We show mercy because Christ is merciful to us. We love because He loved us first.

January 20

"Count it all joy, my brothers, when you meet trials of various kinds, for you know that the testing of your faith produces steadfastness."
-James 1:2-3

When we daydream about what we want our days to look like, we often think about ideal weather, ideal circumstances and the absence to difficulty. For many of us, our sense of joy is tied directly to what is taking place at that point of time in our lives and if everything seems to be going well, we consider ourselves joyful.

Then we look at a portion of Scripture like this where believers in Christ are invited to experience the joy of Christ regardless of our circumstances. How can that be? The truth is, true joy isn't circumstantial at all.

In Christ, our future is secured. In Christ we know that no trial will come into our lives that isn't both for God's glory and our ultimate good. What good could possibly come from our trials and tests?

What if the Lord is using tests of your faith to make your faith stronger and to show you that He is sufficient for all that you need today? What if the trials you're going through will be used by Him to bless those you love? What if He uses your trials as a tool to grant you greater wisdom? As James says in this passage, a tested faith makes a steadfast person.

January 21

"Do not be deceived: God is not mocked, for whatever one sows, that will he also reap. For the one who sows to his own flesh will from the flesh reap corruption, but the one who sows to the Spirit will from the Spirit reap eternal life."
-Galatians 6:7-8

Every day, we're making investments in something or someone. We make investments of time, talents and treasure in other people and projects. We're also making investments in ourselves, but what kind of investments are we making?? What is currently being poured into our lives?

This world wants our attention and it wants us to make investments in our lives that are unhealthy. It wants us to fill our lives, minds and souls with gossip, slander, impurity and all kinds of wickedness. And when we do so, there are natural and spiritual consequences to those decisions. Not surprisingly, the fruit of those investments is sour and spoiled.

But in Christ, we're invited to pour out our lives in worship toward Him and to welcome His presence. He invites us to make investments in our lives that find their source in His life-giving Spirit. What long-term outcomes might we expect from a life that's being invested in with the Word of God, prayer, godly conversation and edifying relationships?

January 22

> *"Ask, and it will be given to you; seek, and you will find; knock, and it will be opened to you. For everyone who asks receives, and the one who seeks finds, and to the one who knocks it will be opened."*
> *-Matthew 7:7-8*

Making a request can be a difficult action for some people to take. When we request something, it forces us to admit that we have a need we can't meet on our own. It forces us to act with humility by causing us to admit that we need someone else's help. Because of this, many people choose to suffer needlessly in life as they would rather hold onto their pride before humbling themselves to ask for help, even when that help is greatly needed.

Jesus knows that we need His help in this world and He invites us to request it through prayer. He invites us to come before Him and bring our petitions for His intervention. We can ask Him for what we need because it isn't a surprise to Him nor does He shame us for coming to Him with our requests.

Just as He first knocked on the door of our hearts when He initiated our relationship with Him, He invites us to knock at the gates of Heaven in prayer. We won't be turned away if we're truly seeking His help and presence. He delights in this expression of our humble trust and faith in Him to provide.

January 23

*" If any of you lacks wisdom, let him ask
God, who gives generously to all without
reproach, and it will be given him. "*
-James 1:5

When most people come before the Lord in prayer,
what do you suppose they pray about? How about us?
What do we usually ask Him for? Comfort? Less pain?
The end to our trials? Financial help?

When we bring our requests before the Lord, He hears
us and He knows how best to answer our prayers.
Sometimes, without realizing it, we ask Him for things
that are outside of His sovereign will or possibly outside
of His moral will.

But there is a request we can make of Him that He will
always say, "Yes!" to. He tells us in His Word that if
we ask Him for wisdom, He will gladly supply us with
it. He will grant us His wisdom, generously.

How often are we asking Him for the wisdom He is so
willing to generously provide? As believers in Jesus
Christ, we have been granted the ability to see things
with His eyes and His mind. Likewise, His Word
makes His will abundantly clear to us. It's clearly His
will to grant the gift of wisdom to anyone who comes to
Him in faith and makes that request.

What will you be asking God for today?

January 24

"Brothers, if anyone is caught in any transgression, you who are spiritual should restore him in a spirit of gentleness. Keep watch on yourself, lest you too be tempted."
-Galatians 6:1

Sin is a persistent struggle in our lives. We wrestle with it every day and if we aren't wrestling with it, that probably means we're giving into it.

Sometimes in life, we come to a place of repentance as the Holy Spirit impresses that desire upon our hearts and we confess our sin and seek the Lord's strength to walk away from what we've been giving in to. Other times, we repent because we've been caught and confronted by another brother or sister in Christ who loves us enough to tell us the truth.

Knowing that we all wrestle with sin and fall short in many ways, how should we respond to our brothers and sisters in Christ who are caught in sin. Should we ignore them? Should we affirm their sin? Should we dismiss it or should we seek to lovingly and gently restore them? We should see to restore them without heaping added shame upon them.

As we do so, let's be mindful of our own weaknesses and just how easy it can be for us to be tempted by the very same things they've been struggling with. Be careful, but for Christ's glory, restore those you love.

January 25

> *"Finally, brothers, whatever is true, whatever is honorable, whatever is just, whatever is pure, whatever is lovely, whatever is commendable, if there is any excellence, if there is anything worthy of praise, think about these things."*
> **-Philippians 4:8**

Have you ever had a difficult time sleeping because it felt like you couldn't "turn off your brain"? How often do anxious thoughts, what-if scenarios, check lists and other stressors swim through our minds? How often do we dwell on the hurtful words and deeds of others? Do we entertain thoughts of revenge? How often do we allow other impure thoughts to take residence in our thinking?

Naturally speaking, there are many unhelpful and unholy things that we can allow to cloud our thinking on a daily basis. But in Christ, we have been given a new mind, new eyes and a new heart. While the rest of the world may feel stuck with dwelling on things that bring them down, you have the option to make a different choice. You have been empowered by the Holy Spirit to spend your mental energy thinking about true, honorable, just, and loving things. This is a gift that Christ delights to see us utilize.

What's on your mind today? What will you be choosing to dwell on?

January 26

"Humble yourselves before the Lord, and he will exalt you."
-James 4:10

We live in a world that loves to puff itself up. As people, we brag about our high moments and conveniently forget about our lower moments. We show off. We pretend we're self-sufficient. Sometimes, we become so full of ourselves that we become unteachable.

Humility is a misunderstood concept. Sometimes people think it means that we need to be self-deprecating or that we need to speak and think poorly of ourselves, but that's not the essence of humility. Humility is all about admitting who we actually are, not pretending to be something we are not.

In the context of our relationship with the Lord, humility involves recognizing that He's in charge. It means admitting that we're sinful, but Christ is sinless. It means that we acknowledge that we need salvation and that Jesus is the only Savior.

As we live that out in relation to each other, we can esteem the needs of others over our own. We can live selflessly as Christ empowers us to do so. We can reflect the heart of Christ to each other knowing that He chose to exercise humility when He willingly took on human flesh and suffered for humanity on the cross. As Christ values others, so too can we.

January 27

"For we do not wrestle against flesh and blood, but against the rulers, against the authorities, against the cosmic powers over this present darkness, against the spiritual forces of evil in the heavenly places. Therefore take up the whole armor of God, that you may be able to withstand in the evil day, and having done all, to stand firm."
-Ephesians 6:12-13

In this world, many people think they have enemies, but the people they mistakenly think are their enemies, aren't enemies at all. Humanity is all in the same boat. We're all children of Adam and we all struggle with sin. When we fight against each other, it's because we're forgetting who our real enemy is.

Satan and his legion of fallen angels work against humanity every day. They seek to blind our eyes to the gospel of Christ and our need for salvation. They promote lies and false doctrines with the goal of causing confusion, division and separation.

But all believers in Christ are blessed with His power. In the midst of the spiritual battles we're facing, He grants us the strength to stand firm. He enables us to see this battle from His perspective so we can stop falling for Satan's schemes. He enlightens our minds with gospel truth so we can reflect His heart.

January 28

"God is spirit, and those who worship him
must worship in spirit and truth."
-John 4:24

Where do we worship God? What contexts are most
appropriate? Is He primarily worshipped in a building?
Is there a location on earth He prefers to be worshipped
from? Is there a certain ritual we're supposed to follow?
What is God's preference?

These were the kinds of assumptions people came to
Jesus with. During the course of His earthly ministry,
some people assumed that God could only be truly
worshipped from the temple in Jerusalem while others
emphasized other locations.

But Jesus emphasized something different. He shows
us that God is looking at the heart and wants us to
worship Him without pretense. Worship is not about
merely going through the motions. It's not about
ceremony. It's not about recitation. True worship
occurs when our hearts, lips and lives are poured out in
grateful appreciation and honor to the Lord.

Worship isn't confined to a location either. God is
spirit. He isn't contained by boxes, buildings or
geography. He is spirit and our efforts to pin Him into a
corner aren't even logical.

Jesus invites us to worship Him with sincerity,
wherever we may be in every activity of our lives.

January 29

And he sat down and called the twelve. And he said to them, "If anyone would be first, he must be last of all and servant of all."
-Mark 9:35

What does it mean to be "first"? Does it mean you're the best at something? Does it mean you're the most prominent? Does it mean you're the most important?

Jesus' early disciples wrestled with this concept. They had given up the lives they were living in order to follow Him. They expected Jesus to establish His rule as King sometime during their natural lives and they wanted to occupy positions of honor in His kingdom. But Jesus showed them a different way.

This world values pushing and shoving to get our way, but Christ isn't thrilled with selfish attitudes or behavior. A heart of service is what He wants His followers to develop with His strength to aid us. Just as He came to serve us, so to should we begin to value Christ-honoring service in our lives.

A good life really isn't about getting our way, sitting at the head of the table or being first in line. Christ's kingdom doesn't operate that way. In His kingdom, the priority involves putting Him first and valuing the needs of the people He brings into our lives.

Who can we serve for Christ's glory today?

January 30

*"with all humility and gentleness,
with patience, bearing with one another
in love,"*
-Ephesians 4:2

People are wonderful. Humanity has been created in God's image and He desires us to reflect His glory. When we think back over the course of our lives, we can all recall people God blessed us with the privilege of knowing who were easy to love and appreciate. We're grateful for the gift it has been to know and relate to such people.

People are also difficult. Our sin impacts the way we think, believe and live. It can and often does damage the way we treat and perceive each other. It makes us cautious and untrusting. We may feel like it's too risky or difficult to spend time with others because of our fear of getting hurt, insulted or burdened.

Jesus came to this earth to take our burdens upon Himself. He invites us to give the things that weigh our hearts down to Him. He also challenges us to respond to others in a way that reflects His heart. That involves bearing each others burdens and treating each other with gentleness and patience, just as Christ is treating us.

During the course of today, you're likely to encounter someone who will test your patience. Rely on Christ's strength to respond to them with kindness.

January 31

"For you, O Lord, are good
and forgiving, abounding in steadfast
love to all who call upon you."
-Psalm 86:5

Understanding who God truly is is something that matters. Many people on this earth are convinced that God's favor must be earned and that He is harsh toward us when we struggle, stumble or drift off the path. But that's not the case at all.

Yes, the Lord is perfectly just. Yes, He is perfectly righteousness. As this Scripture reveals, He is also perfectly good, perfectly forgiving and perfectly loving. It's important that we allow that truth to fully sink into our hearts so we don't forget the nature of our Lord and how He interacts with humanity.

During the course of His earthly ministry, Jesus regularly interacted with people who forgot these truths. He experienced the harsh, unloving attitudes of the religious leaders who seemed more interested in holding on to power than they seemed interested in helping people grow closer to God. He also experienced many people who had spent their lives wandering like sheep without a shepherd. They were unsure of who God is and what He is truly like. But Jesus showed them and He shows us.

Jesus is good, forgiving and the perfection of love.

February 1

"Hear, O Israel: The Lord our God, the Lord is one. You shall love the Lord your God with all your heart and with all your soul and with all your might."
-Deuteronomy 6:4-5

Love is an often misunderstood concept. For many people, love is thought of in a purely emotional way, but there's much more to love than that. In fact, Scripture treats love from the perspective of action more so than from the perspective of emotion.

That means if we are going to truly love someone else, we need to be actively seeking what is best for them even at great personal cost to ourselves. That's the kind of love Jesus has shown us. He actively sought what was best for us, even though it was a costly and painful decision on His part to do so.

In response to who the Lord is and how He chooses to operate in our lives, we're called to love Him, and not just on the days when we emotionally feel like doing so. Rather, we're to make a conscious decision each day to actively seek to honor Him from the core of our beliefs and in the midst of our actions. We're called to love Him with every part of our being; our heart, our soul and our might. With every ounce of energy He grants us, we're to love Him. We do so joyfully as His dearly beloved children who love Him because He showed us love first.

February 2

But, as it is written,
"What no eye has seen, nor ear heard,
*   nor the heart of man imagined,*
what God has prepared for those who love
him"—
-1 Corinthians 2:9

It seems like some days begin in a slump from the moment we wake up. Regardless of the forecast, the sky seems grey, our energy feels drained and it feels like we just can't shake our emotional funk.

This can happen for many reasons, but one of those reasons may be that we've been spending too much time obsessing about our momentary circumstances. Sadly, when we do that, we can lose sight of the beautiful bigger picture of what God has been up to even before He spoke creation into existence.

Our worst days last for just a moment and our best days cannot compare to the glorious future God has in store for all who have genuine faith in Jesus Christ. His word reveals to us that our natural senses cannot even begin to fathom the kind of future He has in store for His children.

We can't predict what may come our way today. Trials. Fun. Sadness. Happiness. But we can rest in the confidence that through Jesus we have a glorious future to look forward to that far surpasses anything that may weigh our hearts down in the present.

February 3

"But I will sing of your strength;
I will sing aloud of your steadfast love
in the morning.
For you have been to me a fortress
and a refuge in the day of my distress."
-Psalm 59:16

How much do you believe you need to carry in this world in your own strength? Are you trying to meet the needs of others and stitch the pieces of their lives together while also trying to manage your own life and family?

Have you ever found yourself trying to keep your emotions under wraps because you were convinced that you needed to be strong for the sake of someone else? Why is it that we routinely pressure ourselves to do the kinds of things only God can truly do?

In Christ, we find the help and hope our hearts are truly looking for. Our burdens are too heavy for us, but His strength is available for our needs. He is steadfast. He is our fortress. He is the one we can run to when we need refuge. These are just a few of the ways Jesus meets the needs of our hearts.

Today, if you're tempted to trust in your own strength, please remember that Christ's strength is a greater remedy for your needs. He is our refuge and in Him we find the help, safety and security our heart's crave.

February 4

"I love you, O Lord, my strength.
The Lord is my rock and my fortress and
my deliverer,
*   my God, my rock, in whom I take*
refuge,
*   my shield, and the horn of my*
salvation, my stronghold."
-Psalm 18:1-2

On what foundation has the Lord called us to build our lives? Scripture reveals to us that Christ Himself is the foundation that is secure and solid. He doesn't waver. He isn't fickle and His love for us is constant.

At times, however, without expressly declaring it, we may attempt to start anchoring our lives to temporary and shaky things. What we own. How we look. What others think of us. How much others value our opinions, etc. When we do that, we're setting ourselves up for failure because all of those things change and are manipulated by shifting circumstances and opinions. Thankfully, our Lord doesn't operate like that.

Through faith in Jesus we are delivered from the brittle foundations we once tried to build on. In Jesus we find a fortress of security for our souls. When we come to Jesus, we come to a stronghold that the forces of evil cannot stand against. He is our refuge, strength and shield and He will never fail to deliver anyone who comes to Him in genuine faith.

February 5

"For the word of the Lord is upright,
and all his work is done in faithfulness.
He loves righteousness and justice;
the earth is full of the steadfast love of
the Lord."
-Psalm 33:4-5

The Father, Son and Holy Spirit have lived in perfect unity and perfect fellowship for all eternity. One God in three Persons. Scripture also tells us that God created mankind in His image. One aspect of being created in His image that we may not always realize is that we've been designed by God to live in relationship with others. We were not designed by Him to live in perpetual solitude.

But relationships with others can be challenging. Many people admit that they find it much easier to get along with their pets than they do other people. Why is that? Part of the struggle is that we often lose sight of how God relates to us, and when that happens, we may neglect to relate to others in ways that mirror His heart.

God's word tells us that He is faithful. He loves righteousness and justice. He fills the earth with His steadfast love. We see all these things perfectly personified in Jesus Christ. As His disciples, He desires to display these attributes of His nature through us to someone else today. Will we let Him?

February 6

"Whoever pursues righteousness and kindness
will find life, righteousness, and honor."
-Proverbs 21:21

We're all chasing something. Your heart craves what it's convinced it needs and the chase continues until the heart finds what it's looking for. If your heart is still convinced that the things of this world will bring it peace and satisfaction, those are the things it will continue to crave. If your heart is convinced that Jesus is all you truly need, then a deeper walk with Christ will be your heart's desire.

True righteousness is found in Jesus Christ. Through faith in Him, we are declared righteous in the court room of God. At the moment we trust in Jesus, His righteousness is added to our account. Having been made righteous through Him, we're called to live righteously for His glory and to share His kindness because our hearts are grateful for having received it.

The older we get, the wiser we hopefully become. We are surrounded by people who are chasing the wrong things, but by God's grace we pray that what we pursue will give Him glory. The energy He grants us today can be spent in many directions, but the counsel of His word invites us to value His righteousness and kindness and to rejoice in the new life and perspective we've been granted through Jesus.

February 7

"O you who love the Lord, hate evil!
He preserves the lives of his saints;
he delivers them from the hand of the
wicked."
-Psalm 97:10

What are your guiding influences in life? What do you invite into your life that has an impact on how you see yourself, others, circumstances and the future? What entertains you? What goals are you pursuing? Is your answer to any of these questions out of line with the revealed will of the Lord as He has made it known in His word?

The truth is, we don't always hate evil. Sometimes we love it. Sometimes we're loyal to it and we welcome more of it. Sometimes we're convinced that various forms of evil in this world will somehow produce a good result in our lives. Even though that isn't logical, we can see that this might be exactly what we believe when our patterns, opinions and practices are held up to the light of Christ's gospel.

Jesus hasn't called us to welcome evil into our lives. He has defeated its power and shares His victory over sin with all who trust in Him. He wants you to recognize the fact that His power is within you to strengthen you, grant you wisdom, make you truly alive and deliver you from the evil in this world.

Love Jesus. Love others. Hate evil. Live in victory.

February 8

> *"You have heard that it was said, 'You shall love your neighbor and hate your enemy.' But I say to you, Love your enemies and pray for those who persecute you, so that you may be sons of your Father who is in heaven. For he makes his sun rise on the evil and on the good, and sends rain on the just and on the unjust."*
> *-Matthew 5:43-45*

There are people in this world that are difficult to love. People that have hurt you. People that have betrayed you. People that have intentionally sought to malign your character or have opposed you when you were doing what was right.

The easiest way to respond to such people is to become bitter and spiteful toward them while fostering feelings of hatred in your heart. But Christ hasn't called His family to take the easy route. He's empowered us to love others, even those who show by their actions that they do not love us.

Why does Jesus call us to do this? Well, it's the very thing He did when He came to this earth. We didn't love Jesus. We weren't looking for Him, but He loved us and rescued us anyway. Now He calls us to model His heart and His life to those He allows us to encounter in this world. This can't be done in our own strength, but Christ's strength can help us to love even the most unlovable people in our lives.

February 9

> *"We ought always to give thanks to God for you, brothers, as is right, because your faith is growing abundantly, and the love of every one of you for one another is increasing."*
> *-2 Thessalonians 1:3*

It is much easier to focus on the negative than it is to notice the positive. It's easier to complain about bad weather, rude treatment, physical pain, and long waiting times than it is to be thankful for the many different blessings we receive through Jesus every single day. Christ wants us to be grateful.

One of the greatest blessings Christ has given us is the union we have with our brothers and sisters in the faith. We have been united together with them in Christ. We are family and the Holy Spirit spiritually equips us to make important investments in each others lives for the purpose of building one another up.

For these reasons and many more, we should always give thanks to the Lord for His people and we should likewise be thankful for the spiritual growth the Lord is producing in the lives of His children.

What kind of difference do you think it might make in the life of another brother or sister in Christ if you took time today to tell them how thankful you were for their presence in your life?

February 10

> *"If I speak in the tongues of men and of angels, but have not love, I am a noisy gong or a clanging cymbal. And if I have prophetic powers, and understand all mysteries and all knowledge, and if I have all faith, so as to remove mountains, but have not love, I am nothing. If I give away all I have, and if I deliver up my body to be burned, but have not love, I gain nothing."*
> *-1 Corinthians 13:1-3*

Jesus is the perfection of love. In love, He lived a sinless life on our behalf. In love, He died on the cross to pay the debt we owed for our sin. In love, He rose from the grave. In love, He shares His victory over sin, Satan and death with all who believe in Him.

As Christ loves, so too has He called us to love. Love is sacrificial, not selfish. If you could possess every natural talent and every spiritual gift, but didn't utilize those gifts with a loving attitude, what good would you really be doing? Would it have lasting value? Would it glorify Christ or would it just make some noise for a few minutes then fade away?

Love isn't about showing off, it's about serving. When we love, we have the privilege of noticing what someone else needs, then meeting that need with the strength Christ supplies and a heart that reflects His.

February 11

> *"Love is patient and kind; love does not envy or boast; it is not arrogant or rude. It does not insist on its own way; it is not irritable or resentful;"*
> **-1 Corinthians 13:4-5**

Do you resent anyone? Is there someone on this earth that you secretly wish bad things would come their way? Maybe someone who has offended you in some way? Possibly someone who has something that you wish you had and now you're feeling jealous of them?

Resentment is the fruit of forgetting that we already have everything we need for life and godliness in Christ Jesus. When we stop dwelling on that truth, our hearts begin to seek some level of satisfaction from lesser things. We become convinced that if we had what someone else had, then we'd truly be content, but that's a lie. Christ is *who* we need. New life through Christ is *what* we need, and our minds and hearts do well when we embrace that truth.

The person you may struggle with resentment toward has probably noticed. Even in subtle ways, our emotions tend to show themselves. Christ will empower you to truly love that person if you want Him to. The truth is, if you're in Christ, you already have that power, you just may not be using it.

Today is the day to display the patience and kindness of Christ to those you've been starting to resent.

February 12

> *"it does not rejoice at wrongdoing,*
> *but rejoices with the truth. Love bears all*
> *things, believes all things, hopes all*
> *things, endures all things."*
> *-1 Corinthians 13:6-7*

Endurance is a much needed trait in many aspects of life. Depending on where you live, this may be a time of year that requires a lot of snow shoveling. It takes endurance to complete a task like that. Successful marriages require endurance. Raising children requires endurance. Making it to the other end of our trials requires endurance as well.

It's also correct to say that loving well requires endurance. There isn't a single day of our lives that we haven't sinned against Christ in some way. Our thoughts, words and deeds often reveal the presence of our old nature, yet our Lord is patient with us. He endures with us in the midst of this process of growth and maturity He's bringing us through. He doesn't abandon us mid-stream, even on our worst days.

If that's how His love operates toward us, should we abandon others who are also in this process of growth? If true love endures all things, is there a line someone could cross that would grant us permission to no longer love them? What would it say about our understanding of Christ's love if we answered "yes"? The love of Christ at work within us is an enduring love and our love is always called to reflect His.

February 13

"For God so loved the world, that he gave his only Son, that whoever believes in him should not perish but have eternal life."
-John 3:16

This is a time of year when the subject of love is fresh on our minds. Some people love this time of year, particularly if they have a "sweetheart" to share the season with. Other people dread this time of year because they feel like they haven't found that "someone special."

The truth is that life isn't about finding that someone special. Life is, however, about being found by someone who is more than special. How often do we intentionally remind our hearts that our loving God came to this earth looking for us?

God the Father sent God the Son into this world on a mission. Because of His love for humanity, He wasn't content to allow us to wander aimlessly in our rebellious and confused state. He loves us enough to rescue us. He loves us enough to be the remedy for our lostness. He came looking for you and me and didn't stop before His mission was complete.

Jesus, the Son of God, offers us the gift of eternal life through faith in Him. The petals don't fall off His gift and the flavor of His salvation never grows stale. Let your heart rejoice in the knowledge that you are deeply loved by Jesus today.

February 14

"A new commandment I give to you, that you love one another: just as I have loved you, you also are to love one another. By this all people will know that you are my disciples, if you have love for one another."
-John 13:34-35

What is the mark of a mature faith? What does it look like for a person to grow strong in their relationship with Christ? Does it mean they will never make mistakes? Does it require a long check lists of "do's" and "don'ts", or is the mark of maturity something different?

Jesus came to this earth to build a family of devoted disciples. He isn't looking for casual observers or club members. He came to help us learn what it means to be His fully devoted followers and as our understanding of what He's looking for grows, we come to realize that His desire is that we love one another as an outpouring of the overflow of His love that is within us.

If we want others to come to know who Jesus is, this is how we can display His nature and heart. We're called to love another. We love by seeking what is best for one another. We love by speaking truth into each others' lives. We love by sacrificially serving one another just as Christ has joyfully done for us. We love because He has first loved us.

February 15

" In this is love, not that we have loved God but that he loved us and sent his Son to be the propitiation for our sins."
-1 John 4:10

There are concepts in the Bible that are so deep and meaningful that they deserve deeper explanation. One of those concepts is mentioned in this passage of Scripture. It's the concept of "propitiation." For most of us, that's probably not a familiar term, so what does it mean?

Scripture teaches us that Jesus came into this world to accomplish something for us that we were completely incapable of accomplishing for ourselves. He came to be the propitiation for our sins which means He came to satisfy the wrath of God toward our sin and permanently reconcile us to God. This was done as an expression of love on behalf of God the Father toward humanity.

This means that if we have genuine faith in Jesus, His payment for sin is applied to our account and we no longer need to live distantly from God.

Today, Jesus invites you to rejoice in the fact that through Him you are welcomed into the presence of God. Your relationship with God is restored. Though you were once an object of wrath, you are now a recipient of mercy. This is the message He invites you to preach to your heart today.

February 16

> *" Whoever isolates himself seeks his own desire; he breaks out against all sound judgment. "*
> *-Proverbs 18:1*

When we're hurting, exhausted, angry or depressed, it can be tempting to avoid interacting with other people. Sometimes, we find a private corner where no one can find us and we disappear from sight. There are certainly seasons when privacy and solitude can be a good thing, but that isn't God's desire for us as the dominant pattern for our lives.

When we isolate ourselves, we not only avoid those we fear might hurt us, we also end up avoiding the company of those who can help us. We retreat to an echo chamber of our own counsel and ignore the insights of those Christ has united us with through faith in Him.

At the moment we came to faith in Jesus, we were united as one body with our brothers and sisters in Christ. Christ has called us to live in loving community with one another and to make investments in each others' lives that are for our good and His glory. But that can't happen if we isolate ourselves.

If you're hurting today, trust Jesus with your pain and welcome the presence of those He has intentionally placed in your life. He loves you. They love you. Resist the urge to avoid your family in Christ.

February 17

> *"Who shall separate us from the love of Christ? Shall tribulation, or distress, or persecution, or famine, or nakedness, or danger, or sword?"*
> *-Romans 8:35*

One of the most depressing or discouraging forms of false belief is the mistaken thought that God is distant from His children. When we trust in Jesus Christ, we immediately and irrevocably become part of the family of God. We are granted a new name, new identity and a place in His kingdom. We are granted the ability to come boldly before Him, confident of the fact that He welcomes us into His presence like a loving father welcomes his dearly loved child.

There is nothing in this world that is capable of separating us from the love of Jesus. Our most painful trials can't separate us from His love. Persecution, distress and danger cannot either. Even we ourselves are not able to divorce our lives from the love of Christ because His love for us is based on His nature, not our circumstances or seasons of life.

The Lord loves us and won't abandon us. When was the last time you allowed yourself to dwell on that thought? When was the last time you truly preached that message to your heart? It can be far too easy for us to become burdened and anxious in the midst of our trials if we forget who Jesus is and how He faithfully loves His family.

February 18

> *"But false prophets also arose among the people, just as there will be false teachers among you, who will secretly bring in destructive heresies, even denying the Master who bought them, bringing upon themselves swift destruction."*
> *-2 Peter 2:1*

The gospel of Jesus Christ is true, helpful, encouraging and valuable. It truly is "good news", so it's sad to see examples of it being mistreated, compartmentalized or misunderstood. Christ's gospel isn't meant to be altered or tucked away. Rather, we're called to delight in it and joyfully apply it to all areas of our lives.

But in every generation there seem to be those who willingly distort the simple message of Christ's gospel to satisfy their own selfish purposes. Typically for their own personal gain, they promote falsehoods that often deny who Jesus is or minimize the work He accomplished on our behalf. This then leads to the worship of the works of our hands instead of sincere worship directed toward Christ.

Thankfully, the Holy Spirit grants us discernment and He inspired words of caution to be included in the Scriptures to forewarn us of this danger. We're never called to leave behind or alter Christ's gospel, but we are invited to dig deeply into it and rejoice in its truth.

February 19

"For the grace of God has appeared, bringing salvation for all people, training us to renounce ungodliness and worldly passions, and to live self-controlled, upright, and godly lives in the present age, waiting for our blessed hope, the appearing of the glory of our great God and Savior Jesus Christ,"
-Titus 2:11-13

For those who are in Christ, we always have something to look forward to. No matter what experiences we may be going through today, we can approach the future with hope because we know that Jesus has promised to return. We have not been abandoned. We are not forgotten. Jesus will come again just as the Scriptures say.

In the meantime, He invites us and empowers us by His grace to live a life in this world that faithfully reflects His heart and character. We're surrounded by temptations to sin, but at the same time, His power is at work within us to enable us to live godly lives in this world. He empowers us to see worldly passions for what they really are -- harmful prisons that wage war against our souls.

No temptation will come your way today that can successfully stand against the power of Christ. Rely on His strength, follow His leading, and keep looking forward to His return.

February 20

> *"Whoever covers an offense seeks love,*
>   *but he who repeats a matter separates*
> *close friends."*
> *-Proverbs 17:9*

It's difficult to make it through a day without being offended in some fashion. We're often offended by the words, actions and attitudes of others. Sometimes, we're deeply offended by those we're closest to when they act carelessly or even maliciously toward us.

When we're offended, we can do a couple different things with that offense. We can hold onto it, internalize it, and grow bitter or resentful toward the offending party OR we can remember the forgiveness we've received from Jesus and choose to forgive those who have sinned against us.

Forgiveness isn't easy, but it is valuable. It's a gift to the recipient and a blessing to the giver. When we forgive, even when it's painful to do so, we resist the temptation to develop a hateful heart and we gain a greater appreciation of the costly gift of forgiveness we have been granted by Jesus.

What words, actions and offenses have latched onto your mind and heart? What have you been holding onto for too long? Jesus invites us to move beyond the offense by forgiving those who have hurt us. Who is He prompting you to forgive?

February 21

> *"But you, O Lord, are a shield about me,*
> *my glory, and the lifter of my head.*
> *I cried aloud to the Lord, and he answered*
> *me from his holy hill."*
> *-Psalm 3:3-4*

There are times when we come before the Lord with polite and quiet prayers and other times when we pour out our hearts with loud wailing and tears. Both are acceptable to Him and each is proper in its season.

If the Lord didn't answer prayer, and if we were left to ourselves, what state would our hearts find themselves in? We'd drift toward a downcast and defeated state because eventually we'd have to wrestle with the fact that we lacked the help that we needed.

Thankfully our Lord both sees and meets our need for help. Jesus saw us wandering in our lost condition and He stepped into our world to redeem us and lift up our sad, lonely heads. He rescued us from a terrible fate of an eternity devoid of His presence.

Now He assures us that we are welcomed into His presence. When our hearts are burdened with the needs and concerns of the day, we can lift those things up to Him and trust Him to handle them with power that far surpasses the power we naturally possess. When we come before Him in our anguish and tears, we can confidently know that He hears us and answers our prayers in accordance with His will.

February 22

"How long will you lie there, O sluggard? When will you arise from your sleep? A little sleep, a little slumber, a little folding of the hands to rest, and poverty will come upon you like a robber, and want like an armed man."
-Proverbs 6:9-11

Rest is a good thing. Physically speaking, it is healthy for our bodies to receive adequate rest. Spiritually speaking, we're reminded that our souls find perfect rest, peace and contentment in Christ. Healthy forms of rest are great investments we can make in our well-being.

But what happens when we distort the blessing of rest into an excuse for laziness? To one degree or another, this is something that we've all probably wrestled with.

The truth is, our time on this earth is very brief and we haven't been given this time to merely observe others use their gifts and talents while we spend decades staring from the sidelines.

The moment you trusted in Jesus, you were equipped to get in the game. You were supernaturally enabled to accomplish the mission Christ foreordained for your life. How are you going to spend today? Will you sit on your hands or will you get in motion?

February 23

> *"Do they not go astray who devise evil?*
> *Those who devise good meet steadfast*
> *love and faithfulness."*
> *-Proverbs 14:22*

Our hearts are often making plans. We think about the future and we project all kinds of expectations, outcomes and timetables upon it. We don't know what will actually take place in most instances, but we're usually trying to move in some sort of an intentional direction.

What is the greater goal of our plans? For those who invest their mental energy in devising schemes to hurt, defraud or take advantage of others, their lives will move in a direction that piles up regret after regret. But those who have made the decision to glorify Jesus with their lives and likewise seek the good of those He has placed in their lives will gain a greater glimpse of His steadfastness love and faithfulness. They will learn to appreciate it more as they live in the midst of it. They will see it's effect on the lives of those they bless with the outpouring of their faith.

We may struggle to be faithful, but Jesus is always faithful. He isn't fickle. He doesn't change or shift. He has been faithful to us through every season of our lives and His steadfast love is being shown to us today. As we make our plans, may our hearts seek His glory and the good of our brothers and sisters in Christ.

February 24

"For I know the plans I have for you, declares the Lord, plans for welfare and not for evil, to give you a future and a hope. Then you will call upon me and come and pray to me, and I will hear you. You will seek me and find me, when you seek me with all your heart."
-Jeremiah 29:11-13

Your life is not an accident. Before He spoke creation into existence, God intended that you would be born, live when you live, live where you live, and be blessed the the talents, gift and relationships He has shared with you. You are part of His plan and He offers you a good life and an eternal hope.

The hope He offers isn't a wish. For those who trust in Jesus Christ, hope is a certainty. We are promised that in Christ, we have a secure future and He grants us the reassurance that all things will work together for good in our lives.

In the meantime, Christ calls us to delight in our relationship with Him. He wants us to live a life that displays a genuine eagerness to be in His presence. He invites us to call out to Him, confident that He hears us. He invites us to seek Him wholeheartedly without holding anything back. Our Lord loves us and is looking out for us. Our lives find meaning, purpose and direction in Him.

February 25

"For I have derived much joy and comfort from your love, my brother, because the hearts of the saints have been refreshed through you."
-Philemon 1:7

If you're the kind of person that has an active faith in Jesus that bears itself out in regular service toward others, don't be surprised if you experience seasons when your energy level diminishes. You may at times feel drained, worn out, or in desperate need of a break. During these seasons, it's a true gift when the Lord brings you the spiritual boost that you need.

Often, Christ will use His people to refresh each another. The kind words, acts of service, and prayers of other brothers and sisters in Christ can have a huge impact on how we feel. These personal, gospel-saturated investments refresh our spirits and contribute toward our ability to continue pressing on in the labors Christ has entrusted to us.

Who has the Lord routinely used to comfort you? Who has He placed in your life to refresh your spirit? Who seems to know the right words to say or actions to take to remind you of Christ's love and continual presence?

If the Lord brings someone to your mind that fits this description, how can you thank them today?

February 26

> *"For where jealousy and selfish ambition exist, there will be disorder and every vile practice. But the wisdom from above is first pure, then peaceable, gentle, open to reason, full of mercy and good fruits, impartial and sincere."*
> *-James 3:16-17*

One of the most remarkable facets of the heart and mission of Jesus is His others-centeredness. Jesus came to this earth, not to be served, but to serve others and to give His life so that all who trust in Him could experience true and everlasting life.

When we trust in Jesus, He helps us see things with His mind. He grants us wisdom, and He fosters an others-centered heart within us. He helps us not to be overly possessive, jealous, or governed by selfish ambition because fostering that kind of mindset creates disorder and hurts those we're called to love.

As recipients of the wisdom of Christ, we can join Him in His mission of opening up the eyes of others. The prevailing thought that governs many hearts is a mindset of selfishness. But as the heart of Christ is displayed in how we speak to and serve others, Jesus can use our lives as a powerful testimony of His transformative power. As Jesus first did for us, let's place the needs of others above our own today and in so doing, display the wisdom and mercy of Christ.

February 27

> " For I tell you, unless your righteousness
> exceeds that of the scribes and Pharisees,
> you will never enter the kingdom of
> heaven."
> **-Matthew 5:20**

Righteousness is a subject that we often think about. The idea of being righteous certainly sounds appealing, but there's a fine line between true righteousness which honors Christ and self-righteousness which definitely does not.

During the days of Christ's earthly ministry, many people looked up to the religious leaders. They were considered examples of righteousness and holy living. They were well-versed in the Scriptures and they carried themselves in such a way that people were convinced they were the standard of righteousness by which all lives could be measured by.

But Jesus challenged that thought and cautioned the people that unless their righteousness exceeded that of the religious leaders, they would not enter the kingdom of heaven. The truth is, Jesus knew that many of those leaders were self-righteous. Jesus, on the other hand, offers us His righteousness as a gift through faith in Him. At the moment we believe, our self-righteousness is replaced with Christ's righteousness and we are justified (declared righteous) in God's court of justice and welcomed into Christ's kingdom. Let's thank Christ for the gift of His righteousness, which surpasses the self-righteousness of the scribes and Pharisees, today.

February 28/29

"for God gave us a spirit not of fear but of power and love and self-control."
-2 Timothy 1:7

What kind of challenges are you facing during this season of your life? What are you wrestling with? What would you consider to be a genuine struggle that seems to regularly sap your strength? Do you feel defeated? Do you feel discouraged? Do you feel like you're being held back by forces you can't control?

You are not the person you once were. At the moment you trusted in Jesus Christ, you became a new creation and the Holy Spirit immediately indwelled you. Now, in the midst of your natural or spiritual struggles, you no longer need to rely on your own strength. You have His strength to rely on and you can be confident that He won't allow anything to come into your life that ultimately cannot be used to make you stronger and bring Him glory.

You don't need to be afraid, because God has not given you a spirit of fear. You don't need to dwell on your weaknesses as if they define you, because you have been blessed with the power of Christ. You don't need to stew in anger because the love of Christ is governing your heart. You don't need to succumb to temptation because you have been blessed with the Spirit-empowered ability to practice self-control. You are not defeated. You are victorious in Christ.

March 1

"Whom have I in heaven but you?
And there is nothing on earth that I
desire besides you. My flesh and my
heart may fail, but God is the strength of
my heart and my portion forever. "
-Psalm 73:25-26

Deep down within us all, there's a part of us that recognizes we have a need. We can sense that something is missing that needs to be found. We can sense that we lack something we desperately crave. Love. Belonging. Acceptance. Family. There is a vacuum for these things that needs to be filled.

People try to meet the need in many ways. Some people believe human relationships can satisfy the longing of their souls. Others believe that prestige or admiration can meet the need. Some try to fill the void by becoming dependent on mind-altering substances that temporarily dull their pain. But only Christ can satisfy the deepest longing of our soul.

We need a Savior and Jesus is the only one who can truly fill that role. There is no one else in heaven or on earth who can fulfill the deepest longings of our souls. He satisfies the greatest desires of our hearts, grants us His strength, blesses us with His presence, and meets our every need both now and in the future. False saviors and false sources of salvation will always let us down, but Jesus never will.

March 2

"But he knows the way that I take; when he has tried me, I shall come out as gold. My foot has held fast to his steps; I have kept his way and have not turned aside."
-Job 23:10-11

In what direction is your life moving right now? What compels you to walk where you're heading? What are your deepest longings? What is your source of motivation? What fruit is coming from the steps you've been taking? Who is calling the shots and setting the course?

Scripture often refers to our relationship with Jesus like it's a "walk" along a path. This is a wonderful analogy because frequently in life, we see that conversations are fostered and relationships are built through taking walks. Families know this. Couples know this. Friends know this. It's part of the rhythm of many relationships.

Jesus invites us to walk with Him. This is a life-long process where we have the privilege of enjoying our relationship with Him, spending time together, listening to His teaching, and letting Him set the direction that our lives are moving in. As our relationship with Him grows, our desire to walk on the path He has placed before us deepens and our reliance on His strength matures - helping us not to step off the path He's placed before us.

March 3

"For my thoughts are not your thoughts,
neither are your ways my ways, declares
the Lord. For as the heavens are higher
than the earth, so are my ways higher
than your ways and my thoughts than
your thoughts."
-Isaiah 55:8-9

There are things in this world that we don't yet understand. We wonder what good could come from tragic circumstances. We scratch our heads with confusion trying to find God's purposes in some of our deepest trials. We often ask God, "Why?"

But the truth is, the Lord hasn't called us to try and figure everything out. What He has called us to do, however, is trust Him. To walk by faith in Jesus, every single day, confident that He is right here with us and certain that He is looking out for us.

Honestly, we should be glad that the Lord isn't easy for us to figure out. His ways are higher than our natural ways. His thinking is higher than our natural thinking. If we could pinpoint every last thing He is doing and every last detail about Him, would we still be walking by faith or would we be walking primarily by sight? Can man with his limitations truly grasp the Lord's omniscience, omnipotence, and omnipresence? Give yourself a break from trying to do that. Enjoy Jesus in all of His splendor and glory today.

March 4

> *"Have I not commanded you? Be strong and courageous. Do not be frightened, and do not be dismayed, for the Lord your God is with you wherever you go."*
> ***-Joshua 1:9***

You are not alone in this world. One of the tricks that our adversary, the devil, likes to try to play on our minds is to convince us that we are alone. He wants us to believe that we have been abandoned and that the only strength we can rely on is our own natural strength. He wants us to believe that we don't have sufficient help, because that results in our hearts gravitating toward fear and eventually, folly.

But we are not abandoned. Our Lord is present with us. When Jesus was speaking to His disciples, He reminded them that He would be with us always AND the Holy Spirit would be sent to us to live within us forever. God is always present with us. He loves us, delights in us, and strengthens us for every task He calls us to complete and every trial we may be called to endure.

I don't know what's weighing your heart down right now, but if you're feeling paralyzed with fear and if you're struggling to approach today with courage, please remember the truth of this passage. As the Lord was with His people long ago, He's with us today to comfort and strengthen us on this journey.

March 5

> *"And these words that I command you today shall be on your heart. You shall teach them diligently to your children, and shall talk of them when you sit in your house, and when you walk by the way, and when you lie down, and when you rise."*
> *-Deuteronomy 6:6-7*

One of the greatest privileges we are granted in this world is the privilege of raising or teaching children the truth of the gospel and what it looks like to put it into practice every day.

Who do you influence? Are there people who look up to you or people who tend to copy decisions they see you making? What are you doing with that influence? Are you pointing them to Jesus?

Sometimes we carve out time to intentionally teach others. Other times, we end up teaching others by virtue of what they observe us practicing. Those we influence learn from us by virtue of what is "taught" by instruction and what is "caught" by observation.

Never waste an opportunity to show your children, grandchildren, students, or anyone who looks up to you, what it means to walk with Jesus. Talk about Him in the car. Talk about Him in the classroom, and model what it means to trust Him. Young people are watching and learning from you.

March 6

*"O Lord, you are my God; I will exalt you;
I will praise your name, for you have done
wonderful things, plans formed of old,
faithful and sure."*
-Isaiah 25:1

One of the easiest things in the world to do is complain. It seems like everyone does it. We tear things down with our words. We cut people down with our criticism. We may even be tempted at times to complain about the work God is doing, but there's a better way to use the words we speak.

It has always been the plan of God to provide for the redemption of humanity. God the Son, Jesus Christ, came to this earth in the fullness of time to rescue us. He lived, died, rose again, ascended, and is returning again to rule and reign. None of this is accidental or reactionary. It has always been God's intention.

We can complain about momentary circumstances, OR we can lift up our voices and praise God for all that He's working together for the good of humanity and His glory. He deserves our praise because He has done, and continues to do, wonderful things.

The Lord's plans are sure, which means they aren't shaky or fickle. This also means your life isn't an accident or a collection of misfortunes. God has a plan for your life and you can praise Him for the wonderful things He's accomplishing on your behalf.

March 7

"Search me, O God, and know my heart!
Try me and know my thoughts!
And see if there be any grievous way in me,
and lead me in the way everlasting!"
-Psalm 139:23-24

How honest and transparent are we? What do we know about ourselves that we think no one else knows? What are we hesitant to admit? To what degree are we open about the desires of our heart?

There is nothing about us that God doesn't already know. He knows every nuance of our personality, every struggle we wrestle with, every thought that produces fear, and every sin we hesitate to confess. He knows all of this, and He also knows that we have a tendency to hold things back from Him. Why?

Sometimes we forget just how deeply we are loved. When we received the gift of salvation through faith in Jesus Christ, we were rescued, redeemed, and sealed as God's child forever. God no longer sees us as we used to be. Now, we are assured that just as the Father loves the Son, so too are we loved.

Knowing we are loved and living like we are loved can be quiet different. If we are convinced of the love of God, we can joyfully open up our hearts to Him and ask Him to search out what's there, cleanse us of any unrighteousness, and point us in the direction He desires us to follow from that point on.

March 8

"Blessed be the God and Father of our Lord Jesus Christ, the Father of mercies and God of all comfort, who comforts us in all our affliction, so that we may be able to comfort those who are in any affliction, with the comfort with which we ourselves are comforted by God."
-2 Corinthians 1:3-4

In every life, there are seasons that weigh so heavily upon us that we're tempted to despair. When these seasons come, and even after they've left, we will find ourselves seeking to find some level of comfort to help us recuperate from the experience.

What are we seeking to find comfort in? What are we hoping will have the power to soothe our souls? There are dangerous things in this world that offer a false promise of comfort and those things eventually turn into compulsions or addictions if we grant them unhealthy access to our minds and our hearts.

Scripture reminds us that true comfort can be found for our grieving spirits. Through Jesus, we are granted access to the Father. He is the source of mercy. He is the provider of genuine and lasting comfort. He is pleased to comfort us in the midst of our afflictions and grant us His power and wisdom that we can utilize in our efforts to comfort others. His comfort is lasting and in Him we find real peace.

March 9

> *"who saved us and called us to a holy calling, not because of our works but because of his own purpose and grace, which he gave us in Christ Jesus before the ages began"*
> *-2 Timothy 1:9*

It's fascinating and truly beyond human comprehension to fully grasp the fact that our eternal, omniscient God loved us enough to rescue us from our own sin and certain damnation. We were doomed. We were without hope. But now, through the atoning work of Christ Jesus, we have been rescued and placed on a brand new path.

The Lord didn't save us because of anything good we had done. We couldn't earn His favor. We couldn't satisfy His wrath. We couldn't offer Him any excuses. Our righteousness was totally insufficient to match His holiness. So Jesus, the eternal Son of God, gave us the gift of His righteousness, and now we are called holy in God's sight.

God saved us for a purpose. We have a calling. The mission of our lives is the bring glory to Jesus. Our words and our actions testify to His love and compassion. The work we do in this world is now empowered by His strength. The ultimate outcome of the efforts He's accomplishing through us is that more people will come to know Him, and those who do know Him will be built up and encouraged. Each day He blesses us with is a gift and each moment has purpose. How will we choose to live out this holy calling today?

74

March 10

"but in your hearts honor Christ the Lord as holy, always being prepared to make a defense to anyone who asks you for a reason for the hope that is in you; yet do it with gentleness and respect,"
-1 Peter 3:15

There is a big difference in the quality of life between those who are living with hope and those who are living without it. When the Bible uses the term "hope", it's describing something that's certain. It's speaking of a promise that's anchored in the Lord's very nature. To live with hope is to live with complete confidence that everything Christ has promised us will come to pass.

Living with hope has a huge impact on our daily demeanor. It fosters an optimistic perspective. It contributes to our ability to keep trials and setbacks in proper perspective. It helps us avoid getting "stuck in a moment" or mistakenly believing that things won't improve. Our futures are secure in Jesus and He has given us everything good to look forward to.

If this is the kind of perspective that dominates your life, you're likely to draw some attention. At some point, someone who knows you well is going to ask you, "What's your secret? How can you be joyful in a moment like this?" When that day comes, gently and respectfully share that the secret to real hope, and the source of your lasting joy is found in Jesus.

March 11

> *"Know therefore that the Lord your God is God, the faithful God who keeps covenant and steadfast love with those who love him and keep his commandments, to a thousand generations,"*
> *-Deuteronomy 7:9*

In most contexts of life, even in the midst of our deepest human relationships, we often wonder if the promises others make to us will be kept. We're used to promises being broken. We've taught our hearts useful strategies to protect ourselves from disappointment for the moments when others inevitably let us down.

God will never let us down. He will never disappoint us. He is true to His word and it's impossible for Him to lie. He is faithful, and when He makes a covenant, He doesn't break it. In fact, He promises to show His steadfast love toward His people forever.

We see no greater example of this than what was displayed by Jesus during the course of His earthly ministry. People reviled Him. People mocked Him. People hurt Him and eventually killed Him, but He willingly endured it all because He knew He was taking the sin of humanity upon Himself so that we could be eternal beneficiaries of His love. In His resurrection, He broke the power of sin, and His love is forever assured to all who trust in Him.

March 12

> *"by which he has granted to us his precious and very great promises, so that through them you may become partakers of the divine nature, having escaped from the corruption that is in the world because of sinful desire."*
> *-2 Peter 1:4*

Knowing Jesus involves much more than just knowing "about" Him. When we truly know Him, we live in continual relationship with Him. Our hearts are made brand new. Our perspective changes. We begin to see things with His eyes. We start speaking with words that He prompts as He teaches us to live in this world like He did.

In fact, when we came to know Jesus by faith, we were granted a new nature. We are partakers of His divine nature and we are no longer held in chains to the corrupt and sinful desires of this world. The appeal they once had over us has been exposed for the destructive influence it truly is. The damage and ruin the sin of this world was trying to do in our lives has been held up to the light of the gospel and now we can see these things like Jesus sees them.

I don't know if you're feeling trapped in your sin right now, but let me assure you that you are not a prisoner to sin if Jesus is your Lord. Through Jesus, you can escape sin's strangle hold. Through Jesus, you have a brand new nature and the indwelling presence of His power. True freedom is yours in Christ Jesus.

March 13

> *"And we know that for those who love God*
> *all things work together for good, for those*
> *who are called according to his purpose."*
> *-Romans 8:28*

Have you ever tried to trace the hand of God at work throughout the course of your life? Sometimes that can be challenging to do in the moment, but it becomes easier to see His hand at work once we've allowed enough time to pass and we can see more of the effects of what He's been doing.

Sometimes, particularly during trying, upsetting, or confusing times, you might be tempted to question what God is up to and if He is truly looking out for you. But when we take a moment to meditate on the truth of the gospel, we are reminded that it was for our good that Jesus experienced earthy life, physical death, and bodily resurrection. He had our well-being in mind when He was walking through that ordeal.

Those who love the Son, love the Father and this Scripture promises us that God is working all things, even messy, difficult, and upsetting things, together for the good of those who love Him. He has called us unto Himself and He assures us that He will not allow anything to come into our lives that ultimately isn't for His glory and our good. No matter what you may be experiencing during this season of your life, you can confidently trust His promise.

March 14

> *"For this very reason, make every effort to supplement your faith with virtue, and virtue with knowledge, and knowledge with self-control, and self-control with steadfastness, and steadfastness with godliness, and godliness with brotherly affection, and brotherly affection with love. For if these qualities are yours and are increasing, they keep you from being ineffective or unfruitful in the knowledge of our Lord Jesus Christ."*
> *-2 Peter 1:5-8*

Through Jesus we have new life. We are a new creation. In Him, we are continually growing in sanctification as the Holy Spirit fosters holiness within us. We have been made part of the family of God and our Lord is continually making investments in our lives that produce growth and spiritual fruit.

Following His lead, we're also called to make investments in our lives. It's not God's desire that we become complacent Christians who spend multiple decades sitting on our hands. He's called us to put His teaching into practice as an outpouring of our faith. As Christ's disciples, we're challenged to fully devote our lives to following Him in every way.

As we do so, we'll be blessed by the result. Our lives will be marked by effectiveness. Each season we live through will be fruitful. Our knowledge of Christ will grow deeper and our reflection of His heart will become more prominent.

March 15

> *"And there is salvation in no one else, for there is no other name under heaven given among men by which we must be saved."*
> *-Acts 4:12*

Everyone is looking for something or someone to bring them a sense of peace, belonging, healing, security, and unconditional love, but only some people have a clear understanding of where those things can truly be found.

We can tell what our hearts are convinced will save us by observing the priorities of our lives. If you're convinced that an earthly relationship, physical possession, financial windfall, personal achievement, or the respect of your peers can bring you a sense of wholeness, then your sense of well-being will become dependent on one of those things. Your time will be spent chasing it. Your sanity will depend on whether or not what you're chasing loves you back.

But seeking to be "fulfilled" by anything or anyone other than Jesus is destined to result in a broken heart and a crushed spirit. There is one name under heaven, the name of Jesus, where salvation can be found. If we're trying to obtain a sense of peace, comfort, or validation through anything or anyone less than Jesus, we're buying into a harmful lie. But, if we truly come to trust that Jesus is everything our hearts are longing for, we'll experience the contentment and joy He offers us today.

March 16

> *"Put on then, as God's chosen ones, holy and beloved, compassionate hearts, kindness, humility, meekness, and patience,"*
> **-Colossians 3:12**

Do you truly know who you are? That's an important question that's worth wrestling with. Too frequently, we tend to answer that question from a worldly perspective. Sometimes, our answers show that we tend to think of ourselves more from a temporary or earthly view than we think of ourselves from God's eternal view. So, how does God see us?

In Christ, we are referred to as God's "chosen ones." We belong to Him, not accidentally or because we chose Him, but because He chose us. In Christ, we are holy, not because we are sinlessly perfect in our flesh, but because we have been cleansed from our sin by Jesus. In Christ, we are loved, not because we deserve to be, but because the Father looks at us and sees the presence of His Son within us.

If this is who we truly are, then how should we choose to live? We should live in such a way that this world can experience the presence of Christ through the demonstration of our new identity. As we have received compassion and kindness from God, let's be lavish in bestowing those things on others. As Christ displayed humility, meekness, and patience toward us, let's be mindful to follow His example.

March 17

> *"The Lord is my shepherd; I shall not want. He makes me lie down in green pastures. He leads me beside still waters. He restores my soul. He leads me in paths of righteousness for his name's sake."*
> ***-Psalm 23:1-3***

What's your favorite description of the Lord that's mentioned in the Scriptures? The Bible uses word pictures to help us understand more about our Lord's nature and the desire of His heart for His people. In this passage, He's referred to as a shepherd.

Like a shepherd, Jesus looks out for us. He guards our steps. He treats our wounds. He protects us from those who seek to devour us. He meets our needs so we don't lack anything that is necessary for life and godliness.

Jesus grants us rest. He is our source of strength, nourishment, and refreshment. He grants us life everlasting. He leads us in the direction He wants us to go, and the path He's directing us to walk in is the path of life and righteousness.

There is no greater love and no more substantial care than that which we receive from Jesus. Jesus laid down His life for His sheep and now we have the privilege of hearing the voice of our Shepherd call us unto Himself.

March 18

> *"May the God of hope fill you with all joy and peace in believing, so that by the power of the Holy Spirit you may abound in hope."*
> *-Romans 15:13*

After having experienced a relationship with God through faith in Jesus Christ, could you imagine going through this season of your life without Him? Even if we tried, we couldn't accurately quantify all the good He has brought to our lives.

When we came to faith in Jesus, we welcomed God's presence into our lives. He is the source of hope. He is pleased to fill us with joy and peace through faith in Him. And the joy and peace we receive from Him isn't dependent on external circumstances. It doesn't rest on whether or not we've had a good day or a bad day. It doesn't require everything to be going perfectly this week or this year. The joy and peace He offers us is anchored in His unchanging nature.

His presence also changes our perspective. Our outlook toward the future is now hopeful. In fact, the Holy Spirit is actively fostering hope within the lives of all believers through the working of His power. And He doesn't supply just a little hope, but rather, He makes it abound in our lives. The Lord is filling us with His joy, peace, and hope as we walk by faith in Him. By His grace, we're living a blessed life.

March 19

> *"But the fruit of the Spirit is love, joy,*
> *peace, patience, kindness, goodness,*
> *faithfulness, gentleness, self-control;*
> *against such things there is no law."*
> *-Galatians 5:22-23*

It is often said that a tree is known by it's fruit. That concept is mentioned regarding people, multiple times in the Scriptures. The essence of our true identity is demonstrated by the fruit that is produced in our lives.

By grace, through faith, we are united with Jesus. He is the vine and we are the branches. Our union with Him is our connection to life. Jesus nourishes and sustains us daily.

Likewise, the Holy Spirit lives within us, and His presence produces a noticeable affect on our lives. He changes us from within to produce Christ-like attributes that He likewise empowers to operate in our lives. These attributes are referred to as "fruit" and they serve as a visible demonstration of our union with Jesus.

The Holy Spirit fosters love, joy, peace, patience, kindness, goodness, faithfulness, gentleness, and self-control in the lives of God's people. The active display of this fruit serves as a powerful testimony of our love for Jesus. It is convincing proof of His power. It goes far beyond our natural capabilities and can be the very thing the Lord uses to convince others to trust Him as well. Where is Christ calling you to display this fruit?

March 20

> *"Like newborn infants, long for the pure spiritual milk, that by it you may grow up into salvation— if indeed you have tasted that the Lord is good."*
> *-1 Peter 2:2-3*

Healthy bodies feel hunger. Hunger is a good thing. It's a sign that our bodies have an appetite for what will nourish us. It's a signal that our brain is giving off that it's time for more nutrients to sustain us.

Even infants are aware of their need for nourishment. God has given them the instinctive ability to cry as a signal to their mother that it's time to be fed. They crave the nourishment their mother's milk can provide and their little stomachs are fed nutrients and antibodies that keep them healthy and help them fight off disease and infection.

In the spiritual sense, God's word encourages us to long for the spiritual nourishment He seeks to provide. As we ingest the content of His word and the counsel of the Holy Spirit, our faith in Christ matures. Our salvation becomes more evident. We progress from spiritual infancy toward spiritual maturity.

There are all kinds of things set before us each day that we may tend to crave and pursue, but if it is our desire to possess a faith in Christ that's growing stronger and healthier, we need the nourishment of His word.

March 21

> *"Blessed is the man who trusts in the Lord, whose trust is the Lord. He is like a tree planted by water, that sends out its roots by the stream, and does not fear when heat comes, for its leaves remain green, and is not anxious in the year of drought, for it does not cease to bear fruit."*
> *-Jeremiah 17:7-8*

Throughout the course of our lives, there are plenty of things that might prompt us to be fearful. Usually, when we trace back the root of our fear, it comes down to something we can't control. We can't control the future. We can't control the unknown. We can't control what other people do to us or say to us. We can't control surprises. It can become rather easy to live in fear because there is so much in this world that is completely outside of our control.

Fear has a cousin named anxiety. We feel anxious about what we fear. We worry. But trust is the antidote to worry and the man who learns to trust in Jesus is blessed. He roots his life, not in the things he can't control, but in Jesus who has everything under His control.

The fruit of fear is worry. The fruit of faith is confidence. Not confidence in ourselves, but confidence in Christ who holds our lives securely in His hand. He loves us. He's present with us, and won't abandon us in the midst of this journey.

March 22

> *"Finally, be strong in the Lord and in the strength of his might. Put on the whole armor of God, that you may be able to stand against the schemes of the devil."*
> *-Ephesians 6:10-11*

It isn't pleasant to think about, but the reality it, we have an enemy that is working against us daily. Our enemy doesn't have flesh and blood. He isn't visible to us, although the fruit of his efforts certainly are. He isn't working alone. In fact, he has legions of individuals who partner with him to conspire our demise. Satan and the demons who align with him continually oppose and scheme against the followers of Jesus.

The Holy Spirit exposes the schemes of Satan. He helps us see and perceive the things that the devil is attempting to do to us. The devil tempts us with the goal of encouraging us to fall into life-long addictions. He enjoys destroying our reputations. He loves hurting our families. And he takes great delight in working behind the scenes in ways that make it difficult to realize he's been scheming against us.

But we are not powerless in this battle. Christ's power is infinitely greater than Satan's schemes. As we trust in Jesus, glean wisdom from His word, pray for His protection, and heed the counsel of the Holy Spirit, we are equipped for this battle. He enlightens our minds to the truth and He plants our feet firmly so we can stand.

March 23

> *"Blessed is the man who remains steadfast under trial, for when he has stood the test he will receive the crown of life, which God has promised to those who love him."*
> *-James 1:12*

Some of the most difficult seasons of our lives contribute to some of the greatest blessings we'll ever experience.

In every life, there are trials and tribulations. When those things come our way, we typically struggle to appreciate them in the moment. But as time progresses, we can look back on those things and acknowledge that the Lord used those experiences to deepen our faith and bolster our perseverance.

Our trials have a way of clarifying our beliefs. It's easy to claim that we trust Jesus in all circumstances, when things are going well, but it's much harder to express genuine trust in Him when trails come our way. Those moments have a way of proving to our hearts just how deeply we believe in Him to begin with.

In the coming days, you'll experience some smaller tests and some greater trials. Jesus will be with you in the midst of it all. As you rely on His strength to remain steadfast in the midst of adversity, He has promised to bless you on the other side of it.

March 24

> *"For the wages of sin is death, but the free gift of God is eternal life in Christ Jesus our Lord."*
> *-Romans 6:23*

What do we truly deserve in life? When we work at our vocations, we do so, in part, with the desire to get paid something that adequately rewards our efforts. We look at that payment and consider it something that we deserve because we've earned it. It feels right to receive it. It feels merited. It feels fair.

What do we deserve from God? If we're truly honest, we should be glad He doesn't give us what we deserve. Because our sin is such an offense to His holiness, we deserve condemnation. We deserve judgment. We deserve separation from all that is good. In fact, the Scripture tells us that the wages or the payment our sin has earned us is death. That's what we deserved. Thankfully, that's not the end of the story.

Our compassionate God looked at us and graciously chose to offer us a gift that is the opposite of what we have earned. We earned death, but He offers us the free gift of eternal life through faith in His Son, Jesus Christ. This gift is free to us, but is costly to Him. Jesus paid the penalty we should have been forced to pay. He died in our place, then defeated death's stranglehold over us when He rose from the grave. There is no gift greater than the gift of eternal life Christ offers all who believe.

March 25

"If we confess our sins, he is faithful and just to forgive us our sins and to cleanse us from all unrighteousness."
-1 John 1:9

We all have areas of our lives, or matters of personal struggle that we aren't very proud of. Secret sins that we struggle with, that would probably feel quite embarrassing to have to admit to someone else. Things that we keep inside and try our best to cover up. Unfortunately, the longer that continues, the worse the problem becomes.

Sin loves the cover of darkness. If it can operate in the dark, it can do damage in our lives for as long as we let it. When it's exposed to the light, however, it loses it's power because it's shown to be the kind of destructive force it's been trying to pretend that it isn't.

Jesus paid for our sins. His death on the cross was sufficient to atone for what we've said, done, thought, and wrestled with our whole lives. If we truly believe in Him, we are forgiven. That means it's safe to confess our sins to the Lord. He already knows them anyway. He's already covered them with His blood. He doesn't want them to continue to operate as a secret destructive force any longer. Christ's desire for us is that we live in the freedom He has secured for us. Therefore, we're called to confess our sin to Him and allow Him to cleanse all unrighteousness from our lives.

March 26

> *"For it has been granted to you that for the sake of Christ you should not only believe in him but also suffer for his sake,"*
> *-Philippians 1:29*

What did you assume the Christian life would be like when you first came to faith in Christ? For most of us, there is an assumption that everything is going to get better and most aspects of life will become smoother. We tend to picture a more comfortable existence in this world. But is this what Jesus has promised us? Is that what His word actually teaches?

It's certainly true that the Lord is working out all things in our lives for our good. It's also true that He is present with us as our Counselor and Comforter. It's even true that He is actively preparing a place for us with Him in eternity that will far outshine anything we have ever seen or experienced as far as a dwelling is concerned. But it would be a mistake to assume that our earthly lives will not also include suffering.

Jesus suffered during the course of His earthly ministry. As we follow Him, we may be called to do likewise. But He has a purpose for our suffering. It may strengthen our confidence in Him and reliance on Him. It may be used as a testimony to unbelievers to help them come to know Him. It may help us shake off the grip of sin and personal idols. Christ has a purpose for our suffering and He's present with us while we endure it. If you're suffering, trust that He knows what He's doing and believe that He's working out His plan for your greater good.

March 27

> *"On God rests my salvation and my glory; my mighty rock, my refuge is God."*
> *-Psalm 62:7*

There are quite a few things that mankind tries to build their lives upon, but a foundation other than Jesus Christ is a shaky, temporary foundation that is destined to disappoint.

On the contrary, the Lord never disappoints His children. A life that is anchored in Jesus is a life that's destined to experience great joy and the peace that passes all understanding.

Our sense of peace, satisfaction, and rest finds its certainty in the Lord Himself. In Him, we find rest for our souls. In Him is our salvation secured. In Him we find real refuge and the kind of protection our souls deeply crave.

The Scripture refers to the Lord as our "mighty rock." He isn't swayed by fear. He isn't moved by the changing whims of human preference. He is our unchanging God and He will always be the perfection of love, grace, mercy, forgiveness, and righteousness. His eternal nature cannot be altered.

There are many things that may change about our daily circumstances, but we don't need to worry. Our souls find rest in Jesus. Our eternal hope is secure in Him.

March 28

> *"For there is one God, and there is one mediator between God and men, the man Christ Jesus, who gave himself as a ransom for all, which is the testimony given at the proper time."*
> *-1 Timothy 2:5-6*

Arguments and disputes can be rather uncomfortable things. We've all experienced them and we've all witnessed the damage they can do to relationships. People hold grudges. People feel cheated. Even close family members can stop talking to each other because of unresolved conflict.

In the spiritual realm, we were in conflict with God Himself. We were sinful and He is holy. We practiced evil, He exercised justice. His kingdom is a place of joy, but we were doomed to an eternity of sorrow.

But then Jesus intervened. Jesus, the Son of God, mediated the conflict between God and man. To satisfy the righteous wrath of God against the sin of humanity, Jesus suffered and died in our place. He gave Himself as a substitutionary sacrifice for us all, at just the right time, and He invites us to receive His gift of salvation, a gift He paid for with His blood.

Now, as people who have been forgiven, we're invited to forgive others. As people who have had our conflict mediated, we're encouraged to show grace and mercy.

> *"For our sake he made him to be sin who knew no sin, so that in him we might become the righteousness of God."*
> *-2 Corinthians 5:21*

When you're a parent, you do things for the benefit of your children, every day, that they often have no idea you're doing. Your thoughts and prayers for their well-being tend to be one of your primary prayer requests. You look out for them in ways that only you can.

Our Heavenly Father looks out for us and has done for us something that only He could choose to do. God the Father has chosen to look at us - we who are sinners from birth - and decided to declare us righteous. How? On what basis has that been done?

Jesus, God the Son, took on flesh and suffered for us. He never sinned, yet He was treated as if He did. He was treated as if He was the one at fault for our sin. Jesus did this for us so that we could experience the joys of forgiveness. He made our problem, His problem. And He solved it once and for all.

Now, anyone who trusts Jesus - accepting the work He accomplished to atone for our sin, is declared righteous by God. The righteousness of Christ is miraculously added to our account and we can live every day, confident of the fact that our Lord loves us and we will be spending eternity in His presence.

March 30

> *"Surely he has borne our griefs and carried our sorrows; yet we esteemed him stricken, smitten by God, and afflicted."*
> *-Isaiah 53:4*

The earthly ministry of Jesus didn't exactly look like some people expected it would. Of the people living at the time who believed in the prophesies regarding the coming Messiah, the majority were primarily looking for Him to rule and reign as a political leader and king. Jesus will one day rule on this earth in that capacity, but at the time of His first coming, His objective was to take the burden of our sin upon Himself. He came to suffer and die for humanity and offer us new life through Him.

Jesus suffered for us in love, but He was mocked and jeered while He did so. The crowds didn't believe He was God. They considered Him afflicted or punished by God. But, with perfect compassion, Jesus bore our sin at the cross willingly.

Just as Jesus bore our sin at the cross, He also desires to carry our burdens and sorrows today. Many of us spend far too many years trying to carry burdens that we aren't capable of carrying instead of giving them to Jesus. His perfect compassion extends to the things that weigh our hearts down today. Do we trust Him enough to handle these concerns or will we spend the rest of our days trying to carry these burdens alone?

March 31

> *"But he was pierced for our transgressions; he was crushed for our iniquities; upon him was the chastisement that brought us peace, and with his wounds we are healed."*
> *-Isaiah 53:5*

How do you know that you're loved? What would it take for your heart to become truly convinced that you are loved in the deepest way possible?

Hundreds of years before Christ accomplished it, Isaiah described, in detail, what Jesus would do for us. This prophecy tells us that Jesus would be pierced for us because of our sin. Every nail that held Jesus to the cross was pierced through His body because He loved us enough to bear the penalty for our sin. The sword that pierced His side and the thorns that pierced His head also testify to the depth of His love and what He was willing to endure for our good.

Jesus was wounded so that we could be healed. He suffered so that we could find forgiveness through faith in Him. He bore our iniquities upon Himself so that we could be released from them and spend all our days as His forgiven family.

Jesus experienced anguish so that we could live in peace. Our punishment was placed upon Him so now we can live free from the bondage of sin.

April 1

The fool says in his heart, "There is no God." They are corrupt, they do abominable deeds; there is none who does good.
-Psalm 14:1

As much as we might try to deny it, there are some things that God has made abundantly obvious to us. By taking a casual look at creation, we can clearly see that it has been deliberately designed in intricate detail. There are systems and laws in place that operate in nature that scream out to us that there must be a God who brought to life the created world around us.

It is foolish to deny God's existence, but even with such obvious evidence of His hand at work all around us, there are those who choose to ignore Him. They choose not to see His fingerprints on every leaf, every creature, and every person. That's tragic.

God has made it clear to us that He wants to be known. He has revealed Himself to us in multiple ways. The ultimate revelation of God is found in Jesus Christ. Jesus is God in the flesh. He walked among us. Healed us. Raised the dead, yet people still denied Him. Even today, there are some who dismiss Jesus completely.

But still there is hope. God delights to save foolish people like we were. Who is He calling you to pray for today? Who still needs to see Him?

April 2

> *And as Jesus was going up to Jerusalem, he took the twelve disciples aside, and on the way he said to them, "See, we are going up to Jerusalem. And the Son of Man will be delivered over to the chief priests and scribes, and they will condemn him to death and deliver him over to the Gentiles to be mocked and flogged and crucified, and he will be raised on the third day."*
> *-Matthew 20:17-19*

Imagine what it would be like to know when and how you were going to experience death. Would you want to know? Would that trouble you?

Jesus knew when and how He was going to experience death. This wasn't a mystery to Him. This was part of the divine plan to rescue mankind from our sin, and because Jesus was looking forward to our salvation, He willingly endured this all.

Jesus also knew that while death would be painful to experience, it wouldn't ultimately defeat Him. He would defeat death. Just as He assured His disciples, He rose from the grave on the third day. Jesus was victorious over death and He shares that victory with everyone who trusts in Him.

If Christ lives within you, there is no worldly trial you need to fear. Jesus is victorious.

April 3

> *"looking to Jesus, the founder and perfecter of our faith, who for the joy that was set before him endured the cross, despising the shame, and is seated at the right hand of the throne of God."*
> **-Hebrews 12:2**

Everyone needs help. We all need the Lord's intervention in our lives. Thankfully, Christ offers us the kind of help we truly need. He's the one we're encouraged to look to.

Jesus is the perfecter of our faith. He helps our faith to deepen and grow strong. He demonstrates the nature of true faith and invites us to walk with Him daily.

Jesus was not unwilling to bear the cross. Looking to the future with joy, He endured the pain and shame the cross brought. He could see that His sacrificial act would atone for our sin and that through Him, we could live forever. That's what was on His mind when He was on the cross. That's why the shame of the experience wasn't sufficient to stop Him from accepting the suffering that was cast upon Him.

Jesus is victorious. He sits at the right hand of God the Father, and He has assured us that in the fullness of time, He will be coming to this earth once again. This has been His plan from eternity past, and by His grace, we have the privilege of being the beneficiaries.

April 4

> *"In him we have redemption through his blood, the forgiveness of our trespasses, according to the riches of his grace,"*
> **-Ephesians 1:7**

There are various portions of Scripture that outline the depths of what Christ accomplished for us, and this is one of those verses. Pause for just a moment to consider what we're being told in this passage...

In Jesus, we have been redeemed. This means He has delivered us from slavery to sin and has granted us freedom from it's dominion in our lives. He has delivered us from future, eternal condemnation, and has blessed us with the gift of His salvation, by grace, through faith.

Christ's blood was the currency He used to pay the penalty for our sin. In our sinfulness, we never could have paid that penalty in a way that would satisfy God's holiness and justice, but Jesus could, so He did.

In Jesus, our sins have been completely forgiven. When we place our trust in Him, we are perfectly pardoned and our sin is no longer held against us. We are forgiven by God, enabled to forgive ourselves, and encouraged to forgive those who have sinned against us. The riches of Christ's grace have been lavishly poured out into all areas of our hearts, minds, and lives.

April 5

> *"For the love of Christ controls us, because we have concluded this: that one has died for all, therefore all have died; and he died for all, that those who live might no longer live for themselves but for him who for their sake died and was raised."*
> *-2 Corinthians 5:14-15*

The prevailing mindset of a genuine believer in Christ stands out as being quiet different from the rest of this world. Many people in this world are being controlled by the passions and desires of the sinful nature. They do its bidding. They submit to its cravings. But those who have experienced Christ's salvation are compelled and controlled by His love. His love motivates their behavior, mindset, and outlook.

Jesus treats us with selfless love. We see that on display in His work on the cross as He willingly died for us. He showed us what it truly looks like to put others before ourselves. He showed us the nature of true, sacrificial love. And He invites us to follow His example - bolstered by the strength He supplies.

While many people in this world may choose to live primarily for themselves, we have been invited to live for Christ. We live for Him who defeated death and rose from the grave. The priorities of our old nature have been defeated so in Christ, we are truly alive.

April 6

"By this we know love, that he laid down his life for us, and we ought to lay down our lives for the brothers."
-1 John 3:16

Years ago, I knew a man who was experiencing kidney failure. If he didn't receive a new, transplanted kidney, he would definitely die. His family, including his extended family, was tested to see if anyone might be a donor candidate. It turned out that his father-in-law was a match, so that man willingly gave his kidney and risked his own life to save the life of his son-in-law.

Laying down our lives for the sake of our brothers and sisters in Christ is a principle that finds its foundation in the work Jesus Christ accomplished for us at the cross. He died so we could live. He gave His life so we could experience everlasting life. He rose to life so we could experience the joys of resurrected life.

Laying down your life is not a naturally easy thing to do. It involves a complete transformation of thinking. It involves valuing the well-being of someone else more than you value your own needs. It requires us to take a good, hard look at what Jesus actually did for us, and it inspires us to gain a deeper appreciation of His sacrifice.

How can we lay down our lives for our Christian family today? Whose needs has Christ called us to prioritize?

April 7

> *"I have been crucified with Christ. It is no longer I who live, but Christ who lives in me. And the life I now live in the flesh I live by faith in the Son of God, who loved me and gave himself for me."*
> ***-Galatians 2:20***

What are some of the distinct lines you can draw in your life? Are those lines marked by major events? Are they marked by changes in your direction or focus? Are they marked by difficult lessons you were forced to learn?

The truth is, if you are "in Christ", you are no longer who you used to be. You're a new person. Your old passions and the cravings of your sinful nature were crucified with Christ. Now, you have a new identity, new priorities, and a new life that cannot be extinguished.

This new life you've been blessed with doesn't operate like your old life did. You used to live for yourself and the lusts of your old nature. You used to practice a form of "self worship." Now, your faith is in Christ and you have found a new source of strength in Him. The Holy Spirit is empowering you to be an effective witness for Christ in this world. He is opening up doors for you to walk through. He is calling the shots and guiding the course of the life He has blessed you with.

April 8

> *"For if while we were enemies we were reconciled to God by the death of his Son, much more, now that we are reconciled, shall we be saved by his life."*
> **-Romans 5:10**

To reconcile means to take something that's distant and bring it near. Often we use the term in reference to relationship that have become distant for some reason. In your life, you may have at one point experienced a relationship that was at one time strained, become reconciled. Reconciliation is a beautiful thing and it's worth striving for.

The perfect relationship man once had with God was damaged in the Garden of Eden when man sinned. At that point, man set himself against God's will and went his own way. In that moment, we became enemies of God. But God chose to reconcile that lost relationship.

Jesus Christ came to this earth to bridge the gap between man and God. Through faith in Him, we experience a reconciled relationship with our Creator. We are transformed from living as God's enemies to living as God's beloved family. We who were far away are brought near to Him.

As God has reconciled us to Himself in Christ Jesus, so too should we be eager to foster an atmosphere of reconciliation within our human relationships. Who is currently distant from you that can be brought near?

April 9

> *"He is the radiance of the glory of God and the exact imprint of his nature, and he upholds the universe by the word of his power. After making purification for sins, he sat down at the right hand of the Majesty on high,"*
> ***-Hebrews 1:3***

"Who do you think Jesus is?" If you asked that question to some people, you might be surprised at the answers you got. Some speak of Jesus as being a good teacher. Others claim He was a prophet. Some believe He was crazy. But what does this Scripture reveal to us about Him?

The first thing this verse tells us is that Jesus, by nature, is divine. Jesus is God who took on flesh. He is the exact imprint of God's nature in all His attributes, abilities, and character. He is the sinless source of life.

By Christ's word, all things were created and all things are currently being sustained. He's holding everything He created together. Without Him, creation would not be upheld.

He is also the one who has purified us from our sins by shedding His blood for us at the cross. Having completed all that was necessary for our salvation, He sat down at the right hand of the Father. Jesus is God, and in love, He accomplished this all on our behalf.

April 10

> *"For while we were still weak, at the right time Christ died for the ungodly. For one will scarcely die for a righteous person—though perhaps for a good person one would dare even to die— but God shows his love for us in that while we were still sinners, Christ died for us."*
> **-Romans 5:6-8**

Who is the most offensive person you've ever encountered? Someone in your family? Someone you've worked with? How offensive are they to you? Do you struggle to pray for them? Could you imagine giving your life for them?

We were offensive to Jesus. Our sinfulness was a complete offense to His holiness and there was nothing we could do to fix that. We were weak and helpless to correct that problem. We were living as Christ's enemies. We were ignorant of who He is. We didn't care about Him in any respect.

But Jesus looked at us with compassion. In the midst of our weak and helpless estate, He extended His strength. He willingly chose to die in our place. While we were still enslaved to sin and still ignoring Him, He shed His blood for us at the cross. There isn't a deeper, more sacrificial form of love than that.

You didn't, and you still don't have to be perfect to experience Christ's love. He loved you before you loved Him. Speak that truth to your heart today.

April 11

> *"He himself bore our sins in his body on the tree, that we might die to sin and live to righteousness. By his wounds you have been healed."*
> *-1 Peter 2:24*

The price Jesus paid for our freedom from sin is beyond our natural ability to calculate. Knowing full well what He was doing, He bore the penalty for our sins in His body when He died in our place at the cross.

Why did Jesus do this? He did this so that we would be healed from the effects of sin. He did this so we would no longer need to be enslaved to sin. He did this to give us a new reason to live. If we truly believe in Jesus, we are no longer under the mastery of sin. We have been made alive through Jesus, and empowered with His strength which enables us to practice righteousness.

The sinful inclinations of our old nature have demanded too much time and mental energy from each of us. We have dwelled on those things long enough. Now, through Jesus, we can be truly productive, and we can fulfill His greater purpose for our lives.

Whatever used to control you before you met Jesus, doesn't need to control you any longer. Were you controlled by anger? Bitterness? Deceit? Lust? Covetousness? Their mastery over you has been broken. Jesus is your Lord and now you live for Him.

April 12

> *"And he said to all, "If anyone would come after me, let him deny himself and take up h i s c r o s s d a i l y a n d f o l l o w me. For whoever would save his life will lose it, but whoever loses his life for my sake will save it."*
> **-Luke 9:23-24**

The things of this world have an allure to us that is difficult to shake. There are all kinds of things that Christ knows we may begin to covet if left to our natural preferences. But He invites us to experience a different kind of life than that. In some respects, it's a harder kind of life, but in all respects, it's a better life than the one we leave behind.

A true follower of Christ gives up the idolization of the best things of this world because they know they have everything they need in Jesus. A true follower of Christ is willing to be rejected in this world because they find perfect acceptance in Jesus. A true follower of Christ welcomes the leading of the Lord in their life and follows His prompting.

There is nothing that this world can offer us that can't be eventually taken away. If we wrap our lives up in temporary things, we're setting ourselves up for failure and disappointment. But if we recognize that Jesus is who our hearts truly long for, we find peace and satisfaction in Him, and He assures us that in Him, we will find the life we truly crave.

April 13

"for all have sinned and fall short of the glory of God, and are justified by his grace as a gift, through the redemption that is in Christ Jesus,"
-Romans 3:23-24

We all start out in the same boat. There isn't such a thing as "good people" and "bad people." From birth, we were all sinners. From the start, we were living in direct rebellion against God. From day one, the desires of our heart were set against Him. Not a single one of us can claim to be sinless. We have all fallen short of God's perfect, glorious standard.

But God being rich in mercy chose to remedy that problem. Through faith in Jesus Christ, we are granted the gift of being justified. That means we're declared righteous by God, even though we were born sinful.

Through faith in Jesus we are redeemed. That means He purchased our freedom from slavery to sin by shedding His blood on our behalf. Jesus died and rose again so we can experience the blessing of new, everlasting life, through Him.

And the beauty of this all is that even though we still struggle with sin, we can have victory over it through Jesus who lives within us. God the Father now looks at us as holy and blameless in His sight because the righteousness of Christ is covering us.

April 14

> *"Now I would remind you, brothers, of the gospel I preached to you, which you received, in which you stand,"*
> **-1 Corinthians 15:1**

Being forgetful is something we all struggle with to a certain degree. You probably write notes to yourself regularly to keep track of tasks you need to complete. You probably ask friends and family members to remind you of things you don't want to overlook or neglect. We all do that. It's a common struggle.

But there is something that God's word makes a special effort to remind us of throughout every book that it contains. The Lord has ensured that all throughout the Scriptures we'll be reminded of the gospel. Through direct teaching, narratives, comparisons, and other examples, we're shown the importance of the life, death, and resurrection of Jesus. This isn't just a message that's meant for unbelievers to read. It's also meant for believers to be dwelling on daily so we don't forget it.

We couldn't live the perfect life, so Jesus lived it for us. We couldn't satisfy God's wrath toward our sin, so Jesus payed the penalty for us. We didn't have hope beyond this life, so Jesus rose from the grave and defeated sin, Satan, and death's power over us. Now through faith in Him, we have a living hope. We need to be reminded of these truths daily. In our darkest or brightest moments, we can never forget all Jesus has done for us.

April 15

"For because of this you also pay taxes, for the authorities are ministers of God, attending to this very thing. Pay to all what is owed to them: taxes to whom taxes are owed, revenue to whom revenue is owed, respect to whom respect is owed, honor to whom honor is owed."
-Romans 13:6-7

If humanity was left to themselves, there would be chaos. Knowing this to be the case, the Lord has established a series of authorities in our lives. He has established governments and other authorities as agents that are in place to do His bidding. Sometimes these authorities are conscious of this privileged responsibility. Other times, they are not. But just the same, the Lord has called us to honor them.

We honor our government by contributing toward its expenses via taxes and other forms of revenue. We honor other leaders by showing them respect because we recognize why God has granted them their position.

We even see this as a pattern during the course of Christ's earthly ministry. He showed respect toward governmental authorities, but also reminded them that they would have no authority if it hadn't been granted to them from above.

How can we be honoring the authorities the Lord has placed in our lives? How should we be praying for them today? How will they know we respect them?

April 16

"Owe no one anything, except to love each other, for the one who loves another has fulfilled the law."
-Romans 13:8

Debt is an issue that many of us wrestle with in our culture. It's not uncommon to have a mortgage, car loans, student loans, credit card debt, and personal loans all at the same time. As our debt grows, how do we feel? Eventually, if it isn't brought under control and eradicated, it starts to suffocate us and produce unhealthy stress.

Debt may be a cultural preference, but it isn't something the Lord encourages us to embrace. This is especially true when we consider the fact that Christ paid the debt we owed because of our sin. He has set us free from that burden. He covered the cost for us. Why become unnecessarily indebted in the natural world when, spiritually speaking, our debt has been cancelled? Wouldn't it be better, as a practical way of acknowledging that Christ has paid our debts, to live without burdening ourselves with financial debts?

If we're going to owe someone anything, it shouldn't be money, it should be love. We should never come to a place where we stop investing Christ-empowered love into the lives of one another. In each of our lives, there are people who need a glimpse of the love of Christ and we are His chosen vessels to display it.

April 17

*"For the word of the cross is folly
to those who are perishing, but to us who
are being saved it is the power of God."*
-1 Corinthians 1:18

Children say funny things. They make up stories,
invent words, giggle over silliness, and entertain just
about everyone with their creativity. And while this can
be comical, rarely does anyone take it seriously. It's
meant to be comedic and creative, and we treat their
stories like "fairy tales."

Sadly, in some respects, the message of the cross is
through of the same way by many people in this world.
The fact that God took on flesh, was born a man, lived a
sinless life, died on a cross, rose from the grave,
ascended back to Heaven, and promised to return,
sounds like folklore or a science-fiction novel to some
people, and that's tragic.

If you believe the message of the cross to be accurate,
the only reason you can see it as true is because the
Holy Spirit opened your eyes to be able to understand
and accept it. That being said, we ought to be praying
that He would do the same for others that we love so
they won't continue to dismiss the very truth of God's
generous offer to grant them life everlasting.

Who specifically has Christ placed on your heart to pray
for today? Lift that person up to the Lord by name.

April 18

"because, if you confess with your mouth that Jesus is Lord and believe in your heart that God raised him from the dead, you will be saved. For with the heart one believes and is justified, and with the mouth one confesses and is saved."
-Romans 10:9-10

Our eternal life comes down to who we recognize Jesus to be and how we relate to Him. It's one thing to know about Him, but it's another thing all together to have a genuine relationship with Him by faith.

The Scripture tells us that we are invited to confess our belief that Jesus is Lord. This means we're confessing that He is our God and has ultimate power over our lives. Do we confess this?

We're also invited to believe that Christ rose from death. This means we believe that He isn't a dead, Middle-Eastern teacher. He's alive and He is the source of our eternal life. He conquered death when He rose from His tomb. Do we believe this?

If we place our faith in our risen Savior, Jesus Christ, we are saved. We are eternally rescued. We are promised a place in God's presence forever. The Lord has revealed these things to us because He loves us. He invites us to receive the gift of salvation through faith in Jesus Christ and to live with confidence in the fact that He is the source of our life and our hope.

April 19

> *"But in fact Christ has been raised from the dead, the firstfruits of those who have fallen asleep. For as by a man came death, by a man has come also the resurrection of the dead. For as in Adam all die, so also in Christ shall all be made alive."*
> ***-1 Corinthians 15:20-22***

Every day we live is another day we should be truly thankful for the resurrection of Jesus. Our life and our faith rest on the fact that He rose from the grave. Jesus was the first to rise with an immortal body and He gives us an example of the kind of future that awaits all who trust in Him. We too will be resurrected.

At one time, we were under the curse of death. We had fear when we looked toward the future because we knew that eventually, we were going to have to face our mortality. Through our forefather Adam who rebelled against God and was the first to experience death, death has also been passed along to all of his natural children.

But Christ defeated death. He didn't just defeat it conceptually, but personally. If you trust in Him, He will make you truly alive and will guarantee that you will be blessed with eternal life in His presence. You don't need to fear the curse of death because Christ took that curse upon Himself so you would be made alive through Him. Live then, as one who embraces this truth.

April 20

> *"The memory of the righteous is a blessing, but the name of the wicked will rot."*
> *-Proverbs 10:7*

People underestimate what the Lord can do through their individual lives. Most people seem to think you have to have some sort of extraordinary talent or skill to truly make an impact on the life of someone else. But the truth is, we are already equipped through the Holy Spirit, to make lasting investments in the lives of others.

As a recipient of Christ's love, show His love to those He places in your life. Every relationship you have is by design. There is no one you know by accident. God foreordained where and when you would live, and He has placed you as His ambassador to your family, friends, co-workers, and neighbors.

How will they remember you? Will you be remembered as someone who took an interest in them? Will you be remembered as someone who sacrificially served them? Will you be remembered as someone who shared a steady dose of encouragement with them?

Here's a question we would be wise to ask ourselves today and every day, *"How does Christ want to display His heart through me today?"* If you spend your remaining years with this as your focus, not only will you be remembered as a blessing, but Christ will also be honored in remembrances of you.

April 21

> *"I give them eternal life, and they will never perish, and no one will snatch them out of my hand. My Father, who has given them to me, is greater than all, and no one is able to snatch them out of the Father's hand. I and the Father are one."*
> *-John 10:28-30*

There is security in our relationship with Jesus.

In the context of human relationships, many of us have experienced people who in one moment seemed to love us, but in the next were quick to abandon us. This dichotomy can make us hesitant to trust others and more apt to keep our hearts guarded.

But Jesus offers us a different kind of relationship based on the most secure form of love possible. Jesus promises us that if we truly believe in Him, He will grant us eternal life and no one will ever, under any circumstance, be capable of snatching us out of His hand. It can't be done, nor will He allow it to be done.

Satan cannot snatch us out of Christ's loving hand. Our circumstances cannot snatch us out of Christ's loving hand. Our fears, our doubts, our worst days, and our failures cannot snatch us out of Christ's loving hand.

Christ's love for us isn't anchored in who we are or what we do. His love is a secure expression of His unchanging nature. He won't let us go.

April 22

"For his invisible attributes, namely, his eternal power and divine nature, have been clearly perceived, ever since the creation of the world, in the things that have been made. So they are without excuse."
-Romans 1:20

Many people in this world are wondering if God exists? Does He? If so, what evidence has He given to confirm that?

One of the clearest forms of evidence that points to the existence of God is His creation. Both a casual and a close look at the created world, testifies to the existence of a Creator.

In this world we observe symmetry, regeneration, reproduction, complexity and intentionality. Why do we have eyebrows? Because God intentionally placed them there to keep sweat out of our eyes. Why do trees shed their leaves before snowy weather comes? Because God designed them to, so that their branches wouldn't break from the weight of the snow sticking to the added surface area. God's creation reveals to us that He, the designer, exists.

And in addition to natural revelation, God sent His Son, Jesus Christ, as the ultimate testimony and definitive proof of His existence. We are without excuse if we choose to reject what He has clearly revealed.

April 23

> *for it is written,*
> *"As I live, says the Lord, every knee shall*
> *bow to me, and every tongue shall*
> *confess to God."*
> ***-Romans 14:11***

Accountability is a good thing. It's something we all need. It helps us to stay focused on what is right, and remain teachable when we need to make corrections. The Lord doesn't want us to isolate ourselves from one another because doing so results in less accountability and less growth.

Ultimately, we are accountable for our lives to the Lord Himself. Both the Old and New Testaments speak of a day when every person is going to have to come before the Lord and give an account for their lives. Those who have received the free gift of salvation through faith in Jesus will also be rewarded in accordance with their faithfulness to Him. Those who have rejected Christ will be condemned and cast away from His presence for all eternity.

It's certainly true that the day is coming when every knee is going to bow before the Lord and every tongue is going to acknowledge who He truly is, but it's also true that we have the great privilege of making that the pattern of our every day lives. Today is another day when we can testify to His mastery over our lives. We bow our knees before the One we're ultimately accountable to.

April 24

> *"knowing that you were ransomed from the futile ways inherited from your forefathers, not with perishable things such as silver or gold, but with the precious blood of Christ, like that of a lamb without blemish or spot."*
> *-1 Peter 1:18-19*

There are all kinds of things we learn from others and all kinds of ways we have been influenced by those who have come before us. Some of those influences have been healthy and productive, but others have been harmful, selfish, short-sighted, and counterproductive.

Jesus accomplished many great things for us in His act of redemption, and one of those things was to rescue us from thinking and living in unhealthy ways like those who came before us.

We don't have to be selfish people, because Christ has blessed us with a new perspective and a new way to live. We don't have to be consumed with unhealthy ways of thinking because Christ has blessed us with a new mind. We don't have to preach false gospels to our hearts because the light of Christ's gospel has been made clear to us and we can walk in that truth.

Christ Himself has enabled us to live a meaningful life that isn't bogged down with unholy, unhealthy, and negative thinking. Our old perspective has been defeated and our minds have been illuminated by Him.

April 25

> *"To them God chose to make known how great among the Gentiles are the riches of the glory of this mystery, which is Christ in you, the hope of glory. Him we proclaim, warning everyone and teaching everyone with all wisdom, that we may present everyone mature in Christ."*
> *-Colossians 1:27-28*

We are privileged to live in the era we live in. Even though there are great challenges with living during this season of history, there are also great blessings. One of the blessings is the fact that the Lord, in His infinite wisdom, has chosen to make known to us things that were unknown to those who lived long ago.

He has revealed that He is present with us, in Christ. He has made it clear that Jews and Gentiles who believe in Christ are united in one body called the church. He has granted us the privilege of watching the further effects of His redemptive plan unfold. We have been privileged to see things that both humans and angels often wondered about, wanting to know more.

And as recipients of this good news, the Lord expects us to grow. He's fostering maturity in our lives so that we will gradually reflect the heart of Jesus Christ more actively and visibly. As this maturation process continues, our faith progresses and Christ is glorified in us and through us.

April 26

"Consequently, he is able to save to the uttermost those who draw near to God through him, since he always lives to make intercession for them."
-Hebrews 7:25

There are things taking place in the spiritual realm, all the time, that we probably don't think about as often as we should. There are things being done for us, every day, that bring great benefit to us, and help us as we seek to navigate our lives.

Scripture tells us that Jesus is doing something for us, right now, that truly matters. He is interceding on our behalf to God the Father. He is bringing our requests and needs before the throne of God.

Jesus, our merciful and faithful High Priest, is a greater priest than those who served in priestly roles during the era of the Old Covenant. They temporarily interceded on behalf of God's people, then eventually died. But Jesus lives forever, and His ministry of intercession is ongoing and without interruption.

Therefore, through Christ our Intercessor, we will experience the full effects and the eventual result of our salvation. He granted us salvation as a gift, He holds us securely in His hand, He lives forever, and brings our requests before the Father. He rescued us and continues to uphold and sustain our lives in Him.

April 27

"For the Son of Man came to seek and to save the lost."
-Luke 19:10

There's a misconception about Jesus that can be resolved rather quickly if we take a look at what He actually taught and said. The misconception is this: many people mistakenly believe that they need to be good enough, righteous enough, faithful enough, and pious enough for Him to pay any attention to them. But that's not the case at all. In fact, we had no capacity to be any of those things, and that's why He came looking for us in the first place.

We were lost. We were wandering through this world without purpose and without hope. We didn't understand God's design for us and we certainly weren't interested in honoring His will for our lives. But Jesus interjected Himself into the mess we had made with the goal of securing salvation for us.

Jesus wasn't seeking the righteous or the healthy because apart from Him, there is no true righteousness or lasting health. Jesus came seeking those who were lost, and when He found us, He granted us salvation as an undeserved gift, through faith in Him.

You don't have to clean your life up first before you can come to Jesus. He came for the lost, and He takes broken people and makes them whole.

April 28

> *"but emptied himself, by taking the form of a servant, being born in the likeness of men. And being found in human form, he humbled himself by becoming obedient to the point of death, even death on a cross."*
> *-Philippians 2:7-8*

What does leadership look like? That question gets answered in many different ways, but when we look at how Jesus conducted Himself in this world, we find the ultimate answer.

As the creator and sustainer of the universe, Jesus could have exercised an authoritarian form of leadership during His earthly ministry. But He chose to do something different instead. He served. He showed us that real leadership looks a lot like sacrificial service.

Jesus also displayed perfect humility. He was joyfully willing to take on human flesh, walk among us as a man, and submissively obey the will of the Father, even to the point of death. Jesus suffered the most humiliating form of death imagined at the time when He gave His life for us on the cross. But He did this in love, and He invites us to mirror His heart in how we live.

Throughout the course of today, there may be multiple opportunities for you to lead. If that's the case, will you mirror Christ's heart of sacrificial service and humility?

April 29

"For I know that my Redeemer lives, and
at the last he will stand upon the earth."
-Job 19:25

Every season of life comes with its challenges. There are trials and experiences that come our way that stretch us emotionally and spiritually. At times, it can be easy to get too caught up in the moment and potentially begin to feel crushed by the weight of our difficulties, but when we pause and look toward the future, we're reminded of all the good the Lord has in store for His children.

Every trial we experience lasts only for a season. There will come a day when life will be just as the Lord originally intended. No more sin. No more sorrow. No more pain. No more grief. This is what Job was looking forward to when the Holy Spirit inspired him to pen these words.

Jesus, our Redeemer, lives. Death could not defeat Him. The weight of the burdens of this world could not crush Him. He brings life, restoration, and peace to all who trust in Him.

We will one day appear before His judgment seat and He will assess our faith in Him, and to what degree we lived out that faith. Is this a day we're looking forward to? Are we comforted by this thought? As men and women who have been rescued and redeemed by Christ, the thought of His return should foster joy within us.

April 30

> *"Rather, speaking the truth in love, we are to grow up in every way into him who is the head, into Christ,"*
> ***-Ephesians 4:15***

By design, words are powerful things. Few things have as much impact on our perspective, understanding, and self-perception as the words that have been communicated to us.

The Lord has given us His word so that we would know Him, know about Him, understand who we are, and understand what He wants to do with our lives. He reveals His will to us and He helps us grow mature in our faith. He speaks counsel to us. He speaks wisdom to us. He conveys the message of the gospel to us.

We can use the words that proceed from our mouths to give Christ glory and build each other up, or we can use our words to tear each other down. If we follow the Lord's pattern, however, we will speak the truth in love to one another with the goal of edifying each other and making investments in each others' lives that point us to Christ.

In your life, you have known people who have hurt you with their words, but you've also experienced others who have shown you love with what they've spoken. How will you make use of the words that proceed from your mouth today? Who will you build up?

May 1

> *"And without faith it is impossible to please him, for whoever would draw near to God must believe that he exists and that he rewards those who seek him."*
> *-Hebrews 11:6*

Faith pleases the Lord. When we read throughout the many books that comprise the Bible, we are shown through direct teaching, biographical examples, inference, poetry, and prophecy, that the Lord desires His children to live in a trusting relationship with Him. He is reliable. He keeps His word. We can confidently believe in Him.

Many of the human relationships we have experienced operate differently than our relationship with the Lord. There are people in our lives who only seemed pleased with us if they're happy with what we're doing for them. The second we stop doing what they want us to do, we lose their favor and sometimes lose their friendship as well. Their affection toward us is contingent on our ability to meet their needs.

But God doesn't operate that way. He invites us to trust in Him and to draw near to Him through faith in Jesus Christ. We don't have to earn His favor or love. He delights to reward those who trust Him completely. He blesses us with the privilege to come close to Him. He grants us eternal life. He assures us that we have a place in His kingdom. And He comforts us by reminding us that He's present with us always.

May 2

> *"And this is the confidence that we have toward him, that if we ask anything according to his will he hears us. And if we know that he hears us in whatever we ask, we know that we have the requests that we have asked of him."*
> *-1 John 5:14-15*

There are people we have met through the years that we have at times felt nervous to talk to. People we admired. People we liked. People who had fame or notoriety. We felt nervous speaking to them because we weren't certain they would accept us or reciprocate our affection.

But God, in His love, delights when we talk with Him. Through faith in His Son, Jesus Christ, we have been granted access to His throne. We are invited to come before Him confidently. We are assured that He hears us and takes joy in answering our requests when those requests are made in deference to His perfect will.

Likewise, we can be confident that His answers are always perfect and are delivered with precision, in His ideal timing. God knows what we need even before we make our requests. He also knows how best to answer us, even though that means His answers may not be exactly what we initially expected. But if we trust Him, we will likewise have confidence that His will is without error. We can rest assured that our concerns aren't trivial to Him. He delights to answer our prayers.

May 3

"Rejoice in hope, be patient in tribulation, be constant in prayer."
-Romans 12:12

Circumstances change all the time. Every day is different than the next. The predictions we make about our future and what our life will look like on this earth are often incorrect, and we're consistently presented with unexpected challenges and trials. Thankfully, our joy isn't anchored in our circumstances. Our joy is anchored in Christ. Therefore, we can look forward to the future, not with fear, but with great hope - knowing that the promises of the Lord will absolutely be fulfilled.

In the midst of our trials, we can likewise rely on the patience we're granted through the presence of the Holy Spirit in our lives. It might be tempting at times for us to lose our cool or to drift toward despair, but that isn't a direction our hearts need to gravitate. We have been supernaturally blessed with the power of God. He lives within us, is present with us, and can foster the expression of patience as one of the fruits that spring forth from our redeemed lives.

In the midst of everything we endure, we're also reminded to remain steadfast in prayer. Our natural strength is not sufficient for our struggles, but the strength supplied through Christ certainly is. Let's be faithful to worship Him, communicate with Him, and listen to Him because He meets our every need.

May 4

> *"if my people who are called by my name humble themselves, and pray and seek my face and turn from their wicked ways, then I will hear from heaven and will forgive their sin and heal their land."*
> *-2 Chronicles 7:14*

By nature, we find it far to easy to rebel against God. Time and time again, He has shown His people just how much He loves them. He grants His children good gifts. He assures us of His presence. He walks with us daily, and yet we tend to grow used to His blessings to the point that we can unfortunately begin to take them for granted.

This process was illustrated frequently in the context of the people of Israel living during the Old Covenant. The Lord made them a nation, blessed them with a land of their own, did miracles among them, sent prophets to them, protected and defended them from enemy nations, and yet they eventually ignored Him and went their own way. They rebelled, just like we all have.

But even still, God is merciful. He sent His son Jesus Christ into this world and offers us a second chance through faith in Him. He invites us to repent of our unbelief. He invites us to live as His family, not as rebellious enemies. And He promises us a future home in His presence that is more beautiful than anything we have ever witnessed. In Christ we are forgiven and healed.

May 5

> *"do not be anxious about anything, but in everything by prayer and supplication with thanksgiving let your requests be made known to God. And the peace of God, which surpasses all understanding, will guard your hearts and your minds in Christ Jesus."*
> *-Philippians 4:6-7*

It's too easy to worry. Throughout the course of our lives, there are many seasons when we try to control the things that only God can control. And when we do that, we foster anxiety within us because we're trying to do a job that we aren't capable of doing.

But the Lord encourages us not to be anxious about anything. He wants us to trust Him. He wants us to rest with confidence in His power to act on our behalf. He wants us to bring our concerns before His throne and have faith that He will accomplish His perfect work for our benefit and His glory.

As we submit our concerns over to Him in prayer, He not only acts on our behalf, He also calms our hearts. Through faith in Jesus Christ, our Intercessor, our anxiety is replaced with His peace. He keeps a watchful eye on our hearts and our minds. He assures us of His presence. He grants us true rest. He enables us to sleep soundly because we know that His love is real, His power is great, and He is relieving us of a burden we were never meant to carry in the first place.

May 6

> *"Therefore, confess your sins to one another and pray for one another, that you may be healed. The prayer of a righteous person has great power as it is working."*
> *-James 5:16*

Sin likes to operate in secret. It gains a foothold in our lives when we cover it up and make excuses for it. It operates in the dark and never wants to be brought into the light because then it will be exposed as the destructive force it actually is.

Through faith in Jesus, we receive forgiveness for our sins. But even though Christ has taken the ultimate penalty for our sin upon Himself and we have been truly cleansed, we still struggle with sin. We're tempted by it and we let it creep into our lives too frequently.

With that in mind, the Lord encourages us to confess our sins to each other. This can be challenging to do because we don't typically like to admit our faults or mistakes. But if we want to move past recurring sin, we need to stop hiding what we're wrestling with.

As we confess, we're giving others the opportunity to know how best to pray for us. The power of God is accessed through the prayers of His children. Through His power we will be enabled to stop giving into the sin we've been wrestling with and we'll be strengthened to walk in the freedom from sin Christ has blessed us with.

May 7

> *"Rejoice always, pray without ceasing, give thanks in all circumstances; for this is the will of God in Christ Jesus for you."*
> *-1 Thessalonians 5:16-18*

Many Christians spend a considerable amount of time trying to figure out what God's will is for their lives. We wonder about where we should live, who we should marry, what career path we should follow, and how best to spend our retirement years. These are valuable things to think about and pray about, but there are aspects of God's will that are much easier to figure out that we should be giving just as much attention to.

As followers of Christ, we're told that God's will for us is that we live in such a way that we reflect the presence of Christ in our lives. We're called to be people who rejoice always. In every circumstance, we have joy because Jesus is the source of our peace and contentment.

Likewise, it's God's will that we be people who continually pray because we're convinced that our Lord hears us and graciously intervenes in our lives.

We're also reminded to be thankful in every circumstance of life. On our best days and our worst days we can be thankful for our new life in Christ, and grateful for the fact that every circumstance we face has a divinely ordained purpose.

> *"Walk in wisdom toward outsiders, making the best use of the time. Let your speech always be gracious, seasoned with salt, so that you may know how you ought to answer each person."*
> *-Colossians 4:5-6*

When we became believers in Jesus Christ, we were divinely equipped to fulfill a new mission for our lives. Christ has sent us into this world as His ambassadors. We represent Him to everyone we meet and interact with. We give others a picture of who He is and what He does in the life of someone who walks with Him. He's making His appeal to a lost world through people like us.

As His family, we're encouraged to utilize the wisdom He supplies when we interact with others. We're called to be thoughtful in how we make use of the brief time we have on this earth. We're called to give thought to how we choose to speak with others instead of being careless with how we engage in conversation.

It isn't easy to represent Christ in the midst of a fallen world. There are people who will test our patience. There are personalities and preferences that we will find abrasive and sometimes offensive. But just the same, Jesus wants those who are currently living as His enemies to become part of His family forever. Are we welcoming Him to speak to them through our words and our lives?

May 9

> *"There is therefore now no condemnation for those who are in Christ Jesus. For the law of the Spirit of life has set you free in Christ Jesus from the law of sin and death."*
> *-Romans 8:1-2*

Before we came to faith in Jesus, we were condemned. We were doomed to be punished forever. We were on our way to an eternity of enmity with God, separation from God, and conscious eternal suffering.

That's not the future God desires for humanity, but that's the future mankind chose when we rebelled against our Creator. We gave up freedom and life, and traded them for slavery to sin and death.

With compassion, Jesus interjected Himself into the mess we had fostered. He who knew no sin was condemned as if He was a sinner when He died on the cross. Jesus took our sin and condemnation upon Himself so that if we would believe in Him, we would no longer be condemned. We now can have hope and a future through faith in Jesus.

Do you believe this? If so, what kind of impact has this truth made on your life and your perspective? Do you still live as someone who has been condemned or have you embraced the freedom from sin you have been granted through faith in Jesus?

May 10

> *"If your brother sins against you, go and tell him his fault, between you and him alone. If he listens to you, you have gained your brother."*
> *-Matthew 18:15*

What do most people do when someone sins against them or hurts them in some way? There are several ways people usually respond. Some people lash out in anger. Some retaliate. Some seek to slander the offending party. Others choose to ostracize the offender.

How does Christ instruct us to respond to one another when we sin against each other? He encourages us to begin the conversation alone with the person who has hurt us. To take the initiative to dialogue, explain how we were hurt, and give them a reasonable opportunity to repent.

Sometimes, to our surprise, we discover that our brother wasn't aware he had sinned against us. Other times we come to learn that there may have been something we did that caused them to feel provoked. There are all kinds of things we can discover when we open up the door to conversation and understanding.

Jesus is perfect, but we still struggle with sin. We offend others and they offend us. Which is better, to brood for decades over an offense or to attempt to handle it with grace and mercy as soon as possible?

May 11

> *"Be kind to one another, tenderhearted, forgiving one another, as God in Christ forgave you."*
> *-Ephesians 4:32*

What has the Lord done for us? What kind of blessings have we received though Christ Jesus?

In Christ we have been blessed with salvation, new life, forgiveness, an eternal family, an eternal home, purpose, cleansing, strength, spiritual gifts, wisdom, and more blessings than we could conceivably count.

Isn't it ironic that after receiving such amazing gifts of grace directly from the hand of God, we sometimes struggle to share the good things He's granted us with others?

As recipients of His kindness, is it too much of Him to ask us to treat others kindly? As beneficiaries of His compassion, is it too much of Him to ask us to be tenderhearted toward others? As people who have had our sins completely forgiven, is it too much of Him to ask us to forgive those who sin against us?

If we're truly grateful for the blessings we have received through Jesus, our relationships with others will change. When our perspective toward His kindness matures, we'll begin to radiate the kindness He's shown us by displaying that same kindness toward the people He has placed in our lives.

May 12

"An excellent wife who can find? She is far more precious than jewels.
-Proverbs 31:10

Marriage is an invention of God. He created it, He designed it, and He describes how it should function throughout the course of His word.

We live in an era when marriage is misunderstood, maligned, devalued, and sometimes intentionally discouraged. The prevailing wisdom of our era devalues the unique roles of men and women as well.

Marriage is meant to serve as a picture of Christ's love for His church. The relationship between a husband and wife should reflect the love, trust, and relational intimacy that is found in Christ's relationship with His bride, the church.

Men who are blessed to find a godly, Christ-loving, supportive wife, are blessed indeed. Such a person feels like a rarity at times, but the truth is, Christ has filled this earth with many godly women who reflect His loving heart.

A woman who loves Jesus and displays His love is one of the greatest treasures on this planet. They should be loved, cared for, learned from, and cherished. A godly woman nurtures the heart of her husband and children. A godly woman conveys the wisdom of Christ.

May 13

> *"Charm is deceitful, and beauty is vain, but a woman who fears the Lord is to be praised."*
> *-Proverbs 31:30*

In this world, many people mistakenly believe their value is based on temporary and transient things. But our value isn't derived from what we do, what we have, or how we look. We are valuable because we have been created by God in His image. Through faith in Christ, we are called by His name. We are adopted into the family of God forever. None of this is based on external or superficial factors.

In our culture, there is a great amount of pressure placed upon women in particular to pay attention to their appearance. In some contexts, women are treated differently based on how they look. Sadly, some women base their entire sense of worth on their continually changing physical attributes.

Physical beauty is a fleeting thing. It lasts for a season, then fades away. It isn't something that can be trusted, and our sense of worth should never come from it. But a woman who reveres and respects the Lord is graced with a lasting beauty that reaches to the core of her being, and doesn't fade like our physical appearance.

In Christ, you are loved, you are transformed, and you are beautiful. His righteousness has permeated your heart and your life is a reflection of His genuine love.

May 14

> *"For you formed my inward parts;*
> *you knitted me together in my mother's*
> *womb. I praise you, for I am fearfully*
> *and wonderfully made.*
> *Wonderful are your works; my soul*
> *knows it very well."*
> **-Psalm 139:13-14**

Scripture reveals to us that all things were created by, through, and for Jesus. His creation testifies to His powerful hand at work. As we observe the intentional way He crafted the human body to operate, we find the intricate details fascinating. Nothing about the human body is an accident. Every detail of how it operates and appears is by God's design.

This is valuable to think about in light of the false messages we are often tempted to believe. At times, it can be tempting to question our value, to question our worth, and to question whether or not God cares about us in a specific way.

Then we look at a portion of Scripture like this that reminds us that God personally knit us together in our mother's womb. We weren't created haphazardly. We didn't come into being by accident. God's fingerprints are all over our lives.

His work is wonderful. Do you believe that? When you look at yourself today, is that a message you'll repeat to your heart?

May 15

> *"As you do not know the way the spirit comes to the bones in the womb of a woman with child, so you do not know the work of God who makes everything."*
> **-Ecclesiastes 11:5**

One of the great fallacies that men promote in every generation is the superiority of human wisdom. It's true that the Lord has created us in His image and has made us able to learn and perceive many things. He has also given us the capacity to record our knowledge and pass it along to generations that come after us so they can build upon what we've studied and learned. But the truth is, there is a depth of knowledge that is far beyond our human ability to naturally comprehend.

God has revealed to us in the Scriptures that He is all knowing. He has demonstrated this to prophets and kings. Jesus made this abundantly clear during His earthly ministry when He accurately foretold what would soon happen to Him and what He would do next.

When we compare the depth of our knowledge to the knowledge of the Lord, it should prompt us to demonstrate a spirit of humility, an attitude of appreciation, and a heart of reverence. God has revealed Himself to us, but there is so much about God that we still need to learn. There is so much about how He functions that we still don't understand. In the meantime, however, He invites us to trust in Him and rest confidently in the work He is accomplishing.

May 16

> *"The Lord your God is in your midst, a mighty one who will save; he will rejoice over you with gladness; he will quiet you by his love; he will exult over you with loud singing."*
> *-Zephaniah 3:17*

How deep is the Lord's love for His children? Just consider for a moment the active role He takes in the lives of His people.

The Lord is in the midst of His people. He isn't a distance off. He isn't inaccessible. He isn't running from us. He is right here with us. This, by the way, is exactly what Jesus promised us after His resurrection.

The Lord saves His people. He rescues us. He redeems us. Through Jesus Christ we experience the gift of salvation and eternal life.

The Lord rejoices over His children. He isn't aloof and uncaring. He notices His people and takes delight in their faith and repentance. We're even told that He sings loudly over His children as He enjoys His handiwork.

The Lord quiets our anxious hearts with His love. What do we truly need to fear in this world when we know that our Lord loves us, rescues us, is present with us, and is pleased to call us His children. The worries and the fears of this world can't stand up to God's love and presence.

May 17

> *"Oh, the depth of the riches and wisdom and knowledge of God! How unsearchable are his judgments and how inscrutable his ways!"*
> *-Romans 11:33*

In every season of life, there are various things that we identify as needs. What we consider to be our dominant needs tend to change depending on our age and circumstances. But what do we truly need? Is there something we're lacking? What can this world give us and how does that stack up to what we already have through Jesus?

In Christ, we are made rich. Not necessarily rich with worldly goods, but rich in righteousness. And in addition to the righteousness of Christ, we are also supernaturally empowered through the Holy Spirit with abilities to serve others and build them up in faith.

In Christ, we also find wisdom. We are granted the ability to see this world through His eyes when we come to know Him by faith.

Truthfully, once we have Jesus, we have everything we need. As our faith in Him deepens, we come to appreciate the depths of His riches, wisdom, and knowledge and our hearts become even more grateful that He has graciously chosen to share these blessings with us.

May 18

"For God is not unjust so as to overlook your work and the love that you have shown for his name in serving the saints, as you still do."
-Hebrews 6:10

Have you ever felt overlooked? Do you ever wonder if God notices you? Does He care about the work you're doing to help others come to know Jesus? Does He see the loving sacrifices you have made to serve your brothers and sisters in Christ?

The Scripture reminds us that God does not overlook our service for Him. He sees us and He takes note of the labor we engage in for His glory. He empowers us by His grace to show love to one another, to serve one another, and to press on in that direction for a long time. When we rely on His power to actively bless others in this fashion, the Lord acknowledges that service.

Salvation is a free gift that was paid for by Jesus. We receive it through faith and are assured a place in God's heavenly kingdom forever. Amazingly, in addition to a home in God's presence, His word tells us that He has additional gifts that will be shared with His children that have a connection to their faithful service to Him during this time on this earth. He notices and He rewards.

How are you using the time the Lord has entrusted to you? What is He empowering you to do? How are you sharing His love with those He has placed in your life?

May 19

> *"But the wisdom from above is first pure, then peaceable, gentle, open to reason, full of mercy and good fruits, impartial and sincere. And a harvest of righteousness is sown in peace by those who make peace."*
> *-James 3:17-18*

There is a vast contrast between the wisdom of this world and the wisdom that comes directly from the Lord.

The wisdom of this world is focused on temporary things. It seeks to be "right" at the cost of the well-being of others. It looks to be rewarded with earthly riches and it creates needless conflict and division.

The wisdom of God, however, is pure. It produces a harvest of righteousness that encourages peace between brothers in Christ. When a believer is exercising godly wisdom, they display the fruit of the Holy Spirit's presence in their life by conveying gentleness, an ability to reason without being arrogant, and a desire to show mercy toward others.

When Christ becomes Lord of your life, this is the kind of wisdom He brings forth from you. He grants you His mind, He transforms your thinking, and He fosters a thoughtful harmony between you and your Christian family.

May 20

> *"May the God of endurance and encouragement grant you to live in such harmony with one another, in accord with Christ Jesus, that together you may with one voice glorify the God and Father of our Lord Jesus Christ."*
> *-Romans 15:5-6*

Living in harmony with our brothers and sisters in Christ sounds like it would be an easy thing to do, but frequently, circumstances arise that make that task quite challenging. Differences of opinion, conflicting preferences, competing passions, and outright sin can all get in the way of the harmony the Lord desires to see present among His children.

Still, our God grants endurance and encouragement to His children with the goal of helping us to reflect the heart of Christ, and glorify Him with one united voice. When we're weary, we need His supernatural endurance. When we're down, we need His divine encouragement. Where would we be without these things?

At some point soon, don't be surprised if you experience something that makes it challenging to live in harmony with your Christian family. What are you going to do when that happens? The solution is to rely on the power of the Lord to work in your heart to love others with the love of Christ so that He will be glorified in our gracious treatment of each other.

May 21

> *"I appeal to you, brothers, by the name of our Lord Jesus Christ, that all of you agree, and that there be no divisions among you, but that you be united in the same mind and the same judgment."*
> **-1 Corinthians 1:10**

Unity is not an easy thing to cultivate. We all have opinions, and one step beyond those opinions are our convictions. What can we do when our opinions or convictions conflict with those of another brother or sister in Christ?

The first thing we can do is pray. The Lord invites us to come before Him in prayer continually. We can pray for His intervention and clarity. We can pray that He would soften our hearts so we remain teachable. We can pray that He would grant us sound judgment in the matter.

From there, we need to hold our opinions and convictions up to the light of God's word. If our beliefs conflict with the clear teaching of the Bible, we need to humbly admit that and make corrections.

Thirdly, to encourage unity, we need to decide to intentionally love our brother or sister in Christ even if we can't come to an agreement. We are one body in Christ. Our disagreements are only for a season. We'll be spending eternity together, so we might as well begin living in unity now.

May 22

> *"For you were called to freedom, brothers. Only do not use your freedom as an opportunity for the flesh, but through love serve one another."*
> **-Galatians 5:13**

Before Christ intervened on our behalf, we were slaves to sin. We were stuck in a state that led to division, depression, and destruction. We were in chains to the lusts of our flesh, and we did the bidding of our adversary, the devil.

But by the grace of God, we have been set free from slavery to sin when we came to faith in Jesus Christ. Sin no longer has mastery over us. Its power was broken by Christ. We no longer need to submit to the cravings of our old nature.

Yet some people are still convinced that giving in to sin is what real freedom looks like. But the freedom we have in Christ is not a license to do whatever we want. It's freedom from living like a slave to unrighteousness, not an opportunity to rebel against the very One who granted us liberty in the first place.

Christ has blessed us with real freedom. We are free to serve one another, sacrifice for one another, love one another, and edify one another. It isn't His will that we hurt or take advantage of each other. His calling on our lives is that we make ample use of the freedom He has granted us to build one another up in the faith.

May 23

> *"Let each of us please his neighbor for*
> *his good, to build him up."*
> *-Romans 15:2*

Who is your neighbor? When the Bible uses this term, what is it getting at? Is this primarily a reference to someone you live near? Is this solely speaking about someone you interact with daily?

If we look at this term in the broadest sense, it's referring to anyone whose life and well-being you have the capacity to impact. Your neighbor could be someone you have known for years, someone you just met, or someone you may never meet.

What does it look like when we focus on the needs or preferences of our neighbors? Well, it means that we stop looking at other people as a means to an end. We stop focusing on what we can "get" from them, and start focusing on what we can "give" to them or "do" for them, for Christ's glory.

Good things come from this kind of mindset. Christ's power is shown to be real when it is utilized in these contexts. The one who is served AND the one who is doing the serving are both strengthened and built up. Meeting the needs of our neighbors is mutually beneficial and it displays the heart attitude of Jesus.

Who has Christ placed upon your heart to build up today? How will you serve them for His glory?

May 24

> *"Love one another with brotherly affection. Outdo one another in showing honor."*
> *-Romans 12:10*

Throughout the Scriptures, there are many admonitions for believers to love one another. These challenges are about more than having deep feelings or warm affections for each other. They're divine instructions for us to seek what is best for each other, even at great personal cost to ourselves.

This is the kind of love Jesus shows us. His love for us isn't just an emotional love. His love is an actionable love, and He showed us the depth of His love when He gave His life for ours at the cross. Jesus placed our eternal needs over His momentary comfort.

That's the mindset the Apostle Paul was seeking to mirror in his encouragement to believers that we "outdo" one another in showing honor toward each other. This is an encouragement to put our own pride and preferences aside so we can effectively build one another up in brotherly love.

What kind of difference do you think Jesus would like you to make in the life of someone else today? Who is He calling you to show this kind of love to? Who is He nudging you to honor? How do you think you'll feel at the end of today if you decide to put the teaching of this Scripture into practice?

May 25

> *"Know this, my beloved brothers: let every person be quick to hear, slow to speak, slow to anger;"*
> **-James 1:19**

The book of James is considered to be one of the most practical books of the Bible. In it, we're shown what it looks like when we put our faith in Jesus Christ into action. A faith that is acted upon is shown to be genuine.

God's word reminds us to be quick to hear. That isn't easy for most of us. In many contexts, our desire to be heard outweighs our desire to listen. Conversations can at times turn into a competition to see who can say the most. Even our prayer life tends to display more talking at God than listening to God.

The Lord invites us, however, to be slow to speak. He encourages us to be very careful with what we say. To give thought and prayer to what we choose to communicate. To be sensitive to how our words will impact others. To realize that what we say, and how we say it, is a reflection of what's going on in our heart.

The Lord also reminds us through the teaching of James to be slow to anger. People require patience. As recipients of the Lord's great patience, He encourages us to show patience toward others. We are called to aim for reconciliation, practice forgiveness, and never become consumed with thoughts of vengeance.

May 26

"For God did not send his Son into the world to condemn the world, but in order that the world might be saved through him."
-John 3:17

Many people remain confused or sometimes blind to the purpose for which Jesus came into this world. It's even possible for Christians to, at times, forget the goal of Christ's mission? Why was Jesus sent to us?

Scripture reveals that answer to us in multiple ways. It tells us what Jesus didn't come to do, and it also tells us what He was seeking to accomplish.

Jesus wasn't sent into this world to condemn us. His goal was redemptive in nature. He looked at us with compassion and could see that we already stood condemned in the court room of God. So Jesus took our condemnation upon Himself at the cross. He died in our place, then defeated the power and sting of death when He rose from the grave.

Jesus came to this world so that we would be saved through Him. The wrath of God was placed upon Him so that through faith in Christ, we would no longer be objects of wrath, but recipients of mercy.

Likewise, as Christians, the heart of the message we preach isn't one of condemnation, but redemption. Everyone who trusts in Jesus Christ will be saved.

May 27

> *"But I do not account my life of any value nor as precious to myself, if only I may finish my course and the ministry that I received from the Lord Jesus, to testify to the gospel of the grace of God."*
> *-Acts 20:24*

What's the hardest thing the Lord ever asked you to do? Is there something He's been impressing upon your heart to consider during this season of your life? When you look back upon your life someday, are you going to be pleased with how you chose to invest it?

It can be tempting to try to hold on to our lives too carefully in the sense that we can become adept at primarily playing it safe, walking by sight, and rarely taking any risks that force us to step out on faith. But that's not Christ's desire for us.

The Lord has granted to each of us a ministry. In our various mission fields, we have been called to represent Him as His ambassadors. We have been equipped to testify to the truth of His gospel. We have been empowered to communicate the hope of salvation into the dark and unreached places in our neighborhoods, communities, and extended families.

Don't waste the life the Lord has blessed you with. Don't be so overly cautious that you miss the blessing of walking by faith. We're only here for a short time. Use this time to share Jesus with those who need Him.

May 28

"Rejoice with those who rejoice, weep with those who weep."
-Romans 12:15

The Lord has blessed us with the privilege of sharing our lives with each other. Through faith in Jesus Christ, we become part of one body, the church. We are united as family in Christ. Scripture speaks of us as being brothers and sisters who share a common name, heritage, and destiny through Jesus.

As family, the things we experience in life should matter to each other. When you're experiencing a season of rejoicing, I shouldn't be jealous of your joy. Rather, I should rejoice with you and you should rejoice with me.

When you're weeping, I shouldn't be callous and uncaring toward your tears. My heart should grieve as well. And when I weep, your heart should be moved with care and compassion. What matters to me should matter to you. What matters to you should matter to me.

Life in Christ isn't meant to be lived in isolation. It's a shared experience with all those who have been redeemed and united to Him by faith. As we learn to value one another and make intentional investments in each others' lives, our joyful moments become magnified and the burdens of our sorrowful moments become lighter as they're shared by those we love.

May 29

> *"But the steadfast love of the Lord is from everlasting to everlasting on those who fear him, and his righteousness to children's children, to those who keep his covenant and remember to do his commandments."*
> *-Psalm 103:17-18*

Fear is a term that we usually think of in a negative sense. We use that term, in most contexts, to describe something that produces terror and discomfort. It doesn't tend to conjure up positive images in our minds.

In multiple places throughout the Scriptures, God's word encourages us to fear the Lord. Because of our negative associations with the word fear, we sometimes misunderstand those statements. But the mindset and practice of fearing the Lord is very beneficial to our lives.

To fear Him, in the biblical sense, means to revere, respect, and honor Him. It shows that we have a proper understanding of His nature and His great power. And because we are conscious of His great might, as well as His ability to work in our lives, our healthy reverence of Him prompts us to live in obedience to Him.

Ultimately, only Jesus could keep the Law of God perfectly. He fulfilled all righteousness on our behalf and now He empowers us with the strength and desire to live with faithful reverence and obedience to Him.

May 30

"In God, whose word I praise, in God I trust; I shall not be afraid. What can flesh do to me?"
-Psalm 56:4

Throughout the course of our days, there are voices we choose to listen to and voices we choose to ignore. There are people the Lord has blessed us with that seek to build us up in our faith in Jesus Christ, and there are people who actively try to tear us down and hurt us.

Are you afraid of those who wish you ill? How much time do you spend thinking about them? Are you worried about something they might say? Are you overly concerned about something they might do?

The big lesson the Lord wants us to learn during the course of our lives is to trust Him. His word matters more than anything anyone else might say. He's the one that should consume our thinking. He's the one we should be dwelling on. He's also the one who is actively protecting and guiding us.

There is nothing someone else can take away from us that we weren't going to lose anyway. And while there may be people in this world who seek to work against us, we don't need to spend our lives in fear of them. The Lord Himself is present with us. He is guiding our steps, and through Jesus Christ, our futures are held securely in His hands. God promises that if we love Him, all things in our lives will work together for good.

May 31

> *"For the Lord himself will descend from heaven with a cry of command, with the voice of an archangel, and with the sound of the trumpet of God. And the dead in Christ will rise first. Then we who are alive, who are left, will be caught up together with them in the clouds to meet the Lord in the air, and so we will always be with the Lord."*
> ***-1 Thessalonians 4:16-17***

Some of our days are difficult. Other days are a breeze. But in the midst of our difficult days, it can be tempting to begin to think things will always be this way. Thankfully, for those who trust in Christ Jesus, there is a glorious future up ahead. This is something the Lord has revealed to us as an intentional source of encouragement during seasons when we might be tempted to despair.

Jesus has promised that He will return for us. We don't know when this will be, but He has told us to be ready for Him to come at any time.

When He returns, He will grant a new, resurrected body to all believers and He will take us to be with Him forever. In His presence, there will be no more sorrow, mourning, or pain. He will wipe away all our tears and will usher us into an eternity in His presence that is far beyond anything we can naturally imagine. Remind your heart of these truths frequently.

June 1

"He will wipe away every tear from their eyes, and death shall be no more, neither shall there be mourning, nor crying, nor pain anymore, for the former things have passed away."
-Revelation 21:4

There are various aspects of our lives on this earth that produce discomfort and pain. Because of the presence of sin and rebellion in our lives, we have invited these things to be part of the human experience on this planet. God would have been perfectly justified in allowing us to wallow in our own consequences for all time if He chose to, but thankfully, He is merciful and gracious.

God has promised that all who trust in Jesus Christ for salvation will experience a glorious and perfect future. He will make His home with us. We will live forever in His presence. The effects of our sin and rebellion will be wiped away and the painful aspects of earthly life we've become accustomed to will be brought to an end.

This means that whatever is grieving your heart right now is temporary. You won't always feel this way. You won't always cry. You won't always mourn. Your pain isn't permanent.

Jesus bore our griefs and sorrows so He could usher us into the kind of future He has always intended that we live in. Let this truth encourage your heart today.

June 2

> *"so Christ, having been offered once to bear the sins of many, will appear a second time, not to deal with sin but to save those who are eagerly waiting for him."*
> ***-Hebrews 9:28***

When Jesus offered His body on the cross as an atoning sacrifice for our sin, He took our sin and bore the weight of its shame and condemnation upon Himself. He did this so we wouldn't be condemned to an eternity apart from Him. He did this so we could be freed from the chains of sin, guilt, and shame. He did this as the greatest expression of love humanity has ever witnessed.

This was a one time sacrifice. No further sacrifice needs to be made. No other sacrifice would be sufficient to pay for mankind's rebellion against our Creator.

After His resurrection, when Jesus ascended back to Heaven, His followers were assured that He was coming back in the same manner. When He returns, it won't be to atone for our sin. That's something He has already accomplished. His second coming involves granting His family the privilege of experiencing the full effects of His gift of salvation. He will take us to be with Him, bless us with new incorruptible bodies, wipe every tear from our eyes, and usher us into a glorious and perfect eternity in His presence.

June 3

> *"A soft answer turns away wrath, but a harsh word stirs up anger."*
> *-Proverbs 15:1*

Throughout the course of our lives, there are going to be times when we will feel provoked. Someone with an arrogant attitude may antagonize us. Someone may unjustly accuse us. Someone may speak to us in anger with the intention of hurting us or getting under our skin. When those moments come, how should we respond?

The Scripture encourages us to be truthful and gracious in our response. It's tempting to lash out and speak harshly when we're being attacked, but the Lord empowers us to live up to a higher standard. We don't have to stoop to the sinful patterns and practices of the flesh. Through faith in Jesus, we have been set free from those shackles.

As Christ has treated us with mercy, kindness, and truthfulness, so too should we respond to others in the same fashion. When we're cursed, we can bless. When we're persecuted, we can pray for the ones who persecute us. This kind of response glorifies Christ and impacts the conscience of those who treat us poorly. It also releases our hearts from holding on to grudges or seeking revenge and retribution.

Let's finish each day, content that we have responded to others in a way that reflects the heart of Christ.

June 4

> *"Yours, O Lord, is the greatness and the power and the glory and the victory and the majesty, for all that is in the heavens and in the earth is yours. Yours is the kingdom, O Lord, and you are exalted as head above all."*
> *-1 Chronicles 29:11*

The chief aim of our lives is to glorify God. While it's easy to lose sight of that or become distracted with all kinds of other pursuits, giving glory to God is what He has designed us to do.

When we give Him glory, we rob the idols in our lives of the power they crave. When we give Him praise, we're testifying to the fact that we understand that we are not the center of our own universe.

Glorifying God involves an acknowledgement of His great power as well. We were powerless to do anything to change our eternal fate, yet Jesus Christ came to this earth to rob sin, Satan, and death of the power they had over us. The power of God is infinitely greater than any other power or force in this world.

It can be tempting, in certain contexts of life, to want to exalt ourselves, but in the end, our hearts will never be satisfied with exalting anyone or anything above our Lord. If ever we're struggling to understand the meaning and purpose of our lives, this is the concept we need to return to. *"Yours, O Lord,...is the glory."*

June 5

> *"Therefore encourage one another and build one another up, just as you are doing."*
> *-1 Thessalonians 5:11*

Depending on the nature of your present circumstances, it can be easy at times to become inwardly focused. Sometimes it seems like the primary thing we find ourselves thinking about is what can we do to bring some level of benefit to our own lives.

But through faith in Jesus Christ, we're encouraged to develop an outward focus. We're invited to begin prioritizing the needs of others. We're taught to make decisions and foster activity that's motivated by love for God and love for His people. Actions that are inspired by the desire to build up our brothers and sisters in Christ.

This requires us to notice what matters to them. To notice what they need. To seek insight from God so we can utilize His wisdom to provide the kind of encouragement and edification another brother or sister is seeking in a particular moment.

It's easy to tear someone down. Anyone can do that. It takes no special skill and it doesn't require very much thought. But Christ's family has been called by Him to encourage and build one another up, and to make this a continual practice for each day of our earthly lives.

June 6

> *"so that Christ may dwell in your hearts through faith—that you, being rooted and grounded in love, may have strength to comprehend with all the saints what is the breadth and length and height and depth, and to know the love of Christ that surpasses knowledge, that you may be filled with all the fullness of God."*
> ***-Ephesians 3:17-19***

What are you rooting your life in? What kind of soil are you seeking to become established in? How far do the roots of your life currently reach?

God's word encourages us to be rooted and grounded in the love of Christ. All aspects of our lives should be firmly anchored in Jesus. What are the benefits of being rooted in Christ?

If our lives are rooted in Christ, there are healthy forms of fruit that will be produced. The way we think will be impacted. The way we live will change. The way we respond to stress will be altered. The way we treat one another will be improved.

When we're rooted in Christ, we will be nourished by Him and will gradually grow mature in our faith. Christ hasn't saved us with the desire to leave us like we were when He found us. He rescued us with the desire to foster genuine growth and maturity within us that fully reflects His loving heart.

June 7

"Before the mountains were brought forth, or ever you had formed the earth and the world, from everlasting to everlasting you are God."
-Psalm 90:2

The eternality of God is a fascinating subject to try to think about, but impossible for us to wrap our minds around completely. We're used to things having a beginning and an ending point. We're used to seeing things start and finish. But God has no beginning point and He certainly has no end. In every direction we can contemplate, from eternity past to eternity future, He is God.

Even though this isn't something we can naturally explain, it brings our hearts comfort when we come to the point where we can accept this by faith. The greater point is, God is higher than us and He has everything under control. Our lives, His creation, and the future is all securely held in His hands. He is God and we are not, nor do we have to try to convince ourselves of the need to be.

Many people live like they're trying to be their own gods. They try to control things they could never control. That desire for control ultimately produces despair and anxiety. But through faith in Christ, we enjoy a better option. We can joyfully accept that He is God and we are not. He sustains what He has created and we can find solace and lasting peace through Him.

June 8

> *"God, the Lord, is my strength; he makes*
> *my feet like the deer's; he makes me tread*
> *on my high places."*
> ***-Habakkuk 3:19a***

What do you consider to be your greatest source of strength? Depending on your perspective, there might be several different ways to answer that question. Some people would primarily choose to answer that question from a physical perspective. Others might reference a personality trait as their strength. Some might even identify a particular talent or a skill. But because those strengths can change over time or be abruptly taken away, they aren't a reliable source of strength in which we can anchor our souls.

This Scripture reminds us that the Lord is our strength. For those who trust in Him, He is the one our lives are empowered by. God's word tells us that all things were created through Christ and that He is currently sustaining all of creation by His powerful word. There is no greater source of power or strength. Attempting to find our strength in anything less than Him will lead to utter disappointment.

Right now, today, you need the strength of Christ. There are people, circumstances, stressors, and trials that are bound to sap your strength. But through Jesus, you have help and hope beyond your circumstances. Ask Him to teach you to rely on the sustaining strength that He joyfully supplies all who trust in Him.

June 9

> *"Enter by the narrow gate. For the gate is wide and the way is easy that leads to destruction, and those who enter by it are many. For the gate is narrow and the way is hard that leads to life, and those who find it are few."*
> *-Matthew 7:13-14*

Many people in this world are on a path that leads to destruction and despair. In their own wisdom, this path makes sense to them, and in many respects, it's likely that they have no idea they are headed in a direction that results in that unfortunate outcome.

But Jesus invites us to enter by the "narrow gate." The narrow gate is a reference to Him. He is the way to life. He is the way to the Father. While there are many ways in this world that people mistakenly believe will lead to salvation, there is no other way to be saved than by grace, through faith in Jesus Christ.

True faith in Jesus results in us following Him with our lives. It's not always easy to follow Jesus in the midst of a world that tries to encourage us to go in a different direction. This world influences us to take short cuts, to sacrifice our integrity, to harm others for selfish gain, and to treat ourselves like we are the god of our own lives. But Jesus has made Himself known to us and the Holy Spirit is testifying to our hearts that Christ is the one we have been called to follow.

June 10

> *"bearing with one another and, if one has*
> *a complaint against another, forgiving*
> *each other; as the Lord has forgiven you,*
> *so you also must forgive."*
> *-Colossians 3:13*

This is an easy verse to read, but a difficult verse to put in practice. What do we usually do when we have a complaint against someone else? Most often, we vent it to a friend we trust who is likely to agree with us. We keep building our case against the person who has offended us and we stoke a fire of bitterness against them in our souls.

As that bitter root takes hold, it eventually becomes hatred, and as Jesus warned us in His Sermon on the Mount, hatred has the same root as murder. Clearly this isn't what our Lord desires for His family.

Rather, the Lord invites us to acknowledge the value of His forgiveness toward us by teaching us to forgive others as well. When we fail to forgive, we hurt others and we hurt ourselves. We can become sour and unpleasant to be around. And we effectively forget all that Jesus has accomplished on our behalf.

But when we forgive others as Christ has forgiven us, we utilize our lives to serve as a visible testimony to the truth, power, and effectiveness of the gospel. This is the kind of life Christ has called us unto.

June 11

"Be still, and know that I am God. I will be exalted among the nations, I will be exalted in the earth!"
-Psalm 46:10

How often do we convince ourselves that for our lives to truly work out, we have to be in control? What happens when we buy into that mistaken belief?

First off, we become anxious. Anxiety comes when we try to control things that we can't truly control. We may fight admitting that fact to ourselves, but the simple fact is that there are many things that we try to control that only God can truly control.

Secondly, we rob ourselves of rest. Our souls ache for peace, but we can't find peace by trying to be our own god. True peace comes when we surrender ourselves to Jesus and recognize that He is Lord.

God's word reminds us to be still and know that He is God. We don't have to do God's job for Him. We don't have to fix the things only He can fix. We don't have to change the lives and behavior of the people we care about. Our job is to be an ambassador of Christ, to pray for the people and situations that we need the Lord to intervene with, and to trust Him for the results.

How are you doing with this? What about your personality or past experience makes it challenging for you to be still and let God be God?

June 12

> *"The heavens declare the glory of God, and the sky above proclaims his handiwork."*
> *-Psalm 19:1*

It has always been God's desire to have a deep, abiding, personal relationship with mankind. He created us in His image. He placed us in a perfectly designed environment. He entrusted to us meaningful work and responsibilities. And He has surrounded us with visible evidence of His power, creativity, and presence.

In every direction we look, we seek the handiwork of God. When we look to the sky, we see birds, stars, planets, and the visible aspects of our atmosphere. God's fingerprints are all over those things. They preach a message to our hearts that God is real and He is glorious. Creation by its very existence and complexity testifies to its Creator.

When we look at ourselves, we see God's hand as well. In our intellect, emotions, and will, we see a reflection of His image. And again, He testifies to us that He is real and He is intentionally making Himself known.

Ultimately, God took on flesh and walked among us. Jesus Christ spoke to us, healed us, died, rose from death, ascended back to Heaven, and promised to return. He made Himself known to us because He desires a relationship with us. Do you feel like you truly know Jesus or do you simply know about Him?

June 13

> *"If you then, who are evil, know how to give good gifts to your children, how much more will the heavenly Father give the Holy Spirit to those who ask him!"*
> *-Luke 11:13*

What do you think about the nature of the gifts the Lord has blessed you with? Do you appreciate them? Do you thank Him for them? Do you even notice them?

Jesus points out something interesting in this passage of Scripture. He acknowledges the fact that mankind, by nature, is sinful. Yet even in our fallen state, we are inclined to give beneficial gifts to our children. How much more so is God, who does not struggle with sin, willing to give good gifts to His children?

Consider for a moment the nature of the gifts the Lord blesses His children with. Through faith in Jesus, we are blessed with the undeserved gift of salvation. We are blessed with His presence and provision. We are blessed with the gift of hope and a future. And, as Jesus points out in this passage, all believers are blessed with the gift of the Holy Spirit.

The moment you trust in Jesus Christ, the Holy Spirit personally indwells you. He becomes your Counselor and Comforter. He marks you as a child of God. He grants you supernaturally enabled abilities to serve others. And He makes the Scriptures clear to your heart. He is the Father's gift to you.

June 14

> *"But our citizenship is in heaven, and from it we await a Savior, the Lord Jesus Christ,"*
> ***-Philippians 3:20***

Because we're so used to living in this world, during this era of history, and in our particular culture, it can be easy for us to mistakenly believe that what we currently see is all there is and all there ever will be. We can look at what's around us and begin to believe that our true citizenship is in a temporary kingdom.

We can also mistakenly begin to look to our human leaders to satisfy a void in our lives that they aren't truly capable of filling. We want them to end our pain and suffering. We want them to usher in an era of lasting peace. We want them to foster all kinds of prosperity, but then we discover they're just human like the rest of us. Presidents and Prime Ministers can't satisfy the deepest longings of our souls.

Only Jesus can meet our deepest needs. He's the King we're truly waiting for. He's the one who will right the wrongs and restore this bruised creation. Through faith in Him, we are welcomed as citizens of His eternal kingdom. In Christ we find our sense of belonging, satisfaction, peace, community, and an unending supply of all we will ever need.

Sometime soon, Jesus will return, and when He comes, He will rule this earth with justice, peace, and love.

June 15

> *"The father of the righteous will greatly rejoice; he who fathers a wise son will be glad in him."*
> *-Proverbs 23:24*

Children are a blessing from the Lord. Certainly there are times when raising them can be quite a challenge, but the long-term fruit of bringing them in the fear and knowledge of the Lord is a great source of joy and encouragement.

Righteousness is a gift from God. Specifically, Scripture tells us that the gift of the righteousness of Christ is freely granted to all who trust in Him. Fathers should encourage their children to understand this truth. Likewise, they should model their faith to their children so the generations that come after them can visibly see a reliable demonstration of what it looks like when a man truly believes in Christ.

Fathers should pray for their children as well. First that they would trust in Jesus and receive His righteousness, and secondly that they would utilize and embrace the wisdom they are granted by the Holy Spirit.

Navigating our lives in this world can be complicated, but thankfully our Lord is present with us, guiding the steps we take. Likewise, we thank Him for earthly fathers who represent Him well and serve as a faithful example of the love, wisdom, and guidance of Christ.

June 16

"As a father shows compassion to his children, so the Lord shows compassion to those who fear him."
-Psalm 103:13

Apart from the Lord's intervention in our lives, where would we be? We would be lost. We would be going about life in such a way that we'd be inevitably piling up regret after regret, struggling to figure out why things aren't coming together for us.

Apart from the Lord, our lives were a mess. We had no hope. We had no sense of unconditional love. Our future was bleak as we were destined for eternal condemnation. Yet He looked at us with compassion and intervened on our behalf.

It's an amazing thing to consider just how precious we are to the Lord. In love, He predestined us to be adopted into His family. In love, Jesus Christ came to this earth and took our sin and shame upon Himself because He knew that was a weight we were incapable of carrying. And our Lord continues to show us His great compassion to this very day.

When we pray to the Lord Jesus, we're praying to one who understands our struggles, perceives our weaknesses, and knows what it's like to walk in our shoes. He delights to show us His compassion and mercy and as He does so, we are drawn closer to Him as the one through whom we find ultimate solace.

173

June 17

"Father of the fatherless and protector of widows is God in his holy habitation."
-Psalm 68:5

We are vulnerable people. We may not like to admit that to ourselves, but it's true. We have weaknesses and limits. We are often the victims of the poor decisions of others. We regularly struggle with the effects of our own mistakes as well as the effects of the mistakes of those we long to be close to. We also bear the personal scars of tragedies that we have had no control over. Our struggles and our problems are real, but in the midst of every personal battle, we can take heart because our Lord is present with us.

The Lord sees our needs. He knows we have struggles. He sees those who have not experienced the love or regular daily presence of an earthly father. His compassionate eye is upon women who have lost their husbands to death.

Our greatest hope isn't in having a life of earthly ease. Our true hope is in Jesus Christ who fills the voids left by the struggles and tragedies we experience on this earth. Jesus Christ alone is the way to the Father. There is no other name under heaven whereby we can be saved.

Our Heavenly Father is the Father to the fatherless. He is the one who holds in His hands a secure future for the widow who trusts in Him.

June 18

"Fathers, do not provoke your children to anger, but bring them up in the discipline and instruction of the Lord."
-Ephesians 6:4

There are people in your life that the Lord graciously allows you to influence. There are people who copy what they see you practice. There are people who make decisions for their lives based on what they have learned from you, whether you have intentionally tried to teach them or not. You have been granted the privilege to be a living example of the presence of Jesus Christ to everyone He graciously puts you in contact with.

Some of the people you will influence most are the people who live in your home. The people we live in closest proximity to are also the people who have the greatest capacity to get on our nerves. We can see their quirks up close and they can see ours. They may have habits and preferences that annoy us. And if you're in a position of authority over them, you may at times be tempted to retaliate against them and provoke them to anger. When those tempting moments come, please choose an alternate path.

Instead of provoking others to anger, model the care, instruction, and leadership integrity that has been demonstrated to us by Jesus. Don't seek revenge. Don't stir up strife. Create a culture in your home that testifies to the heart and mind of our Lord.

June 19

> *"Husbands, love your wives, as Christ loved the church and gave himself up for her, that he might sanctify her, having cleansed her by the washing of water with the word,"*
> *-Ephesians 5:25-26*

Love is a misunderstood word by many people. To some, it's thought of merely from an emotional perspective. In that case, what is thought of as love can begin to take on a selfish tone as relationships gradually become more focused on what is received than what is given.

In the context of marriage, love should take on a deeper expression than mere emotional attachment. True love is sacrificial. It's the kind of love we see Jesus demonstrate to the church. Jesus gave His life on the cross for the eternal well-being of His bride, the church. Through faith in Jesus, we are made holy and we are cleansed from all unrighteousness. And this is all possible because of His act of sacrificial love.

If the Lord blesses you with the privilege to marry, demonstrate Christ-like love to your spouse. Focus more on their needs than your own. Serve your spouse. Make sacrifices of time, energy, and resources for your spouse. Consider yourself privileged to be able to do so, recognizing that even greater things were done on your behalf by Jesus Christ who loved you first.

June 20

"For what does it profit a man to gain the whole world and forfeit his soul?"
-Mark 8:36

We have all spent a portion of our life chasing something. Maybe we're chasing a dream or an ambition. Maybe we're chasing after material possessions or money. Maybe we're chasing after status or power. Maybe we're chasing after someone we think can make us feel complete.

There are all sorts of things in this world we might be chasing after and it's likely that at one point of time or another, we have mistakenly believed we can only be happy or content once we obtained the object of our search. But the things of this earth pass away. There is no logic in placing our ultimate hope in something that can wear out, fade, break, or be taken away.

Is there something in this world that you've been telling yourself you need to obtain in order to truly be content? Is it worth more to you than your relationship with Christ?

The wealthiest people in the world still feel empty if they're missing a genuine relationship with Jesus Christ. Jesus fills the void in our soul. When we have Christ, we can be content. He gives us a sense of lasting peace. He provides rest for our souls. Until we're convinced that He is all we truly need, there will always be a part of us that feels empty and disjointed.

June 21

"He who dwells in the shelter of the Most High will abide in the shadow of the Almighty."
-Psalm 91:1

In every life, there are things that have the potential to produce worry and fear. We fear circumstances we can't control. We fear people who may have poor motives. We fear "what if scenarios" that we've fabricated in our minds. But our lives on this earth don't need to be consumed with fear. Even in the most difficult and puzzling seasons, we have a refuge.

The Lord Himself is our refuge. His word encourages us to dwell in His shelter. To seek protection and provision from Him. To rest confidently, knowing that He watches over our lives.

Living in God's shelter and abiding in His shadow, is evidence of genuine faith. When we come to faith in Jesus, we can approach the coming days with a brand new perspective. We don't have to convince ourselves that we are the ultimate source of our protection and defense. Rather, we are convinced that one of the benefits of being part of the family of God is His assurance that our lives are held securely in His hand.

In every life there are trials, but when your next trial hits, you don't need to walk in fear. Through Christ, you have a true refuge. You are under the protective care and watchful eye of our loving Lord.

June 22

> *"The Lord will keep you from all evil; he will keep your life. The Lord will keep your going out and your coming in from this time forth and forevermore."*
> *-Psalm 121:7-8*

The temptation to sin is an ever present reality during the course of our earthly lives. We are tempted by the lusts of our flesh, the lusts of our eyes, and the boastful pride of life. Opportunities to defy the Lord, reject His word, and ignore His voice as He speaks to our hearts present themselves to us daily. Left to ourselves, we would be in continual rebellion against Him.

But our Lord understands the nature of our temptations. He knows we're surrounded by evil and He provides His strength and protection to make up for the deficit found in our human limitations. He doesn't lead us into temptation, rather, He provides us the way of escape.

Through faith in Jesus Christ we have been granted a new heart, new desires, and new priorities. We have been blessed with the privilege of seeing sin for what it really is. We have been shown that the long-term consequences that inevitably come from welcoming sin into our lives far outweigh the momentary benefits.

Where are you currently being tempted to welcome sin into your life? Are you relying on the Lord to keep you from evil? What route of escape from sin has He opened up for you?

June 23

> *"but they who wait for the Lord shall renew their strength; they shall mount up with wings like eagles; they shall run and not be weary; they shall walk and not faint."*
> *-Isaiah 40:31*

Hope is a concept that is often misunderstood. In modern day, we tend to think of a "hope" as being the same as a "wish." But biblically speaking, that's not the case at all.

Those who "wait" for the Lord are those who "hope" in the Lord. Biblical hope is a confident expectation that the Lord will fulfill His promises and decrees. Hope in the Lord isn't a wish. It's a certainty.

If our true hope is in Christ, we are saved from sin, and strengthened to live by faith. We are granted His help and guidance. We are energized by His power. We can rely on His arm to guide and protect us.

When our hope is in Christ, we won't become overly discouraged with earthly circumstances and momentary setbacks because we'll see those things from the perspective of eternity.

Through Jesus we are granted victory over sin, Satan, and death. Through Jesus we're blessed with the ability to maintain genuine hope in the midst of the highs and lows of our earthly lives.

June 24

> *"But the Lord is faithful. He will establish you and guard you against the evil one."*
> *-2 Thessalonians 3:3*

Every person, to one degree or another, struggles with fears of being abandoned. We worry about family and friends leaving us. We tend to be concerned about being left on our own. For some people this is a minor fear, but for others this can be a major concern particularly if they've experienced abandonment at some point in their lives.

Thankfully, our Lord doesn't abandon His children. He is the perfection of faithfulness and He doesn't leave us to fend for ourselves without His help. He strengthens us, plants our feet on firm ground, and He guards us against the schemes of Satan.

Even though Satan is a powerful adversary, we know from Scripture that he is a defeated foe. When Christ was crucified, He paid for our sin. When He rose from the grave, He defeated the power of Satan. Satan's days are numbered. His doom is certain. As he awaits his pending judgment, he seeks to devour God's family, but the Lord guards us against the schemes of the evil one.

Because Satan is a defeated foe, and we have received freedom from sin's bondage through faith in Christ, we don't need to give in to sin, temptation, or the schemes of the devil any longer.

June 25

> *Keep your life free from love of money,*
> *and be content with what you have, for he*
> *has said, "I will never leave you nor*
> *forsake you." So we can confidently say,*
> *"The Lord is my helper; I will not fear;*
> *what can man do to me?"*
> **-Hebrews 13:5-6**

In our world, money can become a very easy thing to love. We know what we can use it for. It can be exchanged for things that we want to own. It can be exchanged for trips or experiences we'd like to have. For some people, it's a sign of personal value and worth. People live for it. People kill for it. People die for it.

Christians are allowed to have money and be good stewards of it, but we're told to never love it. Be generous with it, but don't covet it. You don't need it as much as you think you do. If you have Jesus, you have everything you truly need in this world.

In fact, we're encouraged to know that we can be completely content in Christ and what He supplies because He will never leave us nor forsake us. And if our Lord doesn't plan to leave us, ignore us, abandon us, or forget us, what trial do we really need to fear? Tough seasons may come, but He is present with us in them all. Money won't fix our problems. It's better to be sacrificially generous with what the Lord entrusts to us than to be selfishly covetous with blessings He always intended us to share.

June 26

> *"sober-minded, self-controlled, respectable, hospitable, able to teach, not a drunkard, not violent but gentle, not quarrelsome, not a lover of money."*
> *-1 Timothy 3:2b-3*

When we come to faith in Christ, we can be grateful that He doesn't leave us in the same condition we were in when He first found us. In Christ, we are made a brand new creation. We are also indwelled by the Holy Spirit who grants us counsel, comfort, and helps us see things from the perspective of God.

The Holy Spirit has been given to us to help us along the way during our brief lives on this earth. The fruit of His presence in our lives becomes visible in all kinds of areas.

This Scripture tells us that such a man will be sober-minded. He will exhibit wisdom, common sense, and will be cautious about welcoming anything into his life or body that has the power to negatively alter his thinking. He will exhibit self-control and not act like a hot-head. He won't be someone who idolizes money or wastes his life vainly pursuing it as his top priority because of the mistaken belief that somehow money can bring ultimate satisfaction to the soul.

A godly man doesn't yield control of his life to unfruitful, unwise, and ungodly pursuits. He is content to yield his life to the control of the Holy Spirit.

June 27

> *"So then, brothers, we are debtors, not to the flesh, to live according to the flesh. For if you live according to the flesh you will die, but if by the Spirit you put to death the deeds of the body, you will live. For all who are led by the Spirit of God are sons of God."*
> *-Romans 8:12-14*

This passage speaks of debts. And it tells us that we aren't debtors to the flesh. What does that mean? It means we are not obligated to live according to the passions and desires of our old, sinful nature.

We've been set free from sin and death through Jesus Christ. We aren't obligated in any way to go back to the manner of living we were once caught up in.

Truthfully speaking, living according to the desires of the old, fleshly nature, results in disease, depression, and ultimately death.

By the grace of God, however, we have a better option. As sons of God who have been adopted into His family, we are now truly alive. We aren't being led by the forces of evil. We're being led by the Holy Spirit. He's providing us divine counsel. He's speaking to our hearts and our minds. He's illuminating the truth of the Scriptures to us. He's pointing us in a direction that is for God's glory and our good.

June 28

> *"When he had said this, he showed them his hands and his side. Then the disciples were glad when they saw the Lord."*
> *-John 20:20*

As Jesus was speaking to the disciples in this room, He showed them His scars. His scars serve as a visible testimony of what He endured in order for our sin to be forgiven and allow us to become part of His family. He showed these scars to the disciples to confirm His identity to them. He was also making sure that they understood that even though He had just walked through a wall to enter the room, he wasn't some sort of ghost. He was physically present with them.

Jesus was doing a rather large favor for His followers here. He was giving them a gift that impacts the core of a person's beliefs. In showing them His scars, He was blessing them with confidence - not in themselves, but in Him. How is this the case?

Jesus was proving to them and to us that death couldn't defeat Him. Nails in His hands and feet couldn't hold Him back. A spear in His side couldn't end His life. And if we have faith in Him, our life is wrapped up in His.

From the later testimonies of the disciples's lives, it appears that this experience may have helped them to be willing to ultimately face death for Christ's glory because they could now see that death had lost it's power over them.

June 29

> *"The Lord will fulfill his purpose for me;*
> *your steadfast love, O Lord, endures*
> *forever. Do not forsake the work of your*
> *hands."*
> ***-Psalm 138:8***

There is a purpose for your life. God's chief goal for you is that you would glorify and enjoy Him forever through faith in Jesus Christ. In the midst of that larger focus, the Lord also has a specific function for you while He works out His master plan for mankind.

He has granted you specific gifts and abilities. He has caused you to live when you live and where you live with the goal to use your life to impact the lives of others for His glory. He has developed your personality and intends to use your life in ways you may not initially perceive.

In the midst of all of this, He reminds you of His steadfast love. His loving nature will never change. His desire to seek the best for you will not be something He reconsiders or regrets. He is the same yesterday, today, and forever.

God intentionally fashioned you in your mother's womb. You are His handiwork. You were created in His image. He is present with you to lead you, guide you, and grant you His counsel. He will not forsake you because you are the work of His hands and the object of His affection.

> *"For everyone who does wicked things hates the light and does not come to the light, lest his works should be exposed. But whoever does what is true comes to the light, so that it may be clearly seen that his works have been carried out in God."*
> *-John 3:20-21*

Integrity is when we do what is right, even when we don't think anyone is watching us. We all struggle to live with integrity, but through faith in Jesus, we are granted His ability to walk as He walked.

Wickedness thrives in the darkness. It gains its best victories when it thinks it can't be seen. It accomplishes its objectives when it's certain that its motives won't be exposed. Those who practice wickedness, love the dark and hate the light.

Jesus is the light of the world. He came to give light to all of us who were living in the darkness of sin and wickedness. He invites us to trust in Him, rely on His power, and walk in the light.

Are we walking with integrity? Are our lives being lived in the midst of the light of Christ? Is there any aspect of our lives that we would be hesitant to hold up to that light? Are we trying to hide anything from others or even from Christ? As followers of Christ, we're encouraged to walk in the light of His truth in every circumstance or situation.

July 1

> *"For by the grace given to me I say to everyone among you not to think of himself more highly than he ought to think, but to think with sober judgment, each according to the measure of faith that God has assigned."*
> *-Romans 12:3*

Conceit is the same as self-idolatry. When we begin to think more highly of ourselves than we ought to, we're essentially preaching a message to our hearts that is the opposite of the gospel.

The gospel teaches us that by nature, we are needy, confused,spiritually blind sinners who were doomed. But Jesus looked at us with compassion, saw our need, and intervened on our behalf by paying for our sin and taking our punishment upon Himself.

When Jesus was cursed by those who rejected Him, He didn't strut or reply with arrogance. Even though He is God, He willingly humbled Himself and graciously chose to serve and suffer for humanity.

When we make the mistake of thinking too highly of ourselves, we miss out on opportunities to serve others because those opportunities start to seem "beneath" us. And when we idolize ourselves, we forget the example Christ set for us of responding to others with humility and a servant's heart.

July 2

> *"The heart is deceitful above all things, and desperately sick; who can understand it?"*
> *-Jeremiah 17:9*

Frequently, people use the phrase, "Just listen to your heart." What do you think about that statement? Is that good counsel for someone who wants to live in faithful obedience to Jesus Christ?

Scripture teaches us that by nature, we are sinners. Sin impacts all areas of our lives including our intellect, emotions, and will. By nature, our heart has the capacity to deceive us and lead us astray. It isn't a reliable voice to listen to.

When we come to faith in Jesus Christ, we are indwelled by the Holy Spirit. We are cleansed of our sin and given a brand new nature that exists along side our old nature. We're also granted the counsel of the Holy Spirit to help lead us in the direction He wants us to go.

When you're being tested and when you're making decisions that impact your life and the lives of those you love, what voice are you listening to? Are you listening to your heart when it's deceiving you or are you willing to listen to the counsel of the Holy Spirit? The Holy Spirit will never lead you astray and will never tell you to do anything that contradicts with the Word of God.

July 3

> *"Righteousness exalts a nation, but sin is*
> *a reproach to any people."*
> *-Proverbs 14:34*

Throughout the course of human history, nations have risen and fallen. Some have become so strong that they seemed to be beyond the ability to fail. Others seemed so weak that it was surprising they lasted as long as they did.

What makes a nation strong? What makes a nation weak?

The only hope for the nations of the world is Jesus Christ. Through Him we find salvation and the gift of righteousness. His presence in our lives helps us see the world differently and treat each other more thoughtfully.

When an individual welcomes Jesus into their life, they experience powerful changes that begin within and eventually work their way into all aspects of daily living. Nations are made up of individuals. The more individuals come to know Jesus, the greater the propensity for the nation they live in to be influenced to practice righteousness.

Where do you live? Is your nation gravitating toward righteousness or sin? How can you be praying for your fellow countrymen? How is Christ using you as His ambassador to your nation?

July 4

> *"For freedom Christ has set us free; stand firm therefore, and do not submit again to a yoke of slavery."*
> **-Galatians 5:1**

Freedom is a beautiful thing. It is a gift from God. It is a blessing that God joyfully bestows on each and every one of His children. But it can be a misunderstood blessing by some.

In certain contexts, people understand freedom to mean the ability to do anything they choose, regardless of the consequences. Spiritually speaking, however, that's not the nature of the freedom the Lord has granted us.

Before we came to faith in Jesus Christ, we were slaves to sin. We were bound in chains to unrighteousness. Through Jesus, however, we are set free from that slavery. We no longer need to go back to living in that kind of bondage. We are free to live a life that brings Christ glory and reflects the genuine nature of our faith in Him.

Jesus has made us free to live in the light of His righteousness. We are free to love as He loves, live as He has empowered us to live, and choose that which would honor Him over that which is dishonorable. His Spirit strengthens us to stand firm in the midst of a sinful world. When we're tempted to rebel against our Lord, His word reminds us that we are no longer slaves to rebellion. Through Jesus, we are truly free.

July 5

> *And you will say in that day: "Give thanks to the Lord, call upon his name, make known his deeds among the peoples, proclaim that his name is exalted."*
> *-Isaiah 12:4*

At present, there are many people in this world who are either intentionally ignorant of who the Lord is and what He has done, or they simply have never been told about the good news of salvation through Jesus Christ. But Scripture reveals that there will be a day when all the nations will worship Christ and call Him Lord. We look forward to that day, and in the meantime, we can live out the fruit of what it looks like to know Him in a personal way.

We have the privilege of giving Him thanks. We thank Him for rescuing us from certain condemnation. We thank Him for His comforting presence with us. We thank Him for the new outlook on life He has blessed us with.

In our times of need and in our times of plenty, we call on His name. We seek His intervention in our lives. We pray for His blessing to be upon others. We ask Him to reveal Himself to those who don't know Him yet.

While we wait for His return, we joyfully tell others of the work He accomplishes among His people.

July 6

> *"Heaven and earth will pass away,*
> *but my words will not pass away."*
> *-Matthew 24:35*

What do we tend to value in life? What do we have that has lasting importance to us?

Many of the things our hearts are inclined to treasure in this world are temporary things. At times, we place increasing value on the very treasures Jesus has cautioned us not to idolize.

Truthfully, much of what our eyes are drawn to and our flesh tends to crave is here for just a moment and then gone. Jesus reminds us that both heaven and earth will pass away. Scripture reveals to us that both are going to be created new. But the words of Christ will remain. His teaching has eternal value.

What has Christ taught us that we're being called to value today? What has He modeled for us that we're being empowered to put into practice?

Creation was spoken into existence by the powerful word of Christ. The universe is being sustained by the powerful word of Christ. If His word is powerful enough to create and sustain the universe, do we have any logical reason to ignore what He has communicated?

Let Jesus speak to you today and listen to what He says.

July 7

> *"We are not commending ourselves to you again but giving you cause to boast about us, so that you may be able to answer those who boast about outward appearance and not about what is in the heart. For if we are beside ourselves, it is for God; if we are in our right mind, it is for you."*
> *-2 Corinthians 5:12-13*

What keeps us from openly sharing the good news of salvation with others? Isn't it most often a fear of what they will think of us or how we think it might make us look? Some Christians in this world are being genuinely and intensely persecuted, but in our country are we being beaten and put in prison for our faith? Are we being fired from our jobs because we're believers? Is there a risk of us being executed because we bear the name of Christ? The worst thing that tends to happen in our context is someone makes a face at us or says something insulting and yet, that's enough to keep many Christians quiet.

One of the dominant, driving forces in our lives and in the lives of those we know is the desire to be thought of well by others. Have we become overly concerned with outward appearances and less concerned with what's taking place in our hearts? Are we concerned with what the Lord wants to do in the hearts of others as they hear the Gospel, trust in Christ, and follow His teaching?

July 8

> *"For the love of Christ controls us, because we have concluded this: that one has died for all, therefore all have died; and he died for all, that those who live might no longer live for themselves but for him who for their sake died and was raised."*
> *-2 Corinthians 5:14-15*

What's the nicest thing that anyone has ever done for us? That's answered in this passage. Jesus Christ died for us. He took on flesh, lived a sinless life and died on the cross because of our sin. Then He rose from the grave and lives forever. He died for us that we too might live, and that this new life, this second chance we've been given, will not be lived selfishly. We're told here that the calling on our lives, or the way we can say "thank you" is by living for Him who died on our behalf and was raised again.

Selfishness is the mindset of this world, but it should never be the mindset of one who has been blessed with new life in Christ. Once our hearts and minds grab hold of what Jesus has truly done for us, that produces a change. It takes selfish dead men like we were and makes us selfless people who are alive forevermore in Christ.

It also changes what compels or motivates us. We are no longer controlled by the passions of our old nature. We're controlled by the love of Christ. We aren't controlled by anger, the need to be right, a political or social philosophy or even fear. Christ's love is now the driving force in our lives.

July 9

> *"so as to walk in a manner worthy of the Lord, fully pleasing to him, bearing fruit in every good work and increasing in the knowledge of God."*
> *-Colossians 1:10*

Scripture uses the concept of "walking" to illustrate something of a deeper spiritual significance. It's a term that refers to how we live and conduct ourselves. Specifically, we're being told in this passage that we are to walk or live in a manner that: 1. Is worthy of the Lord, 2. Is fully pleasing to Him, 3. Bears fruit in every good work, 4. Is increasing in the knowledge of God.

There are two ways to approach a verse like this. One approach is helpful and effective. The other approach will drive you crazy. Many people select the crazy approach.

The crazy or "drive-you-crazy" approach is to try to do this without help. Trying to live your life worthy of the Lord. Trying to please Christ in all things. Trying to do good works. Trying to increase in your knowledge of Him, and do this all without seeking help and with total reliance on your own strength and perceived abilities. That approach will drive you nuts, and it isn't the way of new life in Christ - even though it may look very spiritual to others from the outside.

The effective approach is to come to a place of humility and accept that you can't do any of this without Christ. It is only in the power of Christ that we can walk in a manner worthy of His name.

July 10

> *"And I am sure of this, that he who*
> *began a good work in you will bring it to*
> *completion at the day of Jesus Christ."*
> *-Philippians 1:6*

When we look around our homes, we can find plenty of examples of unfinished projects. Repairs that aren't complete. Furniture that needs to be dusted. Books that we started, but never got around to finishing. We have a bad habit of leaving things undone or incomplete. Thankfully, our Lord operates differently than we sometimes do. When He begins a project, He finishes it.

At the moment we came to faith in Jesus Christ, a divinely empowered work began in our lives. We were immediately indwelt by the Holy Spirit. We were equipped and gifted to serve as Christ's ambassadors. We were rescued from the penalty of our sin. We were saved from death and condemnation.

God is also continuing a process within us called sanctification. He is helping us to grow in holiness. He is training us to value and reflect the heart of Christ in all we do. He is bringing our faith from a place of immaturity to a place of maturity. And He won't quit the work He's doing in us until it's accomplished. When Christ returns for us, we will be given a new body and we will live in His presence, forever, in complete perfection. We will no longer struggle with sin or sorrow because our old way of living will be done away with. The work God began in us will be brought to perfect completion.

July 11

> *"Ah, Lord God! It is you who have made the heavens and the earth by your great power and by your outstretched arm! Nothing is too hard for you."*
> *-Jeremiah 32:17*

Surrounding us in every direction are examples of God's handiwork. In the skies, we see the planets and stars. On the ground, we see the vegetation. In the seas, we see all kinds of complex organisms. God has created a detailed, intricate, purposeful creation, and by His grace, we are part of it.

Scripture also reminds us that all creation is being sustained by the powerful word of Jesus Christ. He upholds that which He spoke into existence, and at the same time, He desires to be an integral and personal part of our individual lives. This is hard to fathom, but the word of God confirms that it is true.

During the course of our lives, there are going to be difficult seasons that come upon us. The answers to our problems won't always seem easy or obvious to us. But in all season and experiences, our Lord desires that we trust in Him. He is the one who redeems our circumstances and uses them for His glory and our good.

The very situations that may seem impossible for us, are not impossible for our Lord who spoke creation into existence. Nothing is too hard for Him. Trust Him to handle what it troubling you.

July 12

> *But he answered, "It is written, " 'Man shall not live by bread alone, but by every word that comes from the mouth of God.' "*
> **-Matthew 4:4**

What are you convinced you need in order to survive? What does your heart long for? What are you currently seeking to supply your deepest level of satisfaction in this world?

All of us, in one way or another, have spent time convinced that what we need from this world in order to be truly content, is more of the physical resources present on this planet. We mistakenly think that acquiring more food will make us content, but it won't. Or maybe we believe earthly riches, stately homes, and romantic relationships are what we really need. But Jesus reminds us that the source of life and contentment can't be found in any of those temporary options.

Jesus is who we really need. When we have Him, we find contentment and lasting peace. His word brings us comfort and hope. His counsel grants us wisdom and understanding. The truth of His gospel brings enlightenment and joy.

If you've been telling your heart that all you need is "one more thing" from this world in order to be content, please remember Christ's teaching in this passage. He is the one we need. His word points us toward Him.

July 13

> *"Therefore God has highly exalted him and bestowed on him the name that is above every name, so that at the name of Jesus every knee should bow, in heaven and on earth and under the earth, and every tongue confess that Jesus Christ is Lord, to the glory of God the Father."*
> **-Philippians 2:9-11**

Throughout the New Testament Scriptures, we're given a picture of who Jesus is and what He is like. The picture we're given is multi-faceted. Some of the biblical examples share historical accounts of the ways in which Jesus responded to people. He showed kindness, compassion, mercy, and selfless sacrifice.

At times, it can be somewhat easy for us to take Christ's intentional meekness and mistakenly assume it was a sign of weakness. But that's not the case at all. His power, glory, and authority are all made clear when we look at the totality of God's word.

The day is soon coming when every knee will bow to Jesus, and every tongue will confess that He is Lord. Those who trust in Him will bow to Him and call Him Lord. Those who have rejected Him will also bow to Him and call Him Lord. The beautiful thing about knowing this ahead of time is that we've been given the privilege to worship Jesus and acknowledge Him as Lord right now. We don't have to wait for a future day to enjoy the blessings, benefits, and privileges of welcoming Jesus to lead and direct our lives.

July 14

> *"If you keep my commandments, you will abide in my love, just as I have kept my Father's commandments and abide in his love."*
> *-John 15:10*

What visible proof is there in our lives that shows we truly love Jesus Christ? If we say we love Jesus, does that provide sufficient proof or is there a more convincing form of evidence?

When we truly love someone, we care about what matters to them. We make decisions and take actions that demonstrate our desire to honor those we love.

Our love for Christ is demonstrated by the fruit of our lives. Because we love Him, His commandments aren't burdensome to us. We delight to follow His direction. We prioritize His revealed will over our fluctuating preferences.

The greatest motivation to live in faithful obedience to Jesus is love. It can seem easy at times to drift toward listening to our own voice and counsel over His, but that doesn't produce the sense of peace, satisfaction, and joy our hearts truly crave.

Jesus invites us to abide in His love, to grow in our awareness of it, to implement it in our everyday interactions, and to recognize that obedience to His teaching isn't a burden to be endured, but a blessing to be enjoyed.

July 15

> *"Therefore put away all filthiness and rampant wickedness and receive with meekness the implanted word, which is able to save your souls."*
> *-James 1:21*

Our new life in Christ is an amazing thing. Before coming to know Jesus, we went about our day-to-day lives, unaware of the wickedness and worldliness we were embracing. We were ignorantly and foolishly inviting things into our lives that we mistakenly believed would bring benefit to us, when in actuality, they were producing death, disease, and depression.

But then Jesus rescued us. He gave us the gift of a new life, a new mind, and new eyes. He teaches us to see things like He sees them and value things that He values. His word reminds us not to invite anything back into our lives that reeks of the sin and corruption that is so prevalent in this world.

As we cast away the very things we once mistakenly embraced, we're also called to receive the truth of God's word into our lives. His word teaches us what to value. His word teaches us how to live by faith. His word shines a light on the creeping nature of sin and exposes its true motives.

The word of God likewise reveals to us that our souls find salvation through no one else other than Jesus Christ. Embrace this truth today and welcome the protective presence of Christ to reign among us.

July 16

> *"For in him the whole fullness of deity dwells bodily, and you have been filled in him, who is the head of all rule and authority."*
> **-Colossians 2:9-10**

There are plenty of people who still debate who Jesus is. It's clear that there has never been another single individual who has had as powerful an impact on the world as Him, but for some people, their mind isn't fully made up on who Jesus really is.

Some call Him a teacher. Some call Him a leader. Some are willing to call Him a prophet. Some dare to call Him a fraud. But who do we say He is?

According to this passage, Jesus is God. Jesus is the "fullness of deity" and He graciously took on a human body in order to live the perfect life we couldn't live, die the death we deserved to die, rise from death to defeat the curse of sin, and offer new life to all who trust in Him.

The Scripture also reminds us that when we have Jesus, we truly do have all we really need in this world. By grace, through faith, we are "filled" in Jesus. We don't need another savior. We don't need another source of salvation. We don't need a new source of revelation. We don't need another source of power. In Christ we find all that we truly need and our hearts must learn to become content in Him.

July 17

> *"For I am not ashamed of the gospel, for it is the power of God for salvation to everyone who believes, to the Jew first and also to the Greek."*
> *-Romans 1:16*

The Bible tells us that the message of the gospel sounds like foolishness to those who are perishing. To those who live in ignorance of their need for salvation, it might sound comical or even fanatical to think that God would take on human flesh and willingly allow Himself to be nailed to a cross in order to atone for sins He did not personally commit.

But that's exactly what Jesus did, so what will we do with that truth? Knowing that there are many people who may regard that message as silly or not applicable to them, it can be tempting to act somewhat timid about the truth of the gospel. Instead of expressing it with joy, it's possible for us to act like we're ashamed of the very message that brings us hope.

We don't need to be ashamed of the gospel. If our hope isn't anchored in earthly prestige or the fleeting praise of men, we can unashamedly and lovingly express that our hearts find great hope and peace through the knowledge that Christ loves us enough to rescue and redeem us.

How audibly does your life and your words express your love for Jesus Christ and your gratefulness for the good news of His gospel message?

July 18

> *"I will praise you with an upright heart,*
> *when I learn your righteous rules."*
> *-Psalm 119:7*

What bothers your conscience? What troubles you or keeps you up at night? Is there any aspect of your life that you'd rather not think about, because if you thought about it, you'd have to make changes?

What do you do when you come across something in God's word that contradicts what you would naturally prefer to believe? Do you ignore it or embrace it? What happens within you when you ignore it?

The word of God points our hearts toward Jesus Christ. We're encouraged to trust Jesus and live to bring Him glory. When we embrace the teaching of God's word, and rely on Christ's strength to put it into practice, our hearts and our consciences experience a sense of peace in knowing we've been obedient to the Lord's leading. When we ignore or reject the teaching of God's word, our hearts and consciences trouble us up until the moment we repent of our rebellion and unbelief.

As people who have been blessed to have access to the wisdom and counsel of God's word, let's not neglect this gift we've been given. Let's welcome the teaching of God's word into our lives. Let's embrace the moments when it challenges cultural preferences and personal preferences. Instead of idolizing our own opinions, let's honor Jesus by keeping His word joyfully.

> *So the Jews said, "See how he loved him!" But some of them said, "Could not he who opened the eyes of the blind man also have kept this man from dying?"*
> *-John 11:36-37*

Have you ever blamed God for your troubles? Have you ever been a little confrontational in your prayers because you didn't think you deserved the trials you were experiencing?

Why does God allow bad things to happen to good people? We may ask that question, but the truth is, there was only one good person, Jesus, and He was crucified. If we possess any righteousness, it didn't come from ourselves. Righteousness is a gift that is added to our account through faith in Jesus.

But still, we like to blame God as if the problems we experience in this world are His fault. He created a perfect world. He made us in His image, without sin. He invited us to love Him above all else. He warned us that if we went our own way, we would invite death and sorrow into our experience. Then we went our own way and ever since, we've been blaming God for the mess we've made.

Our problems are not God's fault, they are ours. Thankfully, that's not where the story ends. God by nature is compassionate, and though our problems are our fault, Jesus offers Himself as the solution.

> *"and when they had called in the apostles, they beat them and charged them not to speak in the name of Jesus, and let them go. Then they left the presence of the council, rejoicing that they were counted worthy to suffer dishonor for the name. And every day, in the temple and from house to house, they did not cease teaching and preaching that the Christ is Jesus."*
> *-Acts 5:40-42*

How hard were these men were beaten? How swollen were their faces? How torn were their clothes? How bruised were their bodies? These men were being punched in the face and yet they left the presence of the council rejoicing.

What were they rejoicing over? Because of their relationship with Jesus, they had joy that could not be diminished by their circumstances. They loved Christ. They taught in His name, and testified to the eternal power that is present in His name. And they delighted themselves in the fact that they were *"counted worthy to suffer dishonor"* in the eyes of men because they lived and taught in the name of Christ.

And just as we're called to do,, they continued to teach others in homes and in public places that Jesus is the Christ. These men rejoiced in their suffering and pressed on with all the strength the Lord had given them.

Likewise, we can also praise Jesus when all seems well and in our times of suffering.

> *"Therefore be alert, remembering that for*
> *three years I did not cease night or day to*
> *admonish every one with tears. And now*
> *I commend you to God and to the word of*
> *his grace, which is able to build you up*
> *and to give you the inheritance among all*
> *those who are sanctified."*
> *-Acts 20:31-32*

The Apostle Paul, who is quoted in this passage, was looking forward to his inheritance in God's kingdom, and on top of that, he was happy to work with his retirement plan in mind. Empowered by the Holy Spirit, he was making investments that would be counted in his favor for all eternity.

Scripture teaches that every believer has an inheritance in Heaven, and that in addition to that, the Lord has rewards in store for believers as a bonus that compliments everything else He's given us.

At times, we're tempted to work for the things of this world as if they're the best of what there is. But why do you suppose God tells us about an inheritance that He has in store for those who are in Christ? In part, it may be an attempt to keep us looking forward in faith to things that we cannot yet see, and motivate us to take our discipleship seriously.

I think it's also part of the Lord's plan to develop appreciative hearts within us. A thankful heart is a sacrificial heart. A thankful heart is a giving heart.

July 22

> *He said to them, "But who do you say that*
> *I am?" Simon Peter replied, "You are the*
> *Christ, the Son of the living God."*
> *-Matthew 16:15-16*

The biggest question we're all being given the option to wrestle with is this, "To you, who is Jesus?" In regard to our eternal destiny, there is no greater question. In regard to our daily walk in the present, there is no greater question.

As we well know, there are many ways people choose to answer that question, but all answers can be boiled down to two primary categories; distant or relational.

If our answer to the question of who Jesus is speaks of Him as if He is a distant, uninvolved, deceased human leader, that means we have chosen to forego His help, assistance, empowerment, hope, and rescue. It means we're on a path that leads to a discouraging present and an unenviable future.

If our answer to the question of who Jesus is mirrors the response Simon Peter gave, we're on the path that leads to hope, joy, forgiveness, and an eternity in the life-giving presence of our Savior and Creator, Jesus Christ.

Jesus is the Messiah. He is God in the flesh. He lives, and He offers new, abundant, purposeful, and eternal life to all who come to faith in Him. He isn't distant. He wants to be part of your life both today and forever.

July 23

but Jesus said, "Let the little children come to me and do not hinder them, for to such belongs the kingdom of heaven."
-Matthew 19:14

One of the great blessings we are able to experience by observing the earthly ministry of Jesus, is the privilege of gaining a deeper appreciation of His heart. We learn more about what motivates Him, what pleases Him, and what He desires to see in our lives.

We also observe how deeply He values the lives of those who are often neglected or marginalized by society. Throughout the gospels, Jesus spoke kindly and respectfully toward women, who at that time were often treated like property. He also treated children with kindness and welcomed them into His presence.

Children don't possess wisdom, but they do display great faith. They are examples of what it means to walk by faith, and Jesus teaches us that unless we trust in Him with the kind of faith we often see expressed by a child, we will have no place in His kingdom.

It can be easy to become impatient with children because they are still in the process of learning and growing mature. But Jesus was patient with them, and He is also patient with us. He loves children. He loves adults. And He invites us all to come to Him with genuine faith and excitement over being welcomed into His presence.

July 24

> *"It is well with the man who deals generously and lends; who conducts his affairs with justice."*
> **-Psalm 112:5**

When the Lord entrusts something to our care, there are several ways we can treat that blessing. We can hoard it and hold onto to it with selfish motivations, or we can share it and take pleasure in blessing others in the same manner we were blessed.

When we give or when we lend, we should do so without expecting something in return. Our motives shouldn't be centered around obtaining earthly riches or privileges. Rather, we should be motivated by the thought of giving Christ glory, and graciously sharing gifts with others because of the gracious and undeserved gift of salvation we have been given by Christ.

If we have Jesus, we already have all that we truly need. We are amply supplied with all that is necessary for true life and godliness. There is nothing we need to covet. There is no earthly thing we need to attempt to utilize to satisfy the longing of our souls. Jesus perfectly fills the void that once existed in our hearts.

What needs has the Lord brought to your attention? Who do you know that the Lord is encouraging you to bless? What brings a greater experience of joy to your heart; withholding blessing or generously sharing a blessing with someone in need?

> *"Do not love the world or the things in the world. If anyone loves the world, the love of the Father is not in him. For all that is in the world—the desires of the flesh and the desires of the eyes and pride in possessions—is not from the Father but is from the world. And the world is passing away along with its desires, but whoever does the will of God abides forever."*
> *-1 John 2:15-17*

Even if we believe in Jesus and are looking forward to an eternity in His presence, it can be difficult to avoid being tempted to over-value the fleeting things of this world. Sometimes we treat temporary things like they are permanent realities. We might even start to place our sense of hope and security in things of this world that have no capacity to last beyond this brief season of time.

Jesus loves the people of this world, but He doesn't love the mindset or values of this world. This world invites us to covet what we don't possess. The mindset of this age teaches us to desire things that compete with our affections for Jesus Christ. The worldview many people we love have embraced is a worldview that drags them down and doesn't build them up.

Instead of embracing the mindset of this world, Jesus invites us to be transformed through faith in Him. As transformed people, the love of God the Father is shown to be present in our lives.

July 26

"Now faith is the assurance of things hoped for, the conviction of things not seen."
-Hebrews 11:1

Walking by sight is the natural inclination of every human. By nature, we tend to trust our eyes. Our confidence is often in what we can see and what we have previously experienced.

But real life goes far beyond natural sight. When we come to trust in Jesus Christ, and receive His gift of salvation, we are spiritually granted a new mind and new eyes. We are blessed with the ability to see things like He sees them and perceive things like He perceives them.

Faith pleases the Lord. It is His desire that His children walk through every day with confident reliance on Him. The faith that He has prompted us to express assures our hearts of things we cannot naturally see. By faith, we confidently look forward to a future where Christ will reign on this earth and restore His creation. By faith, we believe the Scriptures that tell us we will one day be granted a new, sinless body. By faith, we are certain that sorrow and pain are temporary conditions, and the future of all those who trust Jesus will ultimately be filled with abundant joy.

Walking by natural sight isn't God's ultimate desire for us. Living by faith, however, pleases Him greatly.

July 27

> *"Therefore, since we are surrounded by so great a cloud of witnesses, let us also lay aside every weight, and sin which clings so closely, and let us run with endurance the race that is set before us,"*
> *-Hebrews 12:1*

Through faith in Jesus Christ, we have been set free from slavery to sin. We are no longer bound to the sin that once held us in its grips. We are no longer forced to do its bidding or obey its directives. Jesus has removed those binding chains from us and has granted us true liberty in Him.

But that doesn't mean sin won't be a struggle for us during the course of our earthly lives. We are frequently tempted to go right back to the very sin we've already been freed from. Knowing that this is the case, God's word invites us to embrace a better option.

Instead of allowing the sin that tempts us to weigh us down and cling to us, we're invited to lay it aside. In other words, we're invited to leave it behind and not invite it to go on the journey of faith that Christ has us walking on. The things that tempt us might have been welcomed companions during previous seasons of our lives, but they aren't welcomed to be a part of this segment of our journey.

Rather, in Christ, we have been grated the liberty, grace, and endurance we need to run the race He has set before us without being held back by our former masters.

> *"For whatever was written in former days was written for our instruction, that through endurance and through the encouragement of the Scriptures we might have hope. "*
> *-Romans 15:4*

Our Lord has intentionally provided us with a tool to help us grow strong in Him. The tool He has blessed us with is His word. The Scriptures have been given to us to instruct us. The Scriptures have been given to us to help us endure difficult seasons. The Scriptures have been given to us to encourage us. The Scriptures have been given to us to help us cherish the certain hope that is only found in Him.

When God's Word speaks of hope, it's not speaking of wishes. It's not speak of dreams. It's not speaking of possibilities. It's speaking of guarantees. It's telling you and me that we will experience many moments in this world that require more strength and endurance from us than we naturally possess. Yet through Jesus, we can see beyond those moments and can know for certain that the outcome of it all is safely secured by Him. We know the end of the story. We already know it will all work out.

What do you suppose sustained the Apostle Paul in His ministry? What sustained the missionaries, martyrs and every other committed believer throughout the ages? It was hope in Jesus Christ, and that hope beams from every page of the word of God.

July 29

> *"O my God, I am ashamed and blush to lift my face to you, my God, for our iniquities have risen higher than our heads, and our guilt has mounted up to the heavens."*
> **-Ezra 9:6**

Ezra states that this sin makes him blush and feel shame. He speaks of "our" iniquities and "our" guilt. He recalls the patterns he has seen of his people's history, a history of doing this over and over again, and he lays this all before the Lord.

While this is certainly painful to read, it's also a powerful reminder that we as members of the body of Christ would do well to heed. It's easy to feel overly individualistic at times, but the truth is, we're all part of one body. If we believe in Christ, we have been united together as family.

That means if you're struggling, it matters to me. If I'm struggling, it matters to you. If one of us goes in a direction that dishonors the name of Christ, we can't just remove ourselves from caring. We rejoice and we grieve together as a family.

In life, because of both our pride and shame, it can be very tempting for us to try to hold on to our feelings of guilt instead of confessing them to the Lord or to others. But the Lord doesn't want us to go through life that way. He invites us to confess our sin so that we may live, untethered to sin's power. Sin and guilt do their best work in secret, but they are no match for the light of Christ.

July 30

> *"If the world hates you, know that it has hated me before it hated you. If you were of the world, the world would love you as its own; but because you are not of the world, but I chose you out of the world, therefore the world hates you."*
> *-John 15:18-19*

Jesus uses the words "love" and "hate" in this passage, in a much stronger sense than we may initially realize. He cautions us that the world will at times express irrational hatred for His followers just as it has for Him.

Jesus came into this world to teach, model, suffer for, die for, and redeem this world, but because His holiness and the specifics of His teaching challenge the preferences of the human heart, He is irrationally hated by many in this world. And those who bear His name and submit their lives to His lordship, can expect to be irrationally hated as well, even when they're trying to serve others for the greater good.

Jesus also cautions His followers that if we're serious about following Him, we may experience outright persecution.

If the good you're doing in this world is an attempt to be loved by the world, you're going to be disappointed and possibly heartbroken. But if you recognize that the Lord sees you and loves you, you'll find it easier to align your expectations with what Christ has graciously made known.

July 31

> *"As soon as I heard these words I sat down and wept and mourned for days, and I continued fasting and praying before the God of heaven."*
> *-Nehemiah 1:4*

One of the worst things we can do as people when our hearts are burdened is to try to carry those burdens ourselves. Sometimes, we're fearful of burdening others, so we don't share what's troubling us. Other times, it may be that we aren't convinced God will really help us if we bring these matters before Him. But the Lord, His word, and His people can bring us encouragement if we will be willing to humble ourselves and admit our need for it.

Nehemiah took the burden that was weighing his heart down and he brought it before the Lord. He prayed and confessed his sin. He confessed the sin of his people. He confessed their failure to keep the commandments, and he acknowledged that this was why they were frequently in difficult situations like they now found themselves in.

If a person never comes to this kind of admission before the Lord, they will never experience the joy of His salvation. If we keep trying to carry the burdens only God can carry, we'll spend our life on earth, and our eternity, foreign to the mercy of God. But if we recognize that Jesus Christ, the Son of God came to this earth to keep the very commandments we violated, and if we will trust in Him to cleanse us of all unrighteousness, He will lift our burdens from us, having placed them on Himself, and He will set us free to enjoy His gift of righteousness.

218

August 1

> *One day, as Jesus was teaching the people*
> *in the temple and preaching the gospel, the*
> *chief priests and the scribes with the elders*
> *came up and said to him, "Tell us by what*
> *authority you do these things, or who it is*
> *that gave you this authority."*
> *-Luke 20:1-2*

The religious leaders questioned Christ's authority. When we read the gospels, the religious leaders of that era tend to be presented in an unfavorable light. Because of that, we tend to write them off and dismiss their actions. But sometimes, as uncomfortable as it may be, it can be helpful to study their words and deeds with the goal of asking if those same things are present in our lives as well.

Have you ever questioned Christ's authority? I'm not just speaking about the season of your life before you came to faith in Him. I'm also speaking about the season of your life that you're currently in the midst of. Is there anything Christ has ever said that makes you uncomfortable? Have you ever sensed that He was asking anything of you that you felt hesitant to respond to? Is there a false belief that you still cling to because you're trying to soothe your heart with it? Is there a pattern of behavior in your life that Christ has already revealed to you that He is eager to transform?

We may not question Christ's authority outright, but it's entirely possible that we struggle with covertly elevating ourselves as a higher authority in our lives than Him. What will it take for that pattern to change?

August 2

"But be doers of the word, and not hearers only, deceiving yourselves."
-James 1:22

The Lord has blessed us in countless ways. When mankind rebelled against Him in the Garden of Eden, the Lord would have been justified in cutting us off from His presence forever. He could have chosen not to redeem us, not to care for us, and not to bless us with any revelation of Himself.

In Jesus, God was revealed to us in human form. He walked among us, lived with us, died for us, rose from death, and promised to return again. The Lord has also given us revelation through His word. The pages of Scripture point our hearts toward Jesus and teach us the necessity of trusting Him and walking with Him daily.

Many believers, convinced that the Scriptures are divinely revealed by God, spend a considerable amount of time studying them and learning the content of both the Old and New Testaments. This is an important practice for anyone who wants to grow in their understanding of God's heart and God's will.

But the Bible isn't a big trivia book. It's meant to illuminate our hearts and produce life change. We're called to read it, internalize it's content, then put it into practice by actually living it out. God's calling on our lives is that we wouldn't only be people who hear His word, but people who joyfully practice what it teaches.

August 3

> *But the Lord said to Samuel, "Do not look on his appearance or on the height of his stature, because I have rejected him. For the Lord sees not as man sees: man looks on the outward appearance, but the Lord looks on the heart."*
> *-1 Samuel 16:7*

A common pattern that is present in the lives of all people is the tendency to judge or assess others based on outward appearances. We make judgments related to status, wealth, intelligence, and even spirituality based on visible characteristics alone. Sometimes we grant too much credence to those assessments as if they're definitive.

But the Lord doesn't see things from a fleshly perspective. He sees the total person. He knows what's in a man's mind. He knows what's in a man's heart. He can correctly discern what motivates a person's actions, words, and service. He can see if we're motivated by faith in Jesus Christ, or if we're primarily motivated by receiving the praise and glory that should rightfully be directed toward Christ.

What does the Lord see right now when He peers in our hearts? Does He see faith expressing itself in obedience, or does He see selfishness and the presence of lesser motives? What is He inviting us to confess to Him today? How is He leading us toward deeper faith and integrity that's empowered by His grace?

August 4

> *"Thus says the Lord who made the earth, the Lord who formed it to establish it— the Lord is his name: Call to me and I will answer you, and will tell you great and hidden things that you have not known."*
> *-Jeremiah 33:2-3*

Discernment and understanding are gifts that come to those who trust in Jesus Christ. As we submit our will to His will, and seek His guidance, He delights to grant us the kind of wisdom and understanding that can only come from Him.

In the midst of our seasons of joy, He invites us to seek Him. In the midst of our seasons of trial and desperation, He invites us to call to Him. Our Lord hasn't abandoned us to rely on our own limited understanding. Rather, He openly invites His children to come before Him and seek His answers.

The Lord answers the prayers of His family. He reveals things to us that we would never naturally come to an understanding of. He illuminates our hearts and our minds so that we can approach our years on this planet with a Christ-centered perspective.

What do you desire to be made known to you? Have you called out to the Lord and asked Him to make it clear? Have you sought His counsel through His word? Have you asked Him to speak to you through someone you trust?

August 5

> *"The unfolding of your words gives light; it imparts understanding to the simple."*
> *-Psalm 119:130*

One of the greatest blessings the Lord has granted to us during this era of time, is the ability to access information quickly and easily. If we want to know something or learn something, the process has become easier than ever.

Like no generation that has come before us, we have been amply blessed with access to God's word. We own printed copies and can access digital copies in a matter of seconds.

But having access to something doesn't necessarily guarantee that we're using it. Yet, when we do choose to read and internalize the teaching of God's word, we have the privilege of growing in our walk with the Son of God, Jesus Christ.

All Scripture has been given to us by God. Every portion of His word points us to Jesus. His word blesses us with the wisdom and understanding that we desperately need. Through His word, He grants light to those who seek the illumination of His truth. Through His word, He grants understanding to those who crave it.

Never trivialize the blessing of having immediate access to God's word. This is a blessing unique to our generation.

August 6

"While Ezra prayed and made confession, weeping and casting himself down before the house of God, a very great assembly of men, women, and children, gathered to him out of Israel, for the people wept bitterly. "
-Ezra 10:1

Ezra was filled with sorrow for his people and in that sorrow, he came before the Lord in prayerful repentance. Sorrow that grieves the very things that the Lord grieves has a somewhat painful, but very helpful effect. It produces repentance in the life of a believer, and that's a good thing.

Repentance frequently sounds like an unpleasant word, but because we are confident of the abiding love of Christ and because we're confident of that fact that just as our Heavenly Father is well pleased with the Son (whom we are united to), we can be confident that His love for us is unchanging. It is safe for us to repent.

In fact, one of the marks of maturity in the life of a follower of Christ is repentance. We don't need to go through life with the mistaken belief that we need to present ourselves as perfect people who don't make mistakes. We don't need to live under the pressure of trying to convey a false image to one another. We can joyfully repent, apologize, confess, and ask for prayer because we are confident of our acceptance in Christ.

Godly sorrow produced repentance in Ezra's heart and it will produce that fruit in our heart as well. It's easy to embrace sin, but Christ gives us the strength to make the harder choice. Through Christ, we can experience joyful repentance.

August 7

> *"For if there was glory in the ministry of condemnation, t h e   m i n i s t r y   o f righteousness must far exceed it in glory. Indeed, in this case, what once had glory has come to have no glory at all, because of the glory that surpasses it."*
> *-2 Corinthians 3:9-10*

Have you ever taken the time to read the Old Testament Law? If you read it all, you can see that it testifies to the holiness of God and the sinfulness of man. It contains ceremonial, civic and moral regulations, and Scripture tells us that if we break one aspect of the law, we're guilty of breaking it all.

So why did God give us the Law, knowing that we couldn't keep it? He gave it to us to make it clear just how much we needed Jesus. Under the Law, we were condemned, but Jesus kept the Law for us, was condemned in our place, and offers us His gift of righteousness if we will believe in Him. He is the Savior and He came to this earth to rescue those who were sinful and under condemnation. In Him, there is no condemnation. In Jesus, we find life.

That's why Paul states that the New Covenant has a greater glory than the Old Covenant. We haven't been given a ministry with a fading glory. We haven't been given a ministry of condemnation. We have been entrusted with the privilege of testifying to the undeserved righteousness of Christ that He grants to all who come to Him by faith.

August 8

> *"So then, brothers, we are debtors, not to the flesh, to live according to the flesh. For if you live according to the flesh you will die, but if by the Spirit you put to death the deeds of the body, you will live. For all who are led by the Spirit of God are sons of God."*
> *-Romans 8:12-14*

We've been set free from sin and death through Jesus Christ. We aren't obligated in any way to go back to the manner of living we were once caught up in. Truthfully speaking, living according to the desires of the old, fleshly nature, results in disease, depression, and ultimately death.

As sons of God who have been adopted into His family, we are now truly alive. We aren't being led by the forces of evil. On the contrary, we're being led by the Holy Spirit. He's providing us divine counsel. He's speaking to our hearts and our minds. He's illuminating the truth of the Scriptures to us. He's pointing us in a direction that is for God's glory and our good.

Generally speaking, as you assess your life, what are the dominant voices you're listening to? It becomes evident that we truly are God's children as we practice listening to His voice. Those who are led by the Spirit are sons of God. He loves us enough to lead us. He loves us enough to counsel us. He loves us enough to choose not to abandon us. He loves us enough not to leave us here to try to figure this all out ourselves.

August 9

> *"Are not five sparrows sold for two pennies? And not one of them is forgotten before God. Why, even the hairs of your head are all numbered. Fear not; you are of more value than many sparrows."*
> *-Luke 12:6-7*

What message do you typically preach to your heart? Is it a message of hope and encouragement, or is it a message of shame and despair?

Throughout the Scriptures, the Lord makes it clear to us that we are precious to Him. He created us in His image, revealed Himself to us, walks with us, redeems us, forgives us, and offers us an imperishable inheritance in His kingdom through faith in Jesus.

But, unfortunately, we don't always preach this message to our hearts. Sometimes, we let ourselves believe that we are forgotten and forsaken. We feel overlooked and unloved. Yet Jesus reminds us that we are of more value to God than anything else in His creation.

When our hearts become convinced that we are truly loved by our Lord, our perspective toward the future begins to experience a drastic change. We latch on to genuine hope. Our intrinsic fear is replaced with confident faith.

What message will you be preaching to your heart today? Despair or hope? Abandonment or love? Fear or faith?

August 10

> *"God is our refuge and strength, a very present help in trouble."*
> *-Psalm 46:1*

There are seasons of life when trouble seems rather prevalent. Sometimes it seems to come in waves. Other times it may hit us like a brick. Most of us aren't looking for trouble, but it manages to find us anyway. How do you handle your seasons of trouble?

When trouble comes, there are healthy ways and unhealthy ways to deal with the emotions that come with it. If we're honest with ourselves, we will probably notice times when we have attempted to ease our pain and discomfort by utilizing something unhealthy. We take what seems to be the easiest way to soothe our pain, only to find that the easy solution we pursued wasn't effective.

Through Jesus, we have the help we need. He is present with us and within us. He is sufficient to heal what weighs our hearts down. He is compassionate toward us and can completely understand our struggles.

The Scripture tells us that the Lord is our refuge. In Him we find safety and security. We're also told that He is the source of our strength. He will uphold us when we feel weak. He is present with us to help us. He isn't distant from us. We have not been abandoned in the midst of our trouble.

August 11

"For godly grief produces a repentance that leads to salvation without regret, whereas worldly grief produces death. "
-2 Corinthians 7:10

Grief is one of the most difficult things for us to deal with in this world. Typically, it's a word we associate primarily with loss. We grieve when we drop our phone and the screen smashes. We grieve when our company closes and we lose our job. We grieve when someone we love passes away. It's unwise and unhealthy to hold grief inside while pretending it isn't real or genuinely painful. There are quite a few unhealthy habits that we can form when it comes to failing to handle grief in a healthy way.

From a spiritual standpoint, there are two different kinds of grief. Paul differentiates in this passage between godly grief and worldly grief and there's a big difference between the two. Worldly grief comes from trying to hold on to or possess something unhealthy or something we never really had the power to hold on to. It can also develop into a form of self-pity.

Godly grief operates differently. Godly grief is a healthy thing that is the fruit of a conscience that has been awakened to the heart of God. A person who is wrestling with godly grief comes to a point where they recognize that something in their life isn't honoring to Christ, and as the Holy Spirit develops that conviction in their heart, they finally come to a place of repentance. They turn back to God, experience His cleansing from their sin, and walk forward with a renewed sense of the love of Jesus and His divine design for their life.

August 12

"Or do you not know that your body is a temple of the Holy Spirit within you, whom you have from God? You are not your own, for you were bought with a price. So glorify God in your body."
-1 Corinthians 6:19-20

Of the blessings the Lord has granted us, our bodies are one of the most obvious and visible. We are advised in Scripture to treat our bodies well, and to use our bodies to bring glory to Jesus Christ.

The Scripture reminds us that we are stewards of our bodies, not owners. The manner in which we use or abuse our bodies reflects the nature of our trust in Jesus Christ. Do we believe Jesus paid the ultimate price for us? Do we believe that we ultimately belong to Him?

The moment we came to faith in Jesus, the Holy Spirit indwelled us. He lives within us. He counsels us, empowers us, and directs us. His presence within us produces the fruit of righteousness. Through Him, our bodies become instruments of love, joy, peace, patience, kindness, goodness, faithfulness, gentleness, and self-control. It is God's intention that our bodies be used for these purposes.

This world encourages and promotes a mindset that fosters careless mistreatment and bodily harm. Christ, on the other hand, challenges us to care for our bodies and bring Him glory with how our bodies are used.

August 13

> *"For we are his workmanship, created in Christ Jesus for good works, which God prepared beforehand, that we should walk in them."*
> *-Ephesians 2:10*

You are not an accident. You have been intentionally designed by God and created in His image. Before you were born, He fashioned you in your mother's womb and He has an unfolding, beautiful plan for your life.

When you came to faith in Jesus, you likewise became a new creation. In that moment, you were born spiritually, and God continues to foster your growth and maturity.

When Jesus saved you, He didn't do so with the intent that you would become a museum piece, merely to be stared at. His desire is that you would devote yourself to the good works He has intentionally equipped you to do. There are people He wants you specifically to connect with. There are tasks that He has specifically equipped you to do in order to help others, and serve as a visible testimony of His power and presence.

We can devote ourselves to many things in this world, but God's word encourages us to be devoted to Him, and to walking with Him. Use the efforts of your mind to glorify Christ. Use the actions of your hands to glorify Christ. Without grumbling and without reservation, serve others in His name.

August 14

> *"Behold, I stand at the door and knock. If anyone hears my voice and opens the door, I will come in to him and eat with him, and he with me."*
> *-Revelation 3:20*

We were created to live in perfect fellowship with the Lord. God did not create us to live at a distance from Him. We were made in His image and likeness, and blessed with the opportunity to come to know Him in a personal, relational way.

Is your heart open to this kind of relationship? Jesus implores us to open our hearts to Him, but that's something most people struggle to embrace.

For a growing Christian, what does it look like to live in fellowship with Christ? It involves many things, but for starters, it requires us to genuinely trust in Him. As we trust Him, we're blessed with His peace which guards our hearts and guards our minds against welcoming the anxieties of this world to dominate our lives.

Living in fellowship with Christ also involves subjecting our will to His. Where He calls us to go, we go. What He calls us to do, we do. Our desire is not to ignore the prompting of the Holy Spirit as He illuminates our hearts and points us to Jesus.

Can we hear the voice of Christ in our lives? Are we open to growing in fellowship with Him?

August 15

> *"For if we live, we live to the Lord, and if we die, we die to the Lord. So then, whether we live or whether we die, we are the Lord's."*
> *-Romans 14:8*

A mistake that many of us find rather easy to make is the mistake of believing our lives belong to us. We treat our lives as if they find their source in us, are completely governed by us, and are operating on our exclusive timetable.

But that's not the case at all. We were dead in our trespasses and sins until Jesus found us and granted us new life. Jesus purchased us with His blood at the cross. We don't belong to ourselves, but to Him.

When we become convinced of this spiritual reality, we start to realize that the goal of each day of our lives is to live that day in such a way that Christ receives honor and praise. We live to honor His priorities. We strive to be about the work He has equipped us to accomplish.

Likewise, we also live with a conscious understanding that our time on this earth is brief. There will come a day when our present body will stop functioning and our breathing will cease. But even in that moment, we can glorify Christ by approaching the reality of that season with great hope, knowing that He holds our future in His hands and has promised us an incorruptible inheritance in His eternal kingdom.

August 16

> *"Peace I leave with you; my peace I give to you. Not as the world gives do I give to you. Let not your hearts be troubled, neither let them be afraid."*
> *-John 14:27*

God's Word is comforting and encouraging, and Jesus knew that His followers would need comfort and encouragement. He also was well aware of our heart's desire for peace, and in this same conversation promised us peace through Him.

This world tells us that we will have peace when we have enough resources, but money and possessions are useful tools, not the source of lasting peace. They go away too quickly and are not eternal in nature. This world also tells us that we will have peace when our circumstances become ideal and we're free from trouble or surprises. But that's not the case either because in this world, we regularly have trouble, and we cannot control many aspects of our circumstances.

So Jesus offers lasting peace. The peace that He offers is genuine and not fleeting. Some people find this peace, but many others reject the notion of it being real because they still believe in the world's false promises. The kind of peace Jesus offers isn't based on resources or circumstances. His peace is based on a relationship with Him. When we come to faith in Him, He assures us that though our circumstances may often look confusing or troubling in this world, we do not need to be troubled or afraid because He is with us.

August 17

> *"Let the one who boasts, boast in the Lord." For it is not the one who commends himself who is approved, but the one whom the Lord commends.*
> *-2 Corinthians 10:17-18*

There are few things as unappealing as being forced to listen to someone boast or brag about himself. To be in the presence of someone who thinks so highly of himself that he dominates the conversation with story after story of the great and impressive things he has done is both irritating and revolting.

Boasting can be a form of pride and self-worship. It reflects the arrogant heart of Satan, more so than the humble character of Christ. But there is one form of boasting that is healthy and proper to practice. God's word invites us to boast about who the Lord is and what He is actively accomplishing.

Pause for just a moment to reflect on some of the amazing things Jesus has done in your life. He has made you a new creation. He has transformed the way you think. He has blessed you with a certain hope and a glorious future. He carries your burdens, comforts your heart, gives purpose to your life, and shares the victory He secured in His resurrection with everyone who trusts in Him.

If we're going to boast, it shouldn't be about ourselves. Any boasting we do should be about our Lord, how wonderful He is, all the good He has done for us, and all the good He has in store for us.

August 18

> *He said to them, "Then render to Caesar*
> *the things that are Caesar's, and to God*
> *the things that are God's." And they were*
> *not able in the presence of the people to*
> *catch him in what he said, but marveling at*
> *his answer they became silent.*
> *-Luke 20:25-26*

Every generation complains about the government to one degree or another, but biblically speaking, the government is one means the Lord uses to promote justice and restrain sin. There will be no perfect government until Jesus is ruling and reigning on this earth, but in the meantime, we're called to show respect to government authorities out of reverence for the Lord.

Humanity, by nature, is rebellious. It's easier for us to challenge authority than it is for us to submit to authority. But Christ calls us to be good citizens who remember to pray for our leaders. We're called to obey the law, so long as the law doesn't conflict with our devotion to Christ. And even if we do choose to object because of an issue of conscience, we need to accept that there may be earthly consequences for that decision.

This wasn't what those who questioned Jesus wanted to hear. They just wanted to cause trouble for Christ, but He gave them the answer they truly needed to hear in that moment. Have you ever had a similar experience in your walk with Christ? Have you ever made a request of Him, waited for an answer, received His answer, but didn't like what He had to say? What do you suspect He may be trying to teach you through moments like that?

August 19

"Obey your leaders and submit to them, for they are keeping watch over your souls, as those who will have to give an account. Let them do this with joy and not with groaning, for that would be of no advantage to you."
-Hebrews 13:17

If the Lord is calling you to leadership, please understand that it can certainly be a joyful experience, but it definitely isn't easy. And if the form of leadership you're being called to is specifically within the context of the local church, it can be helpful to remember the content of these verses. The task of church leadership is to keep watch over the spiritual well-being of the church family, with the understanding that the day will come when you'll give an account to the Lord for how seriously you prioritized that task.

The essence of Christ-like leadership is service. Jesus came to this earth to humbly serve and graciously give. Good leaders keep His example in mind when they lead. Good leaders look for opportunities to serve those they have been called to lead, always remembering that they have been sent on a mission as Christ's ambassadors.

The writer of Hebrews was encouraging the Hebrew Christians in the early church to make the responsibilities of their leaders a joy to carry out. Most leaders wrestle with various insecurities. They also get tired. They hear a lot of complaints. They are the targets of regular criticism, yet they probably don't whine about it very much. Many leaders internalize the majority of their struggles. For this reason, the Holy Spirit inspired this Scripture to be written to remind us all to make the task our leaders have taken on a joy. We are called to be men and women who are a joy, not a drain, to serve.

August 20

"I have set the Lord always before me; because he is at my right hand, I shall not be shaken."
-Psalm 16:8

One of the most difficult things to avoid in this world is fear. For some people, the older they get, the more fearful they become. Because of a series of difficult circumstances, tragedies, or unpleasant events, they begin to worry about what might be coming along next. They frequently wonder if misfortune awaits them in the near future.

There certainly are difficult things we'll endure during our lives, but if fear becomes our dominant emotion, we'll find ourselves operating from an unhealthy and unhelpful perspective, instead of the perspective we're encouraged to adopt in God's word.

In Jesus, we find strength. In Jesus, we find hope. In Jesus, we find guarantees that should put our hearts at rest. He will never abandon us. He is working all things together for our good. He is sustaining us. He isn't ashamed to call us His own.

During this season of life, what has the most potential to shake your confidence in Christ? What seems to produce the most fear? If you can identify it, what will you do with it next? There may be many things in this world that have the potential to produce fear in our hearts, but through Christ, we are not shaken.

August 21

> *"May the God of hope fill you with all joy and peace in believing, so that by the power of the Holy Spirit you may abound in hope."*
> *-Romans 15:13*

Hope is a gift from Jesus that is worth embracing. He has blessed us with the understanding that we can be completely confident that He will fulfill every promise He has delivered to us in His word.

There are many people in this world who live without hope. Some even do so willingly as they actively reject the hope that is secured by trusting in Christ.

Through faith in Jesus, we are blessed with a confident hope that is designed by God to overflow from our lives. Scripture also reveals to us that with hope, we're blessed with joy, peace, confidence, and power. Each of these blessings are supplied to us in abundance through Jesus when we trust Him, stop working against what He's trying to teach us, and stop working against what He's trying to do within us.

Our future hope directly impacts the quality of our present life. Each day seems more purposeful when we acknowledge all that Jesus holds in store for us. Even our trials have a silver lining because we know they are being used for our good, and will not last forever. Let God cause your hope in Him to overflow from your life, and be used to bless those He has surrounded you with.

August 22

> *"He who did not spare his own Son but gave him up for us all, how will he not also with him graciously give us all things?"*
> *-Romans 8:32*

God knows how to give good gifts to His children. He isn't stingy or selfish with us. He delights in giving us the best of what He has to offer, and He is pleased to secure for us a permanent inheritance in His kingdom. Our Lord is the perfection of generosity.

The Lord knows everything there is to know about us. He is well acquainted with our needs even before those needs become apparent to us. Knowing that our greatest need was the restoration of our relationship with Him, the Father sent the Son to bring healing, forgiveness, and eternal reconciliation.

Salvation is a gift that is freely offered to us, but it came at great cost to the Lord. The Father willingly gave His Son who, for the joy set before Him, paid for our redemption with His blood. There is no greater cost that could be imagined than what Jesus paid in order to secure our freedom from sin and its effects.

When was the last time you reminded yourself of this truth? What else does your heart need for it to become fully convinced of the depth of your value to God? God's love for you isn't a trivial thing. Let His word remind you of this truth today.

August 23

> *"When the cares of my heart are many,*
> *your consolations cheer my soul."*
> *-Psalm 94:19*

What keeps you up at night? What robs you of joy during the day? What creeps into your mind and makes you feel fearful or anxious?

We all experience things that have the capacity to influence us to feel worried. Sometimes it begins to feel like those areas of worry are starting to pile up. We may even begin to believe that the concerns that are weighing our hearts down will continue to amass in a heap until they eventually crush us.

Jesus invites us to give Him our burdens. The concerns that are dragging us down feel so heavy to us, but to Him, they are light and momentary. In fact, He invites us to also adopt that perspective toward the cares of our hearts.

At times, it can be easy to feel weighed down with a load of care. That weight seems even heavier when we insist on trying to carry it alone. Has that been your experience? Is that a pattern you're noticing in your life?

Look around you. Who has the Lord placed in your life to help you? Look up. What will it take for you to unload your burdens on Jesus and trust in the strength of His arm to carry you through this season?

August 24

> *"I love the Lord, because he has heard my voice and my pleas for mercy. Because he inclined his ear to me, therefore I will call on him as long as I live."*
> *-Psalm 116:1-2*

One of the greatest privileges we've been given as people who trust in Jesus Christ, is confident access to the Lord in prayer. He invites us to come into His presence. He assures us that we are welcomed near to Him. He shows us repeatedly that it isn't His desire that we live at a distance from Him.

In our seasons of weakness and despair, it's comforting to know that the Lord hears us when we call out to Him. He knows that we need His mercy and He delights to shower us with it. Before we came to know Jesus as our Savior, we were under the wrath of God. But now, through faith in Jesus, we have become His beloved children, and we're shown mercy in more ways than we could easily count.

The psalmist insists that he will call on the Lord as long as he lives. That's a practice we're encouraged to implement as well. It's foolish and fruitless to spend the bulk of our days ignoring the help our Lord is offering us. He invites us to embrace His mercy. He offers us His power. He grants us His wisdom. He supplies us with His comfort. Call out to Him in prayer, and enjoy the divine blessings only He can supply.

August 25

> *"So have no fear of them, for nothing is covered that will not be revealed, or hidden that will not be known. What I tell you in the dark, say in the light, and what you hear whispered, proclaim on the housetops."*
> *-Matthew 10:26-27*

Are there people in your life that you find intimidating? Have you ever met people who, as a pattern, attempt to intimidate others? What do they typically do? Sometimes they stand uncomfortably close to you when they're talking to you. Sometimes they raise their voice. Sometimes they become unfairly critical of you. Why do they do this? Usually it's done in an attempt to assert themselves, influence others to bend to their will, and then eventually get whatever it is they're seeking.

As Jesus was preparing His disciples for the nature of the ministry He was entrusting to them, He warned them that they would encounter people who would attempt to work against them, intimidate them, and influence them to feel afraid. But Jesus directly told His followers not to fear people like this, no matter what kind of pressure or pain they attempted to inflict. Why didn't Christ's disciples need to fear? They didn't need to fear because they were aligned with the truth.

Sin and poor motives can't stand to be brought out into the light. They resist it because they can't tolerate the scrutiny that comes with being exposed. Jesus was clear when He said, *"for nothing is covered that will not be revealed, or hidden that will not be known."* In time, the truth will be made known. Motives will be made plain. That which He has favored will be revealed.

August 26

"For as in one body we have many members, and the members do not all have the same function, so we, though many, are one body in Christ, and individually members one of another."
-Romans 12:4-5

When you look in the mirror, what do you see? Are you grateful for the way the Lord has intentionally fashioned you, or is your mind flooded with comparisons when you look at your reflection? Do you primarily notice areas you think are deficient, or can you see God's handiwork in the details of your design?

In Christ, we are one body. He unites all who trust in Him into one family, and He gives us strengths and abilities that are intentionally different from one another. These abilities are meant to be complimentary, and are to be used for building each other up.

Christ intentionally gives us different gifts to help foster humility within us. He unites us as a family, then reminds us that we can never say we don't need each other. For each of us to grow spiritually mature, we need the help and assistance of our brothers and sisters in Christ.

The world, the devil, and even your own attitude might try to keep you discouraged about ways you wish you had been created differently. But the truth is that Jesus has designed you and gifted you in a purposeful fashion. Use your gifts to glorify Him, and serve others with gratefulness.

August 27

> *"You keep him in perfect peace whose mind is stayed on you, because he trusts in you."*
> **-Isaiah 26:3**

Most people, when they're asked what this world needs most, will give the answer, "peace." We see wars going on all around us. There's conflict on our streets. We hear leaders express threats toward other nations, or we're forced to listen to other nations when they threaten us. There's a great amount of turmoil in this world, so it's easy to see why peace would be desired. But how is peace really obtained?

Likewise, when we take a close look at what's going on within our hearts, it's easy to spot the presence of inner conflict. Many people admit struggling to sleep at night because of the presence of anxious thoughts. Some of us find ourselves worrying for a considerable portion of the day. What's the solution for this?

Jesus is the ultimate solution to our need for peace. He has the power to end conflict between nations, and He promises that He will indeed do that one day. He also has the power to calm the fears and worries of our anxious hearts.

The Lord invites us to trust in Him. Trusting in Him involves handing over to Him the things that cause us to fear. He can handle it all. He can calm our minds and hearts. What is He prodding your heart to hand over to him today?

August 28

> *"Command and teach these things. Let no one despise you for your youth, but set the believers an example in speech, in conduct, in love, in faith, in purity."*
> *-1 Timothy 4:11-12*

Paul told Timothy not to let anyone look down on him just because he was young. Rather, he was challenged to set an example for others of what it meant to be a fully devoted follower of Jesus Christ in multiple areas. The counsel Timothy was given fully applies to us as well.

Believers are encouraged, in this passage, to set an example, first of all, in our speech. The words we say and the way we say them work like a mirror into our soul. We can use our words to build others up or tear them down. We can use our words to communicate the heart of the gospel, or we can speak in such a way that we misrepresent Christ. A follower of Christ that wants to demonstrate spiritual maturity will keep a close eye on their speech.

Believers are also called to set an example with our conduct. The idea conveyed here is that the way we live will back up the words we speak. If we claim to love Jesus, our life should match that claim.

We're also called to set an example in love, faith, and purity. We could elaborate on each of these at length if we chose to, but the point is that our lives should be empowered by the Holy Spirit to serve as a living example of the presence of Christ within us. That's an example that the Lord can foster through our lives, regardless of our age. It's something He wants us to value and prioritize.

August 29

> *"There is neither Jew nor Greek, there is neither slave nor free, there is no male and female, for you are all one in Christ Jesus."*
> **-Galatians 3:28**

If someone asked you the question, "Who are you?", how would you answer?

Our answer to that question typically reveals what we are trying to find our sense of identity in. Some of us may be trying to find our sense of identity through our nationality, our social status, our gender, our occupation, our education level, or a talent we've developed. But each of these areas are cheap imposters for the real identity we've been blessed with in Christ.

Through faith in Jesus, we become a new creation. The old has gone. The new has come. Our identity isn't tied to temporary things. Who we really are is permanently anchored to Christ. He blesses us with a new identity that doesn't shift, change, or diminish.

In Jesus, we are forever loved. In Jesus, we are made holy. In Jesus, we are adopted into the family of God. In Jesus, we are secure.

There are all kinds of labels you may be tempted to adopt in an attempt to find a sense of worth. But please remember, our value isn't tied to temporary titles. In Jesus, we become permanent members of the family of God with a new and better identity that's found in Him.

August 30

"Now when the wall had been built and I had set up the doors, and the gatekeepers, the singers, and the Levites had been appointed, I gave my brother Hanani and Hananiah the governor of the castle charge over Jerusalem, for he was a more faithful and God-fearing man than many."
-Nehemiah 7:1-2

There is no truly great task that ever gets accomplished alone. Buildings are built by people who have mastered different trades. Great songs and albums are team efforts between band-mates, writers, producers and promoters. Great works come to pass as the Lord raises up, and lends gifts and talents to people who work together in a synergistic fashion to accomplish something greater than any one of them could accomplish alone.

It's clear that the Lord inspired Nehemiah to build the wall around Jerusalem, and it was entrusted to him to oversee that responsibility, but that wasn't a task he could complete alone. God also surrounded him with various people who shared his calling, vision and desire to be obedient to the Lord. And now, with the wall completed, there was a great need for this work to be sustained. This would require ongoing support and partnership with godly people.

This kind of activity is something Christ wants to see taking place in His church. He desires that His church be built up, brick by brick, like this wall around Jerusalem was. A major facet of how the church is built up involves identifying and entrusting more and more followers of Christ with roles and responsibilities. Who is Jesus calling you to entrust responsibilities to? Who is He enabling you to help equip?

August 31

Jesus answered them, "This is the work of God, that you believe in him whom he has sent."
-John 6:29

The nature of many of the relationships we have on this earth can sometimes confuse us when it comes to understanding the kind of relationship our Lord wants to have with us.

Many of the people we know show us love or concern, primarily based on what we have the capacity to offer them in return. It's a conditional form of love, which means it really isn't love at all.

With so many of our human relationships being connected to what we do, it isn't surprising to realize that many people mistakenly believe God operates in the same way. It's too easy to believe that God loves us based on what we do, even though Scripture reveals to us that God's love for us is based on His perfect nature, not our perfect behavior.

Jesus addressed this very issue when speaking to people who thought of God's love or His favor primarily as something that can be earned and deserved. But God's love can't be earned. We can't be good enough to receive it or good enough to keep it. Our only hope is to trust in Jesus who fulfilled all righteousness on our behalf. That's what Jesus communicated thousands of years ago, and that's what He's still telling us today.

September 1

> *"But I have this against you, that you have abandoned the love you had at first."*
> ***-Revelation 2:4***

Jesus speaks of love in this verse. Love is one of, if not the most misused or misunderstood words in the English language. We like to say, "I love that song, game, movie, color, etc." People claim to be "in love" and "falling out of love." All we're really doing in these contexts is using the world "love" in place of "enjoy" or "appreciate", but biblical love goes much deeper than momentary affection.

Biblical love is a love that reflects the love of God. God's love isn't selfish. He loves unconditionally. And Jesus expresses in this passage that the Ephesian church had abandoned the love they had at first. What is the love they abandoned? Love for others? Love for Christ? Both? It's probably fair to say both. Instead of living with an appreciation for the love of Christ, and then extending that love toward others, they were focusing primarily on other priorities.

Think back for a moment on how you came to believe in Jesus. Before you came to believe in Him, there was a loving person who first showed you what it was like to follow Him in a loving way.

When a person comes to appreciate the unconditional love they have received from Christ, it fosters gratitude, appreciation, and reciprocation. Christ wants us to have solid beliefs anchored in Scripture coupled by genuine love for Him that translates into genuine love for others.

September 2

> *"Train up a child in the way he should go; even when he is old he will not depart from it."*
> *-Proverbs 22:6*

Children are a blessing. They can be a great source of joy in our lives. They can also be a major source of anxiety, depending on our perspective toward them. While children are often great examples of faith, they are not typically strong in wisdom. For that reason, the Lord has blessed them with the wisdom and protection of their parents.

If the Lord blesses you with children, you are given the opportunity to shepherd their young lives and help them understand more about the nature of the love of Christ.

Training our children is one of the highest priorities of our lives. We're called to help them understand what it means to walk with Jesus and obey His teaching. We're encouraged to lovingly correct them when their lives are going in an unhealthy or unsafe direction. And we're encouraged to come before the Lord in prayer as we will need His strength for this often emotionally exhausting task.

We can also rest confident that the investments we're making in their lives will bear fruit. It may take time, but a harvest of righteousness will be produced in the life of a child that is lovingly invested in with the gospel.

September 3

> *So Peter opened his mouth and said:*
> *"Truly I understand that God shows no*
> *partiality, but in every nation anyone who*
> *fears him and does what is right is*
> *acceptable to him.*
> **-Acts 10:34-35**

Peter was in a very unique situation. He had grown up avoiding Gentiles. He was taught by the words and examples of others to look down on Gentiles and it took the intervention of God, and the admonition of the Apostle Paul to shake Peter out of that mindset.

Now he was in a room, surrounded by Gentiles who desperately wanted to hear what Peter had to say. He was surrounded by sincere people who wanted to hear God's truth proclaimed. They were open vessels. They were ready to have their false beliefs challenged so that they could come to know the Lord of all Creation, Jesus Christ. So Peter opened His mouth and proclaimed Jesus.

Every day, we are surrounded by people who need Jesus. They may not yet realize how much they need Him and maybe we don't always realize how much we need Him either, but their hearts are heavy and they're weighed down with burdens and anxieties that they don't know what to do with. Their hearts desperately need to hear and believe some good news, but at present, they remain in their downcast state. If no one will take the risk to open their mouth and make to joyful truth of Christ's gospel known to these folks, they will never know the joy He freely offers. Will you be the one to open your mouth?

September 4

"Follow the pattern of the sound words that you have heard from me, in the faith and love that are in Christ Jesus."
-2 Timothy 1:13

Words are powerful things. What we say to others can often have a bigger impact on their heart than we may realize. The words that proceed from our mouths should bring glory to Christ and should reflect the fact that He has changed our hearts and transformed our pattern of thinking.

Hopefully, in your life, you have been blessed with a few good examples of how a believer should use their words. In this Scripture, the Apostle Paul reminded Timothy of the example he had been to him of how a believer should speak. If the Lord has blessed you with the privilege to spend time with people who have been followers of Christ for a longer period of time than you have, take note of how they speak. How do they use their words? Can you see evidence of spiritual maturity and the fruit of the Holy Spirit in their conversations?

As Paul mentions in this Scripture, the way we speak should testify to the faith Christ has prompted in our hearts and the love He has poured out into our lives. Every day we're given a brand new opportunity to build others up in the faith and love of Jesus Christ as we intentionally use our words to reflect His heart.

September 5

> *"Go therefore and make disciples of all nations, baptizing them in the name of the Father and of the Son and of the Holy Spirit, teaching them to observe all that I have commanded you. And behold, I am with you always, to the end of the age."*
> *-Matthew 28:19-20*

Your life has a purpose. As people who have been blessed by Jesus with the privilege to know Him, trust Him, love Him, and follow Him, He has commissioned us to help others come to know Him as well. He invites us to share the good news of His gospel in every context He places us in.

Likewise, as others come to know Him, He teaches us to remain involved in their lives as leaders, mentors, or teachers. What He wants to see happening is seasoned, mature Christians, making intentional investments in the growth and maturity of newer Christians.

What's the mark of a mature Christian? A mature Christian loves Jesus enough that they actually obey the counsel of His word instead of idolizing their own ideas and preferences. This is something Jesus wants mature Christians to help those who are new in the faith to also come to understand.

Likewise, Christ gives believers the privilege to identify with Him in baptism as a visible expression of the faith and devotion He has fostered within us. This is a privilege He wants us to share with as many people as we possibly can.

September 6

> *Jesus answered him, "If anyone loves me, he will keep my word, and my Father will love him, and we will come to him and make our home with him."*
> *-John 14:23*

This world is full of people who, in a casual or cultural sense, might call themselves "Christians", yet when their lives are observed, there is very little difference in their manner of living or personal beliefs that differentiates them from the culture they live in.

True Christians have an authentic love for Jesus Christ. They trust Him, seek Him, follow Him, and obey Him. They look for ways to put Him first in their lives instead of seeking ways to creatively avoid His presence or influence.

A true believer in Jesus Christ wants Him to be close to them, not distant. One who loves Jesus will keep His word, not reject what He taught. Those who trust in Him will rely on His strength to enable them to make this the pattern of their lives.

Many people in this world complain that they feel like the Lord is distant from them. Could it be that God feels distant, not because He seeks to be, but because we work rather hard to keep Him at the margins of our lives? How would our lives look differently if love for Christ and obedience to His teaching became our priority?

September 7

> *"Each one must give as he has decided in his heart, not reluctantly or under compulsion, for God loves a cheerful giver."*
> *-2 Corinthians 9:7*

What is your attitude toward giving? In his second letter to the Corinthians, Paul was trying to help that church understand and experience the joy of generous giving. They lived in a decadent culture that certainly had examples of wealth and poverty. We get the impression that there were examples of both within the Corinthian church as well. It can be tempting at times when the Lord blesses you with something, to try to hold on to that blessing in a stingy way, even though it may be that He shared that blessing with you to grant you the privilege of sharing it with others.

Our God is gracious and generous. He gives gifts to us that we don't deserve. He is a cheerful giver and our hearts should reflect His. We're told here that God loves a cheerful giver. He is pleased to see His children trust Him enough to step out on faith and bless others with the blessings He's bestowed.

Paul was trying to help the church understand this concept. This was more than just a momentary action he was trying to prompt. It is a way of life for the growing follower of Christ. Generosity isn't something that's only practiced when it's prompted by force. Rather, the principle Scripture teaches is that we should seek the Lord's direction in this area and give as He leads.

September 8

"Therefore, confess your sins to one another and pray for one another, that you may be healed. The prayer of a righteous person has great power as it is working."
-James 5:16

What are you holding onto that you struggle to admit to others? Is there something that you've allowed to creep into your life that isn't in line with God's will? Even though you've been set free from sin's grip on your life through faith in Jesus, is there something you're still allowing to dominate your life, or your thinking, in an unhealthy way? Why do some of these sinful things lurk in our lives for so long? Why do we struggle with them for years and sometimes even decades? Could it be because we refuse to expose them to the light?

James indicated that one potential cause of sickness could be unconfessed and unrepented sin. Certainly not every case of sickness is the result of unconfessed sin in a person's life, but biblically speaking, we're told that there are some illnesses and other issues that come into people's lives that are the direct result of unrepented sin.

The Lord invites us to pray in conjunction with the confession of our sin. We can confess to each other. We can confess to Him. And this shouldn't be overly scary to us or resisted by us, because the alternative is spending years and years feeling like we're being bound and defeated by the very things Jesus already defeated when He rose from the grave. Jesus defeated sin. There's no reason to let it defeat us any longer. The prayer of a person who has received the righteousness of Christ as a gift has great power. Pray for Christ's strength to live in the victory He has already secured for you.

September 9

> *"Older men are to be sober-minded,*
> *dignified, self-controlled, sound in faith,*
> *in love, and in steadfastness."*
> *-Titus 2:2*

God's word give us excellent counsel for every season of our lives. Children are encouraged to listen to the instruction of their parents and not act in a wild or disobedient way. Adults are encouraged to be examples of faith and to display the fruit of the Holy Spirit in their interaction with others. Older men are likewise encouraged to be examples of what it looks like to trust in Jesus Christ.

When Jesus becomes your Lord, He leads and directs the course of your life. Through faith in Him, your outlook and temperament changes. The way you react to stress and conflict matures, and the steady nature by which you carry yourself is used by the Lord to bless others who look to you as an example.

An older man who follows Jesus should have a sober mind that isn't overcome by disorienting substances or worldliness. He should display dignity in how he speaks to women and those who are younger than him. His faith and love should serve as a testimony to his desire to use his life as an ambassador of Jesus.

Someone is copying you. Someone looks up to you. Someone may be modeling their life after what they see in you. Is your life pointing that person to Jesus?

September 10

> *"even to your old age I am he, and to gray hairs I will carry you. I have made, and I will bear; I will carry and will save."*
> *-Isaiah 46:4*

During the years of our lives, there are things we become more gradually convinced of. One such thing should be our confidence in the Lord to carry us through every trial or calamity we face.

We don't have the ability to predict what may come our way. We may currently be experiencing a season of reprieve or we may be in the midst of one of the greatest trials of our lives. But just as the Lord carried His people in the past, so too can we be confident that He is present with us now. We can lean on Him. We don't have to rely on our own strength.

That's particularly helpful for us to remember as we age. When our bodies are at their peak strength, it is sometimes too easy for us to become overly self-reliant. But as we mature, one of the lessons we learn is that our body has the capacity to fail, but the Lord can be the source of strength we find refuge in.

Our Lord delights to save His children. In Jesus, we find help and hope. In Him we find comfort and salvation. Regardless of the season of life we may currently be in, Jesus is the Rock we can come to and the hope we can trust.

September 11

"In this you rejoice, though now for a little while, if necessary, you have been grieved by various trials,"
-1 Peter 1:6

The process of growing up can be a painful experience, and for most of us it is. As you're tested and you experience certain difficulties for the first time, it can be difficult to cope with them. It's also sometimes difficult to see beyond them. It's easy to feel like they may never end.

Thankfully, the joy we have in Jesus is not dependent on circumstances. As Peter was speaking to these believers, he reminded them that even though for a little while they were experiencing pain, they could still rejoice in Christ. And even still, the Lord would bring great things out of the trials they were experiencing so that even their most painful experiences in life could become occasions through which they could praise God.

The perspective we're invited to adopt in this passage is to begin looking at the trials of life as things that only last for a "little while." The unpleasant things we experience in life are only for a season, then they're done.

But while we wait for our trials to pass, we can be confident that the Lord is using them to have a great effect on our lives and our faith. The adversity we experience in life tests our faith and makes it stronger. Our seasons of difficulty help demonstrate whether our faith in Christ is genuine or not. There's value in our faith being tested.

September 12

> *"Rejoice in the Lord always; again I will*
> *say, rejoice."*
> *-Philippians 4:4*

If you asked most people what they want more than anything in this world, many of them would probably tell you they want to find happiness. On the surface, that doesn't immediately sound like a bad thing, but the truth is, happiness can be a very circumstantial and fleeting emotion.

For those who have genuine faith in Jesus Christ, we will certainly experience happiness, but we'll also experience something different and deeper. In Jesus, we find joy. We find contentment and delight in Him that isn't dependent on our circumstances. In the midst of our darkest days, we can rejoice in Christ. In the midst of our brightest days, we can rejoice in Christ. In fact, we're specifically told to do that very thing.

Why can we rejoice in Christ regardless of our circumstances? Well, first of all, we can rejoice in Him because of His unchanging nature. We can also rejoice in Him because His love for us isn't based on our ability to earn it or cultivate it. We can rejoice in Him because He is present with us in the midst of every life experience. We can rejoice in Him because He holds our future in His hands and He has promised it will be glorious.

There are many things in this world that may test your faith and even temporarily dampen your spirit, but regardless of your circumstances, always remember to rejoice in Christ.

September 13

"Finally, all of you, have unity of mind, sympathy, brotherly love, a tender heart, and a humble mind."
-1 Peter 3:8

It is far easier to be concerned about yourself and your well-doing than it is to show genuine concern for someone else. It's easier to prioritize your opinion, your comfort, and your preferences, than it is to prioritize those of others.

Yet, in Christ, we've been united into one body. We have one Savior, one faith, and a common future. With that in mind, we're encouraged to foster unity within the church, even though it can often be rather difficult to do so.

If it was easy for us to be united, the Lord probably wouldn't have bothered to tell us to work toward it. If it was easy for us to by sympathetic toward each other, He probably wouldn't have encouraged us as often as He has, to adopt that mindset.

Pride comes more naturally to us than humility, but in Christ, we've been equipped and empowered to live in humility toward each other. We're invited to adopt the mindset of a servant as we interact with our Christian family, recognizing that the Lord is only asking us to practice something that He graciously demonstrated toward us first.

September 14

"Jude, a servant of Jesus Christ and a brother of James,
To those who have been called, who are loved by God the Father and kept by Jesus Christ:"
-Jude 1

We are loved by God the Father. That is a truth that we would do well to meditate on every day because when we truly believe this to be true, our hearts, lives and internal motivations are impacted in the most powerful way. People live and behave differently when they know they are loved. We live and behave differently when I know I am loved.

We all know the difference it makes to be loved. When we're loved, we feel welcomed and accepted. We feel at liberty to be ourselves and not feel like we're walking on egg shells. We don't live with the constant fear that if we make a mistake we'll immediately become "unloved" or "unwelcome." Knowing that truth deep down has a big affect on us. It produces boldness and confidence.

Looking again at this passage, Jude reminds us that we are *"loved by God the Father."* What difference can that truth make for us? If we truly believe that, it will impact every area of our lives. If in Christ Jesus, we're unconditionally loved by God, we'll find joy in that relationship. We'll delight in loving Him. We won't buy into the false teaching that tells us we need to earn His love. We won't spend our lives trying to fill a void for love by seeking to earn love from others because we know for certain that God the Father loves us.

September 15

> *"And do not fear those who kill the body but cannot kill the soul. Rather fear him who can destroy both soul and body in hell."*
> **-Matthew 10:28**

What's your greatest fear? How much time do you spend worrying about what others might do to you? During the era Jesus was ministering in, as well as the centuries that came immediately after, Christians were regularly threatened for their belief in Christ. Some were threatened with the loss of their homes and jobs. Some were threatened with punishment or imprisonment. Others were threatened with death. Yet Jesus reminded His followers that we don't need to fear those who only have power to kill the body. They cannot kill the soul. They cannot take your eternal life from you. If we're going to fear anyone, it should be God, but our fear of Him should be the healthy reverence that shows we respect His power.

The truth is, we're of great value to the Lord. Sadly, we aren't as convinced of this as we should be. Isn't it ironic that we as Christians can theologically acknowledge that God the Father send God the Son to this earth to die in our place, demonstrating our great value to Him, yet we struggle to think anything nice about ourselves when we look at ourselves in the mirror? We can acknowledge our value to God theologically, but we struggle to acknowledge our value to God emotionally. That disconnect needs to be rectified.

God sees us, notices everything about us, loves us, and holds our lives securely in His hands. Never minimize your value to God.

September 16

> *"Who is wise and understanding among you? By his good conduct let him show his works in the meekness of wisdom."*
> *-James 3:13*

Wisdom is something the Lord invites us to pray for. He delights to answer that prayer with an emphatic, "Yes!" He wants His people to walk in wisdom that is supplied by the indwelling presence of the Holy Spirit, and through the counsel of the Scriptures.

During the course of His earthly ministry, people marveled at the wisdom of Jesus. Even from a young age, they were amazed at the level of understanding He possessed. Now, through faith in Christ, we're offered His wisdom as a gift of His presence within us.

As possessors of godly wisdom, what should we be doing with it? What kind of impact does the wisdom of God have on our lives? How does His wisdom correlate to our daily conduct?

A person who walks by faith in Jesus Christ, utilizing the wisdom of the Holy Spirit, will conduct their life in such a way that obedience to the teaching of Christ will be one of their top priorities. They will be empowered to say no to ungodliness. They will treat others with the patience and love they have received from Jesus, and they will see this world and its temptations with new eyes. The manner in which a believer lives their life gives great testimony to the presence of Christ within them.

September 17

> *"Therefore be imitators of God, as beloved children."*
> *-Ephesians 5:1*

From the earliest seasons of their lives, children begin to imitate their parents. They imitate the way their parents speak. They copy the way they act toward people. They often tend to show an interest in some of the same things their parents are interested in.

Through faith in Jesus Christ, we have become children of God. We are part of His eternal family and we are deeply loved by Him. As His deeply loved children, we are encouraged to be imitators of Him. What are some of the ways this works out in our lives?

As the Lord is loving toward us, we can reflect His love toward others. As the Lord shows us great patience, we can show others, and even ourselves, patience. As the Lord blesses us with mercy, even though we deserve condemnation, we can be merciful toward others. He invites us to imitate Him in all these areas and more. He is the ultimate standard by which our lives should be measured.

And not only has the Lord called us to imitate Him, He has empowered us to do so as well. We aren't required to rely on our own strength to do these things. That's not even possible. Our ability to live as imitators of God is directly enabled by His presence within us.

September 18

> *"Whoever has the Son has life; whoever does not have the Son of God does not have life."*
> *-1 John 5:12*

The major question we need to have settled in our mind and our heart during the course of our earthly life is, "Who is Jesus?" If you asked that question to a large group of people, you would most certainly be offered several different answers. Some would probably speak of Jesus as an important historical figure. Some might say Jesus was a revolutionary. Others might say He was a prophet, but who do you say He is?

When we look at what the Scriptures teach about Jesus, we can clearly see that He is spoken of as being God in the flesh. His nature is divine. He is eternally self-existent, and He lives in perfect union with the Father and the Holy Spirit. All creation was spoken into existence by His powerful word, and at present, He continues to sustain what He has created.

It is Christ's desire that we live. He wants us to experience new life. He wants to bless us with eternal life. He makes this offer to mankind, but only some accept this gift. Yet for those who will trust in Him, Jesus grants the blessing of everlasting life in His presence. Before knowing Him, we were dead in our trespasses and sins, but once we come to faith in Jesus, the Son of God, we are blessed with true life from the very source and sustainer of life, Jesus Christ.

September 19

> *"Let no corrupting talk come out of your mouths, but only such as is good for building up, as fits the occasion, that it may give grace to those who hear."*
> *-Ephesians 4:29*

The words that come out of our mouths have a profound effect on those who hear them. One of the primary ways we influence or encourage others is through the words we speak. Conversely, one of the primary ways we discourage and tear others down is also through the words we communicate.

The things we choose to say grant others a window into what is going on in our minds and our hearts. What can be learned about our hopes, motivations, goals, and worldview from our speech? Can our love for Jesus be perceived from what we verbalize?

Followers of Christ are encouraged to be thoughtful and intentional about the manner is which they speak. Our communication should be empowered by the Holy Spirit and reflective of His presence within us. That way, we won't adopt the course jesting or degrading talk that is so prevalent in the world.

When we speak, it should be to edify those who hear. We can encourage, challenge, correct, and instruct, but whatever comes forth from our mouths should sincerely reflect the heart of Jesus.

September 20

> *For which of you, desiring to build a tower,*
> *does not first sit down and count the cost,*
> *whether he has enough to complete*
> *it? Otherwise, when he has laid a foundation*
> *and is not able to finish, all who see it begin to*
> *mock him, saying, 'This man began to build*
> *and was not able to finish.'*
> **-Luke 14:28-30**

The first, and most obvious step to a building project is figuring out if it's affordable to complete it. How much will materials cost? How much will labor cost? What about insurance and permits? Jesus said that an incomplete building project results in mockery when people see a foundation in place, but nothing sitting on it because it wasn't funded. The cost wasn't properly evaluated.

The crowds that were following Jesus at this point in His ministry weren't following Him to give something, share something, or to spend something. They were following Him because they wanted to get something. This was a common problem among the crowds that followed Him during that day, and it's also a problem that is present among modern day believers as well.

But Jesus makes clear that there is a price we will pay to follow Him closely and sincerely. What is that price? Is it financial? Relational? Experiential? Emotional? Will there be a return on this investment or is that the wrong question?

Let's be honest, there is a cost to follow Jesus, but the investment will be worth it forever. The truth is, we always invest in what matters most to us.

September 21

"The grace of the Lord Jesus Christ and the love of God and the fellowship of the Holy Spirit be with you all."
-2 Corinthians 13:14

We have one God who exists in three persons. The Father, Son, and Holy Spirit live in perfect unity. From eternity past, they have shared perfect fellowship, purpose, and love. We, as recipients of God's gift of salvation, are blessed with their presence in our lives in special ways.

We're reminded, by this Scripture, that God the Father loves us. His love for us isn't passive and distant in nature. He is the perfection of love, and His love for His children is deep, abiding, and active. He has a plan for our lives, and He is directing human history toward the restoration of all that has been damaged by sin.

The Lord Jesus Christ has shown us His grace. He bestows His undeserved favor upon us. We don't deserve all He has done for us, nor do we deserve the ways in which He is actively building us up at present, but He continually brings blessings into the lives of those who walk by faith in Him.

The Holy Spirit has united us in perfect fellowship. He opens our eyes to see things we wouldn't naturally see, comforts and counsels us, speaks wisdom into our hearts, and reminds us that we are one family with our brothers and sisters in Christ. What a blessing it is to worship our God who is willing to do all of this for His glory and our good.

September 22

> *"Therefore welcome one another as Christ*
> *has welcomed you, for the glory of God."*
> *-Romans 15:7*

Jesus has shown us what it looks like to live with an others-centered perspective. Our natural inclination is to primarily pursue what is in our best interest without considering how others might be impacted by the decisions we make. But Jesus has shown us that it is better to give than it is to receive. It's better to bless others than to selfishly covet those blessings for ourselves.

In some ways, it would be nice if people always made it easy to bless them, serve them, and be kind to them, but that's not typically the case. Ironically, those who are often hurting the most, or possibly have the greatest need for assistance, can sometimes seem the least appreciative and may even lash out at you when you're trying to assist them.

That kind of response usually puzzles us, but when we consider the process Jesus went through to help humanity, it makes sense. Jesus healed and He was tortured in return. Jesus encouraged and He was hit in the face. Jesus offered hope and yet He was mocked. Jesus grants the gift of eternal life and yet He was murdered.

Christ has welcomed us and helped us, even though He suffered to do so. For His glory, He invites us to emulate His example.

September 23

> *"Put on then, as God's chosen ones, holy and beloved, compassionate hearts, kindness, humility, meekness, and patience, bearing with one another and, if one has a complaint against another, forgiving each other; as the Lord has forgiven you, so you also must forgive."*
> *-Colossians 3:12-13*

This passage is calling us to approach life and relationships with a visible demonstration of the new heart that Jesus granted you when He called us and chose us. Believers are called "holy and beloved" in this passage. This means that we are objects of Christ's love and we have been set apart to give Him glory. When He set us apart to display His glory, He likewise granted us new hearts. Hearts that aren't motivated by self-interest or dominated by worldly ambitions, but hearts that reflect His loving heart.

So, what difference does this new heart make in our lives? How does the redemption Christ has accomplished in our lives impact the way we relate to others?

According to this passage, the fruit of a new heart will become evident in the way we forgive one another. We're called here to bear with one another. This means to put up with one another's weaknesses and failings. This means we're to stop demanding perfection from each other. This means we aren't to keep track of each other's offenses or hold grudges. When Jesus saved us, He gave us the power to let go of grudges. He gave us the ability to forgive as we have been forgiven by Him. And binding all of this together is love...love for Jesus and love for those He loves. This is His calling on our lives and relationships today.

September 24

"My little children, I am writing these things to you so that you may not sin. But if anyone does sin, we have an advocate with the Father, Jesus Christ the righteous."
-1 John 2:1

Through faith in Jesus Christ, we are granted His power to overcome the chains of our old, sinful nature. He delights to see us walk in freedom. He delights to foster spiritual maturity within us and watch us grow. But He also knows we will experience setbacks along the way. There will be seasons when we may stumble back into the sin we've been freed from.

In those moments, it can be easy to preach a false gospel to our hearts. We can start condemning ourselves, calling ourselves names, berating ourselves, and believing that we'll never experience victory over our areas of weakness. It can even be tempting to start believing that God may stop loving us, or that we've gone too far this time for Him to still welcome us into His family.

But Scripture tells us something different. We're told that if we sin, we have Jesus Christ to speak on our behalf before the Father. Christ has paid the penalty our sin deserved. His body still bears the scars of His torture. The Father declares us righteous, holy, and blameless in His sight, and graces us with eternal life that is secured for us by Jesus, not by our ability to deserve it.

September 25

> *"Therefore, preparing your minds for action, and being sober-minded, set your hope fully on the grace that will be brought to you at the revelation of Jesus Christ."*
> *-1 Peter 1:13*

The counsel we're given here as followers of Jesus Christ is to first of all, prepare our minds for action. We're being challenged to not just be people who dwell in the muddy waters of theories and speculation, but to use our minds in an active manner.

But, as we well know, there are plenty of things that challenge or even inhibit us from using our minds in an active and healthy way. Peter reminds us to be "sober-minded." A sober-minded man is someone who yields their mind over to the Holy Spirit, and as a result, their mind is disciplined, focused, and morally straight.

Instead of yielding our minds over to competing affections, Peter encourages us to be hopeful people. Specifically, we're challenged to set our hope on Jesus Christ and the grace He delights to bring into our lives. This is particularly good counsel when something comes your way that seems to have a depressive effect. God's word reminds us that our true hope isn't in our circumstances. True hope is found in Christ. For that reason, we're encouraged to set our minds fully on the grace that is brought to us by Jesus.

September 26

> *For we know him who said, "Vengeance is mine; I will repay." And again, "The Lord will judge his people." It is a fearful thing to fall into the hands of the living God.*
> *-Hebrews 10:30-31*

It's healthy and wise for us to recognize that our Lord is gracious and merciful. He delights to bestow His favor upon His children, even though we don't deserve it. He has joyfully given His Son, Jesus Christ, who came to this earth to satisfy the righteous wrath of God by taking it upon Himself. He has also told us that He is not ashamed to associate with us or call us His family.

In the midst of so many blessings, it can be easy to forget something else that's true of the Lord. He is the ultimate authority and judge. He calls us and equips us to walk in holiness, and He holds us accountable when we choose not to.

In some contexts of life, we may feel like we've been wronged by others. If that's the case, it can be easy to want to seek revenge, but the Lord has told us to leave vengeance up to Him. He's the only one who can truly judge fairly. He who has no sin can give the fairest determination.

He also cautions us to be mindful of how we choose to live, lest we rebel against Him and invite Him to take disciplinary action in our lives. He has assured us repeatedly that He loves us enough to admonish, intervene, and correct should we choose to veer in the wrong direction.

September 27

> *"But seek first the kingdom of God and his righteousness, and all these things will be added to you."*
> *-Matthew 6:33*

There are plenty of things in this world that vie for our attention and compete for our affections. There are things we would like to own, places we would like to visit, and experiences we would like to have. Some of these things are fine, but others have the potential to become personal idols if we aren't careful.

Jesus knows that we are interested in these things, but He reminds us not to pour out our lives in the pursuit of them as our primary objective. There's something of eternal value we're encouraged to seek first. Specifically, Jesus tells us to seek the kingdom of God and the righteousness that He generously supplies.

A kingdom mindset is one that is focused on the greater mission of Jesus more so than on the trivial objectives of this world. A kingdom mindset delights to give glory to Jesus more so than seeking personal glory or the accumulation of worldly goods.

When the kingdom of God and the righteousness the Lord supplies are our primary objectives, the rest of life will fall in place. The things He desires us to own, places He wants us to go, and experiences He wants us have will come to pass. But even greater than these things is our contentment in knowing that when we have Jesus, we have all we truly need.

September 28

> *"The natural person does not accept the things of the Spirit of God, for they are folly to him, and he is not able to understand them because they are spiritually discerned."*
> *-1 Corinthians 2:14*

There are certain things we can understand about God just by observing what He has created, but there are specific details that we will only understand after we come to faith in Jesus Christ, and the Holy Spirit unveils our eyes so we can truly see.

Those who live in this world without faith in Christ are walking in spiritual blindness. In that state, they reject spiritual truth. They don't accept what God has revealed, and they treat the truth of the gospel as if it is a fable. They lack discernment. They believe lies, and they look down on those who have accepted the truth the Holy Spirit reveals through Scripture, and to the hearts and minds of those who believe.

When we're confronted with this kind of experience, what should we do? How should we interact with those who disparage our faith? In those contexts, it's important that we pray for the Holy Spirit to remove the blinders from the eyes of their heart so that they can see the truth of the gospel. It's also vital that we remain patient, recognizing that at one point, we were in the same situation. The Lord was gracious to allow us to see what we couldn't initially see. With hope, let's entrust those we care about to Him with the expectation that He will help them understand as well.

September 29

> *"For everyone who does wicked things hates the light and does not come to the light, lest his works should be exposed. But whoever does what is true comes to the light, so that it may be clearly seen that his works have been carried out in God."*
> *-John 3:20-21*

Sin likes to operate in secret. It doesn't want its motives exposed. It prefers to lurk beneath the surface where it can get away with its destructive activity without being caught. This is why sin sometimes finds itself able to stick around for a long time in a person's life. The more it's allowed to exist in the shadows, the longer it remains.

Those who belong to Christ are invited to experience something better than bondage to sin. We're invited to walk in the light of Christ. Instead of covering our sin, we confess it. Instead of idolizing our sin, we crucify it. Instead of welcoming sin, He empowers us to abhor it.

Jesus is doing a work in the lives of those who trust in Him. He wants to do great things through His family and He doesn't want anything to inhibit us from experiencing the kind of life He has planned for us. If we're holding on to secret sin, He invites us to expose it to the light, confess it to Him, and repent of it, so it will lose its dominance over us. As we do so, He delights to empower us to carry out the real mission He has designed our lives to fulfill.

September 30

> *"And it is my prayer that your love may abound more and more, with knowledge and all discernment, so that you may approve what is excellent, and so be pure and blameless for the day of Christ,"*
> **-Philippians 1:9-10**

The Lord has called us to be people of prayer. He invites us into His presence, encourages us to come before Him boldly, and grants us the privilege of receiving His counsel and leading.

Many of the prayers we bring before Him are on behalf of other people. We pray for their salvation. We pray for their healing. We pray for their protection. And as the Apostle Paul illustrates in this passage, we can also pray for their spiritual growth and the fruit that will come from it.

On behalf of those we care about, we are shown the importance of praying for brotherly love to abound. This is how the world will ultimately know we're followers of Jesus. We're also shown the importance of praying for knowledge and discernment, so that we can see beyond the tricks and traps of worldliness.

We do this all while keeping in mind that Jesus will return someday. What if He returned today? What would we be involved in? How would we be spending our time? Would our lives show that growing in the maturity of our faith was high on our list of priorities?

279

October 1

> *"Blessed are you when others revile you and persecute you and utter all kinds of evil against you falsely on my account. Rejoice and be glad, for your reward is great in heaven, for so they persecuted the prophets who were before you."*
> **-Matthew 5:11-12**

Naturally speaking, it makes sense to desire an easy, conflict-free, kind of life. It's understandable why most people enjoy being liked by others. It's also perfectly logical to recognize that most people strongly dislike being hated or treated poorly.

But the reality is that followers of Christ may experience poor treatment at the hands of others during the course of their time on this earth. Many people simply do not love Jesus, nor do they support those who worship Him and obey His teaching.

Jesus sought to make us aware of this reality, and He encouraged us to remain joyful even in the midst of difficult circumstances. If someone treats us poorly because of our faith in Him, we can take some comfort in the knowledge that we aren't alone in this struggle. Believers who came before us also endured this same kind of experience, and the Lord was faithful to see them through it.

Jesus reminds us that our greatest rewards aren't earthly in nature, they're heavenly. He has great things in store for us and He intends to reward those who remain faithful to Him in the midst of persecution.

October 2

> *"The fear of man lays a snare, but whoever trusts in the Lord is safe."*
> *-Proverbs 29:25*

Some people can be scary. Others seem to excel at intimidating others. Certain people may even intentionally try to bully others or push them around. How do you respond to people like that? What makes you afraid of certain people?

When we fear others, we reveal something about our own hearts. At the center of unhealthy forms of fear is the presence of insecurity. We're intimidated by others because there's a part of us that feels inadequate.

But in Christ, we have perfect security. In Him, we find our true sense of identity. In Him, we find love that isn't conditional in nature. In Him, we are granted strength and wisdom that exceed what we can naturally develop.

An unhealthy "fear of man" can be a major detriment to our life and faith. It can lead to rebellion against the Lord. It can result in us valuing the temperamental opinions of our peers over the unchanging revelation of the Lord.

If you're currently wrestling with the fear of man, give that struggle over to the Lord. Trade the desire to be "self-confident" for the blessing of finding your confidence in Him, and let Him be the audience you care about pleasing most.

October 3

> *"So put away all malice and all deceit and hypocrisy and envy and all slander. Like newborn infants, long for the pure spiritual milk, that by it you may grow up into salvation— if indeed you have tasted that the Lord is good."*
> *-1 Peter 2:1-3*

What kind of life is a follower of Christ called to live? We're called to put away the fruit of sinfulness, meaning, we're supposed to be tossing it in the junk drawer of our lives so it gets lost and forgotten because we've been made a brand new person. Scripture tells us we've experienced a new birth in Christ, and our walk with Him begins with a form of spiritual infancy.

Generally speaking, what do infants want? They tend to want rest, comfort, and food. If any of those things are missing, they usually make a point to scream until the situation gets rectified. And when it comes to eating, once they discover that they enjoy food, they tend to crave it more and more.

Our relationship with Christ operates in a similar way. Once we taste the goodness of His grace, the depth of His love, and the comfort our souls find in Him, we tend to crave those things more and more. We want to be nourished by what only He can supply, and as we welcome the various forms of spiritual nourishment He offers, we grow more mature in our faith. As He pours into our lives from His word, from fellowship with other believers, through prayer, and with His peace that is beyond human understanding, we are built up and made strong in Him.

October 4

"Do not boast about tomorrow, for you do not know what a day may bring."
-Proverbs 27:1

To one degree or another, we're all making plans. Maybe we're planning for an upcoming vacation or holiday. Maybe we're planning out our grocery list based on the food we expect to eat during this coming week. Maybe we're making long-term financial or retirement plans. Planning in and of itself isn't a bad thing, but we always need to keep in perspective the fact that we don't control the future. Even our best plans can be drastically altered when we least expect it.

God is sovereign and we are not. He's the one in control. We should never boast about the plans we have made for the future because the truth is, there are too many variables for us to know if our plans will actually come to pass. This doesn't mean we shouldn't make plans. It simply means we shouldn't idolize the plans we make.

Some people don't mind going through life without much of a plan. Others would find it very stressful to approach each day without one. The good news is, whether you're a planner or not, God is. Those who have faith in Jesus Christ can rest with confidence, knowing that God has a plan for their life that He will bring to fruition. If we're going to boast about anything, it should be about the gracious and generous nature of Jesus, not our attempts to minimize His sovereign role as Lord of our lives.

October 5

> *"Seek the Lord while he may be found;*
> *call upon him while he is near;"*
> **-Isaiah 55:6**

Our time on this earth is rather brief. Even the longest of lives, naturally speaking, is like a mist when compared to the duration of eternity. During this brief season, our Lord has mercifully granted us the privilege to call upon Him. Scripture implores us to trust in Jesus Christ and receive the new, abundant life He graciously offers.

But of course, this is not an option some people take seriously. There are many people on this earth who would rather remain focused on lesser, and more temporary things. Mankind has a tendency to value the idols of our momentary pleasures and worldly temptations over the life-giving presence of Jesus Christ.

Knowing that the time is short, our Lord has blessed those of us who do know Him with the privilege of making Him known. He has commissioned us as His ambassadors and He has sent us out into this world to testify to the delight of walking by faith in Him.

Light triumphs over darkness. The light of the gospel of Jesus Christ overcomes the deception of Satan and his attempts to keep humanity in perpetual blindness. Now is the time to answer Christ's invitation and respond to His call.

October 6

> *"We have spoken freely to you, Corinthians; our heart is wide open. You are not restricted by us, but you are restricted in your own affections. In return (I speak as to children) widen your hearts also."*
> *-2 Corinthians 6:11-13*

The Apostle Paul had an interesting relationship with the church at Corinth. His heart was open to them, but they were withholding love and respect for him. As family united in Christ, Paul invited them to widen their hearts also in love toward him and those who labored with him.

Who are our hearts open to? What are we opening our hearts up to? Are our hearts open to the presence and power of Christ? Are our hearts open to our brothers and sisters in Christ who love us with Christ's love and desire to make healthy investments in our lives?

Or are our hearts open to the false assurances and false comforts of the momentary idols that tempt us? These are valuable questions to wrestle with because there's always something competing for the affections of our hearts.

As followers of Christ, we're encouraged to cultivate hearts that are open to His leading, open to His teaching, and open to the input and admonition of our Christian family.

October 7

"O God, you are my God; earnestly I seek you; my soul thirsts for you; my flesh faints for you, as in a dry and weary land where there is no water."
-Psalm 63:1

What are you convinced will truly satisfy the longing in your soul?

This is a question we're all wrestling with, whether we realize it or not. Throughout this world right this very moment, billions of people are spending their time, energy, and resources, seeking to fill a void they can sense is present in their soul.

This void, or this longing for something to bring us peace, joy, comfort, and rest, is often described in scripture as a "thirst." David, the writer of this Psalm, was blessed by the Lord with the privilege to see that the deepest longings of his heart could only be satisfied by the Lord. He thirsted for the Lord and found contentment in Him.

Jesus told us in the gospels that the thirst of our souls is satisfied by Him. He made it known that once we find contentment in Him, our souls will recognize that our search for life and nourishment is now complete. We don't need to continue to crave lesser substitutes because in Jesus we find true life, true contentment, true joy, and lasting peace.

October 8

"I, I am the Lord, and besides me there is no savior. I declared and saved and proclaimed, when there was no strange god among you; and you are my witnesses," declares the Lord, "and I am God."
-Isaiah 43:11-12

Humanity seems to have an intrinsic sense that we need to be rescued. That's the theme of many popular movies, books, and songs, and it's also the motivation behind many social and political organizations. We're looking for someone or something to save us, but are we looking in the right place?

The Scriptures reveal our need for the Savior. From the earliest pages of the Bible, we read promises that He would one day come. In the books of prophecy, we read and learn more details about Him. In Isaiah's book, we're reminded that the Savior we need, and the only one who can accomplish what is necessary for our salvation, is the Lord Himself.

Our Lord Jesus Christ offers salvation as a gift to all humanity. He invites us to cast aside the false sources of salvation we've attempted to rely on in the past. No social or political organization can rescue us. No elected leader can restore peace on this earth or save our soul. Only Jesus can rescue us. Only He can provide the help we truly need. Trusting in anyone or anything less than Him to do the job only He can do would be foolish.

October 9

"You shall walk after the LORD your God and fear him and keep his commandments and obey his voice, and you shall serve him and hold fast to him."
-Deuteronomy 13:4

We're all taking direction from someone. There is a primary voice we're all listening to when it comes to making decisions. For some of us, that voice is the voice of our heroes. For others, that voice might be our own. But for believers, the voice we're called to listen to and obey is the voice of the Lord our God.

The challenge for obedience that He gave to the people of Israel long ago, is a challenge that we would also do well to heed. We're called to follow Him with our lives. We're called to live with sincere reverence toward Him. We're called to obey what He has revealed in His word. We're called to listen to Him when He impresses His will upon our minds and hearts. We're called to use our lives to serve Him, and we're invited to hold closely to Him in the midst of every storm or season of life.

This is the calling of God for every believer in Jesus Christ. The Lord seeks to direct the course of our lives. He wants to lead us with His wisdom, love, and perfect counsel. He wants to produce holiness and joy in our lives. But for any of that to be the case, we need to submit to Him instead of embracing the rebellious whims of our drifting hearts. His voice needs to be the one we listen to when we're in need of direction and counsel.

October 10

> *"Listen to advice and accept instruction,
> that you may gain wisdom in the future.
> Many are the plans in the mind of a man,
> but it is the purpose of the Lord that will
> stand."*
> *-Proverbs 19:20-21*

One of the blessings the Lord has granted to us is the privilege to be surrounded by other believers in Jesus Christ. By design, the path to spiritual maturity requires the input and instruction of others who love Jesus. The Lord has not designed us to operate autonomously. Just as the Father, Son, and Holy Spirit live and work in perfect community, so too should the people of God work together and welcome the wisdom that can be invested in our lives as other believers speak to us and offer us their assistance.

Some of the world's most foolish people are those who are "wise in their own eyes." When someone becomes overly self-reliant, they run the risk of idolizing themselves, over-inflating their own opinions, and falling flat on their face due to their lack of teachability.

God's word, however, instructs us to be people who are adept at listening to advice and instruction, even if it challenges our assumptions. When a brother or sister who loves Jesus takes the time to impart their knowledge and experience to us, we should consider it a great blessing. Remaining teachable is key if it's our desire to grow mature in our walk with Christ.

October 11

> *"And if anyone forces you to go one mile, go with him two miles. Give to the one who begs from you, and do not refuse the one who would borrow from you."*
> *-Matthew 5:41-42*

We've all probably been encouraged to "go the extra mile" at some point in our lives. Did it ever occur to you that that phrase finds its origin in the teaching of Jesus from His "Sermon on the Mount"?

In that message that Jesus shared with those who were in His hearing, He encouraged those who followed Him to approach life in a different way. In this world, people strive to get ahead of each other. In this world, people seek to get back at one another when they feel like they've been wronged. But as an expression of our faith in Jesus, we're encouraged to give, help, serve, and love those who sometimes act in rather unloving ways toward us.

In the context of the passage we're looking at today, Jesus teaches us to meet the needs of those who come to us looking for help when it's within our power to do so. Because Jesus has been generous with us, He invites us to follow His example by expressing generosity toward others. He's also teaching us not to idolize our possessions or to value objects over people.

Christ went the extra mile for us, even though we didn't deserve it. Who is He calling us to go the extra mile for?

October 12

*"Hear, my son, your father's instruction,
and forsake not your mother's teaching,
for they are a graceful garland for your
head and pendants for your neck."*
-Proverbs 1:8-9

The are several ways in which the Lord has chosen to speak to mankind throughout history. He has, on occasion, spoken with an audible voice. He speaks to our conscience by the Holy Spirit. He speaks to us when we read His word. He also speaks to us through the counsel of people who love us enough to tell us the truth.

Some of the people that the Lord has often used to teach, instruct, counsel, admonish, and advise us, have been our parents. Our fathers and our mothers have served as vessels through which the Lord has communicated His will.

As followers of Christ, there are multiple things we should be known for, and one of those things should be the fact that we honor and respect our parents. Our parents aren't perfect and neither are we, but, out of reverence for the Lord and His sovereign direction of our lives, we should value the helpful things we've been blessed to learn through the parents He has graced us with.

The simple truth is that those who listen to the godly counsel of their parents tend to live longer and healthier lives than those who ignore the wisdom being offered to them. Do you value their loving instruction?

October 13

> *"For to this you have been called, because Christ also suffered for you, leaving you an example, so that you might follow in his steps."*
> *-1 Peter 2:21*

If we call ourselves followers of Christ, we're called to follow in His steps. During His earthly ministry, Christ left us an example of what it looks like to live, love, and serve. During this era of history, He is living within us and empowering us to walk as He walked.

One of the things He is empowering us to endure is the very real possibility of suffering. We may suffer in our personal lives. We may suffer in the context of our employment. We may suffer where we are called to serve. Suffering isn't something we naturally look forward to, but Christ can use our experience of suffering to glorify His name and teach us to appreciate new things.

Consider for a moment the redemptive aspects of suffering. When Jesus came to this earth, He did so with the intent to suffer on our behalf. When we endure suffering for His glory, we continue to operate with a mindset that reflects His. Interestingly, He will likely use our suffering to teach us to pray with sincerity, make us stronger, show others an example of His power at work in our lives, and help us clarify what's really important in this world.

Following in the steps of Christ can be a difficult path to walk, but it also produces the kind of fruit in our lives that the Lord desires to see present among His children.

October 14

"knowing that he who raised the Lord Jesus will raise us also with Jesus and bring us with you into his presence."
-2 Corinthians 4:14

The Apostle Paul's faith wasn't in himself. His faith was anchored in the Lord who holds the power of the resurrection. The Lord resurrects. He brings the dead to life. Just as Jesus rose from death, so too will all who believe in Him. That's God's guarantee to you and me, and we're reminded elsewhere in Scripture that the same Spirit that rose Jesus from the dead is already at work within us.

We weren't originally designed by God to die. He created our fore-parents, Adam and Eve, to live forever. Death only became part of the human experience once they sinned. Now, it's a curse we're all under, but by design, death isn't something we were originally created to be able to mentally process or dwell upon.

Thankfully, our gracious God didn't let the story end there. In Adam's sin, humanity as a whole experiences death. But in Christ's life and resurrection, everyone who trusts in Him is granted eternal life.

This fact changes the way we live. When we know that the power death once had over us has been broken, that produces joy, thanksgiving to God, and confidence in God's work in our lives that directly impacts our perspective in the midst of every circumstance.

October 15

> *"For this light momentary affliction is preparing for us an eternal weight of glory beyond all comparison, as we look not to the things that are seen but to the things that are unseen. For the things that are seen are transient, but the things that are unseen are eternal."*
> *-2 Corinthians 4:17-18*

The afflictions we experience in this world are temporary in nature. This Scripture speaks of those afflictions, which, humanly speaking, tend to feel like a big deal, as if they were but a small matter. Afflictions are called "light" and "momentary", meaning, from the perspective of eternity, our trials and struggles in this world aren't as heavy as we give them credit for being, and they only last a short while.

What difference do you suppose it would make if we could start seeing our afflictions from that perspective? In this moment, if something is afflicting you, could you call it light and momentary? And could you give yourself permission to begin seeing it from the perspective of eternity as something that is preparing you for the eternal glory Christ has reserved for His followers?

Most people in this world are over-consumed and over-burdened with temporary things that they treat like eternal matters. Maybe we find ourselves doing that frequently as well. But real life, the kind that we're granted through a relationship with Jesus, isn't temporary or transient. It's everlasting and eternal. God has given us this portion of His word to make us aware of that truth, and remind us of it often, particularly in the midst of our afflictions.

October 16

> *"And as they were speaking to the people,
> the priests and the captain of the temple
> and t h e S a d d u c e e s c a m e u p o n
> them, greatly annoyed because they were
> teaching the people and proclaiming in
> Jesus the resurrection from the dead."*
> *-Acts 4:1-2*

The Scripture tells us here that Peter and John were communicating in two ways. They were **teaching** the people, and they were **proclaiming** the resurrection of the dead through Jesus. When we share our faith in Christ with others, there are likely going to be times where we're asked to do one or the other, or both.

Teaching often includes interactive or conversational discussion, while proclaiming tends to be a different form of communication. When you proclaim something, you're announcing a statement of belief. It's an effective form of communication, but it doesn't typically involve dialogue. Preaching is a form of proclamation. Some people prefer learning in a context of proclamation. Others prefer learning in a more teaching-centered context. Both are valuable and both have their place in the communication of the gospel to others.

Which approach do you prefer to take when sharing about your faith? Do you prefer conversation? Teaching a small group in an interactive setting? Making a proclamation to a crowd? Writing or typing the message? All are valuable approaches and every single one is infinitely more valuable than the approach of not saying anything. Sometimes we teach. Sometimes we proclaim because a growing disciple of Christ desires to share the hope He has given them with others.

October 17

> *"This Jesus is the stone that was rejected by you, the builders, which has become the cornerstone. And there is salvation in no one else, for there is no other name under heaven given among men by which we must be saved."*
> *-Acts 4:11-12*

The Scriptures encourage us in many places to verbally share our faith in Christ with others. We're told that this is God's ordained method for His gospel to spread, and that without men and women to speak the truth, people will unfortunately not hear it.

The event surrounding this portion of Scripture involved Peter and John being brought before the religious rulers in Jerusalem. This, by the way, was the same ruling council that condemned Jesus to death. Peter and John were questioned as to what name, or by what power they had performed a miracle in which a man had been healed.

Peter responded to their questions. The Scripture tells us that the Holy Spirit filled him, guiding the words he would say and how he would say them. Peter spoke plainly, clearly and piercingly. He made it clear that this miracle was done in the power of Jesus, the same Jesus they crucified and God raised from the dead. And He also made clear that salvation can be found through no one else other than Jesus.

For Christ's glory, speak plainly, honestly, and courageously of Him when He brings you before others who need to know Him.

October 18

> *"A new commandment I give to you, that you love one another: just as I have loved you, you also are to love one another. By this all people will know that you are my disciples, if you have love for one another."*
> *-John 13:34-35*

Love is a word that we use with regularity, but we often mean several different things by it. Sometimes we use that word to describe something we really enjoy. Other times we use that word when we're describing something that brings us comfort. But Jesus is using the term "love" in a much deeper way than it is commonly used in the English language.

Jesus is speaking about a kind of love that reflects His heart toward humanity, and when He uses the term "love" in this passage, He is speaking about an action, not merely a feeling. He's encouraging His disciples to practice love. Specifically, He's commanding us to seek what is best for one another, even at great personal cost to ourselves.

Jesus describes His teaching here as a "new commandment." The commandments of Scripture have always been about loving God and loving people, but there's something new about what Jesus was teaching His disciples that we would be wise to observe.

Jesus was teaching His followers to love one another just as He has loved us, and that in doing so, the world would know that we are His disciples. Christ desires that our lives point others toward Him because people are going to believe what they see in your life, particularly when you're under stress or opposition, before they're going to consider your words credible.

October 19

"Restore to me the joy of your salvation, and uphold me with a willing spirit."
-Psalm 51:12

What's the worst thing you've ever done? How often do you think about it? Does it come back to your mind time and time again? Do you frequently beat yourself up about it? Are you struggling to move beyond it?

It's normal and healthy for a follower of Christ to experience sorrow and remorse in regard to mistakes we've made or sins we've committed. We regret the fact that we've sinned against the Lord. We're bothered by the fact that we've caused others to experience pain or shame.

But beating ourselves up about past mistakes isn't a healthy spot to sit in over the long-term. If we've confessed our sin, repented of it, and are walking in step with the Spirit, we don't need to keep revisiting the bad decisions we've made. Jesus took our sin, shame, and guilt upon Himself at the cross. He knows that isn't a burden we can stand to bear. He knows that the weight of it would crush us. He bore it for us so we could live in the freedom of His gracious forgiveness.

In Christ, we find restoration for our crushed spirits. In Christ, we find encouragement and the opportunity to begin again. Our Lord who has purchased our freedom and has granted us new life, is the one who brings us lasting joy that overcomes our tendencies to brood over the past.

October 20

"Delight yourself in the Lord, and he will give you the desires of your heart."
-Psalm 37:4

What is the substance of most of your prayers? When you come before the Lord, do you praise Him for who He is? Do you confess your sins to Him and seek His cleansing? Do you thank Him for what He has done in your life? Or do your prayers primarily consist of asking God for various things that you're convinced you need?

How many of our "needs" are actually necessary? If we took a hard look at some of these things, what we'd probably find is a collection of items that we're trying to rely on to bring a sense of peace and satisfaction to our hearts. We're convinced that money will bring us peace, so we ask God for it. We're convinced that the absence of physical pain will bring us peace, so we request it. We're convinced that fewer trials will bring us peace, so we express that longing as a "need".

Yet the Scriptures reveal to us that we can be content in Christ. When we have Jesus, we truly do have all we really need. He invites us to be satisfied in Him and through Him. He encourages us to delight in Him. As we delight in Him, He is pleased to grant us the desires of our hearts, but interestingly, delighting in Him helps us to realize that Christ is who our heart really needs. The Lord doesn't intend to give us the idols we once longed to worship. Rather, He has given us Himself and is teaching us to find contentment in Him.

October 21

"I delight to do your will, O my God;
your law is within my heart."
-Psalm 40:8

One of the great blessings that we experience as believers in Jesus Christ, is the presence of the Holy Spirit within us. At the moment of our salvation, we were indwelled with the Spirit, and He counsels, instructs, encourages, and directs us every day of our lives going forward.

As we walk with the Spirit, our manner of thinking is gradually transformed. Before coming to know Christ, we operated like creatures of instinct. We were prone to over-emphasize our selfish desires and elevate our will above the Lord's. But that's been changed. We see things differently. We've been granted the mind of Christ, and the desires of our hearts are being brought in line with His will.

At one point, we would have balked at the idea of following God's will or obeying God's law. Now He's blessed us with a longing to do both. As we've learned to trust Him, we've also learned that what He makes known to us is accurate, true, and beneficial. Once we taste and see how good the truth of His word really is, we begin to crave it more and more.

The law of the Lord isn't burdensome. Rather, in His teaching, we find freedom from the deceptive beliefs that we used to embrace. He grants us new clarity, and the counsel He has blessed us with the privilege to embrace continually points us toward Him.

October 22

> *"For though we walk in the flesh, we are not waging war according to the flesh. For the weapons of our warfare are not of the flesh but have divine power to destroy strongholds."*
> *-2 Corinthians 10:3-4*

Scripture makes it very clear to us that there is a battle taking place all around us. We don't always notice the battle at first, but we can definitely see its effects. There is a spiritual battle taking place for the hearts and minds of mankind. Christ invites us to believe His gospel and live it out. Satan tempts us to reject Christ's gospel and walk according to the flesh. To make decisions based on worldly calculations. To idolize ambitions that have little to do with God's glory and much to do with our own.

The spiritual battle taking place around us is a real thing, but by God's grace, we haven't been left powerless. As believers in Jesus Christ, we've been blessed with His indwelling power. We have His strength to access as He lives within us. We can stand against our spiritual enemy and his schemes because we are protected by God's armor.

When we're waging spiritual battles and seeking spiritual victories, we need to recognize where our true power is found. It's found in Jesus Christ. Death could not defeat Him. Sin could not overtake Him. Satan could not stop Him. By grace, through faith in Him, His victory is generously shared with us as well. His power is what we truly need.

October 23

> *"We destroy arguments and every lofty opinion raised against the knowledge of God, and take every thought captive to obey Christ, being ready to punish every disobedience, when your obedience is complete."*
> *-2 Corinthians 10:5-6*

Every behavior in your life is tied to a belief. In this era we live in, information is everywhere and it's never been easier to access. There are all kinds of ideas and philosophies being proposed every day. There are all kinds of arguments and ideologies being debated continually. Everyone seems to want a label and everyone seems to take pride in belonging to one camp or another.

And just like we see today, so too was it in Paul's time that lofty sounding arguments were often being presented against the true knowledge of God. Sadly, it can even be easy for uninformed Christians to buy into some of these worldly philosophies and arguments. For that reason, Paul encourages the church to take every thought captive to obey Christ.

Effectively, what this means is that we're called to hold what we believe up to the light of the gospel. If our core beliefs don't match with the redemptive message of God's word.... If our personal philosophies conflict with the good news of Christ's grace.... then we need to repent of those false beliefs and embrace the profound truth of Christ's grace, mercy, forgiveness, and righteousness once again.

Do our personal beliefs line up with that message? Christ wants us to experience the joy of living in spiritual victory. Every belief we attest to needs to be held up to the light of the gospel. At your core, what do you believe?

302

October 24

> *"Bear one another's burdens, and so fulfill the law of Christ."*
> **-Galatians 6:2**

Every season of life presents new challenges to us. There are concerns that have the potential to burden our minds when we're young, and there's a different set of concerns that have the potential to burden us when we're old. If left unaddressed, these concerns can lead to depression and despair.

Thankfully, our Lord Jesus Christ desires to take the weight of our burdens upon Himself. He isn't calling us to fend for ourselves and He isn't calling us to try to be overly self-reliant. He reminds us of His presence and He offers us His strength.

He has also blessed us with the church, which is our Christian family. He surrounds us with brothers and sisters in Christ who help us grow in our faith by making intentional investments in our lives. He also reminds us that our Christian family is there to help us when we have burdens that are too heavy for us to carry alone.

Christ has called us to love one another. A powerful expression of this kind of love is our willingness to bear one another's burdens. Christ calls us to help each other through trials, encourage one another when we're down, and pray for one another when we need strength. Not only is this a powerful form of help for brothers and sisters in need, it's also a visible testimony to the unbelieving world of what it truly looks like to follow Jesus.

October 25

> *"addressing one another in psalms and hymns and spiritual songs, singing and making melody to the Lord with your heart, giving thanks always and for everything to God the Father in the name of our Lord Jesus Christ,"*
> *-Ephesians 5:19-20*

The relationships the Lord has initiated within the church are helpful, inspiring, and edifying. Many of us can quickly speak of people that the Lord has introduced us to, through our common faith in Christ, that have gone out of their way to remind us of the joy and truth of His gospel.

As our hearts rejoice over the underserved blessings we have received from Jesus, it's logical that that would begin to overflow in our conversations. The Scripture encourages us to direct this overflow toward each other so that the church would be mutually encouraged and built up.

Because of the hardships and challenges we regularly face in this world, it can be somewhat easy to adopt a sour countenance in response. But the joy we find in Jesus supersedes everything this world throws at us. Our joy isn't dependent on our circumstances because it's anchored in Christ. Therefore, we can be people who are internally grateful, and externally expressive about the thankfulness we feel. Let the joy of Christ expressively flow from you toward others today.

October 26

> *"All Scripture is breathed out by God and profitable for teaching, for reproof, for correction, and for training in righteousness, that the man of God may be complete, equipped for every good work."*
> *-2 Timothy 3:16-17*

Unlike the generations that lived before us, we have been blessed to live in what has often been referred to as "The Information Age." We live during a time in human history when communication happens rapidly. Ideas are exchanged and thoughts are communicated in "real time." And being part of this era, we also have greater access to God's word than our forefathers. So what are we doing with it?

The Bible isn't merely a helpful series of stories, laws, and morals. It is the collection of divinely communicated Scripture. It has been communicated to us directly by God and penned by human writers that the Holy Spirit carried along so that they would accurately write down what He was revealing.

The word of God points us to Jesus. It tells us of our fallen condition and our need for the Savior. It makes known to us things that we would never naturally surmise. It challenges us in areas that we need to be challenged in. It's used by God to comfort us and remind us of the secure hope we find in Him. God's word is a tool that He uses to equip those who follow Him so that we would be trained and prepared to fulfill His calling on our lives. As much as it depends on you, never let a day go by without spending some time reading and reflecting on the truth of the Scriptures.

October 27

> *"For t h e w o r d o f G o d i s l i v i n g*
> *and active, sharper than any two-edged sword,*
> *piercing to the division of soul and of spirit, of*
> *joints and of marrow, and discerning the*
> *thoughts and intentions of the heart."*
> *-Hebrews 4:12*

When followers of Christ get serious about spending time reading through the content of God's word, and giving careful and prayerful thought to the content, they begin to experience some notable changes in their lives and in their perspectives.

God's word cuts to the heart of the issues it addresses. He uses His word to grant us insight into the issues present in our own lives, as well as the issues that may be present in the lives of those we interact with. God's word forces us to examine our motives and hold them up to the light of the gospel.

The word of God is used by Him to convey wisdom to us. By nature, we are prone to drift toward embracing folly, but the Scriptures help us to value wisdom, obtain it, and convey it to others.

Above all else, the word of God points us to Jesus Christ. It reveals our need for Him and shows us that He is the only solution for filling the void in our hearts. There's a road from every portion of Scripture to Jesus. Is that something you see when you're reading God's word? Can you discern the many ways the Scriptures are seeking to point your heart toward Christ?

October 28

"If I must boast, I will boast of the things
that show my weakness."
-2 Corinthians 11:30

What's one of the surest ways to fall into sin and temptation? What's a big contributor to the downfall of many Christians who at one point conveyed an impression that they were strong and had their act together? One of the biggest contributors to that downfall is to pretend that you don't have weaknesses. To pretend like there aren't areas of temptation that you're still struggling with. To convince yourself that you're somehow immune to falling into sin or that some of the things you wrestled with in the past have no chance of surfacing again in this season of your life.

When we look at the Apostle Paul's words in this passage, we can see that he emphasized his weaknesses. While others at the time were boasting about their supposed strengths, Paul displayed that Christ's strength was sufficient for him in the midst of his human weaknesses.

The truth is, we can spend the few brief decades we have on this earth doing one of two things. We can try to make ourselves look good, or we can point people to Christ who actually is good. We can try to pretend like we don't have any weaknesses, or we can display that Christ's strength is sufficient for us in the midst of our human weaknesses. We can carefully craft an image that centers around acting like we've got everything figured out, or we can testify that real wisdom is granted by the Holy Spirit through faith in Christ. He's got it all figured out. Life isn't about trusting ourselves. It's about trusting Him, and walking with Him daily.

October 29

> *"I appeal to you therefore, brothers, by the mercies of God, to present your bodies as a living sacrifice, holy and acceptable to God, which is your spiritual worship."*
> *-Romans 12:1*

Our bodies are fascinating to observe and constructed with intricate detail. They have been intentionally designed by the Lord to function on this earth and in this environment. Our bodies are amazingly complex and they serve as a visible testimony that points to the reality of the existence of our Creator.

Scripture tells us that we have been created in the image of God. As we use the bodies He has blessed us with, we can choose to honor Him or we can choose to scoff at Him. We can subject our bodies to distasteful and dishonorable practices, or we can use our bodies to bring Christ glory.

In the Old Testament era, it was required of the people of Israel to ceremonially sacrifice the bodies of various animals to the Lord. With that practice in mind, the Lord implores us to offer our bodies to Him as well, not as a blood sacrifice, but as a living sacrifice. This means that as we live, we would do so with the understanding that we aren't living for ourselves, but rather for our Lord who gave life and breath to our bodies in the first place.

Christ sacrificially gave His body on the cross to atone for our sin. Now He calls us to treat our bodies like an offering of worship unto Him, by living in such a way that He is glorified in how our bodies are used and cared for.

October 30

"And he said to all, "If anyone would come after me, let him deny himself and take up his cross daily and follow me."
-Luke 9:23

Many of the people who showed interest in Him during His earthly ministry were looking at Jesus primarily through a political lens. Some wanted to follow Him because they were certain He was going to raise the nation of Israel to a place of prominence like it enjoyed under King David. But Jesus isn't speaking of following Him in those kinds of terms in these verses. He tells those within His hearing that *"If anyone would come after me, let him deny himself and take up his cross daily and follow me."* That's the reality of following Christ.

Jesus teaches us to deny ourselves. This doesn't mean to punish, starve, or demean ourselves, but it does mean that we should let go of our selfish desires and the constant search for earthly security that competes with Christ's invitation to walk by faith in Him.

Jesus teaches us to take up our cross. In saying this, He's inviting us to assess the depth of our commitment to Him. Would we be willing to suffer persecution for His name? Would we follow Jesus, even to the point of death? Jesus is telling us that there's no turning back when we become His disciple.

Jesus teaches us to follow Him. Belief in Christ is where discipleship starts, but it continues and grows deeper as we daily follow Christ. Our life needs to be going in the same direction as His. He calls us to follow Him and journey through life confident of His presence, power, wisdom, and encouragement that He will continually pour into us.

October 31

> *"Be sober-minded; be watchful.*
> *Your adversary the devil prowls*
> *around like a roaring lion, seeking*
> *someone to devour."*
> **-1 Peter 5:8**

Life isn't a joke. Our lives have been given to us as a gift from the Lord. He has graciously blessed us with the privilege to live in this world for a season, and has promised us an inheritance in His kingdom forever, through faith in the Son of God, Jesus Christ.

During this season of our lives, however, we have an adversary to be aware of. At times, it might feel like other people are our adversaries, but the truth is, they aren't. Our real adversary is the devil himself. The devil looks for people to devour. He is more than happy to help those who don't take life seriously to essentially ruin or waste their earthly lives. He delights in defaming humanity because we bear the the image of God.

While we await the return of Jesus Christ, we're encouraged to be vigilant and faithful. We're admonished to be "sober-minded." Nothing should be invited into our lives that has the capacity to hinder our judgement or damage our testimony. With the wisdom, clarity, and strength the Lord supplies, we can be watchful for any scheme the devil might be using to hurt or hinder us.

Is there anything in your life that Satan might be using against you to hinder or cloud your judgement? What is the Lord bringing to your attention that might need to be removed in order for you to walk with Him more closely?

November 1

> *"having the eyes of your hearts enlightened, that you may know what is the hope to which he has called you, what are the riches of his glorious inheritance in the saints,"*
> **-Ephesians 1:18**

When you come to faith in Christ, the Holy Spirit transforms you from living, walking, and thinking in darkness, to being able to walk in the light and see things from a new, godly perspective. This world looks different once we're blessed with the mind of Christ. Certain things that once seemed important or valuable are no longer as important to us. Other issues that may not have stood out to us in the past, now begin to seem paramount in importance.

As the eyes of our hearts have been enlightened, we have come to know the hope we've found in Jesus Christ. We have a deep and abiding confidence toward the future as we await the fulfillment of the promises our Lord has made to us. We trust Him to do what He has said He would do. We're certain that He can be counted on with complete reliance.

In Christ, we've been blessed in so many ways. Through Him we've been granted a future inheritance that is being held securely for us. No matter what we may experience in the here and now, we have good and glorious things to look forward to. Our best days during this season of our life will pale in comparison to the future the Lord holds in store for all who trust in Him.

November 2

"Do not repay evil for evil or reviling for reviling, but on the contrary, bless, for to this you were called, that you may obtain a blessing."
-1 Peter 3:9

Consider for just a moment how Jesus has chosen to bless us. Scripture tells us that we weren't looking for Him, so He came looking for us. We were content to go our own way and wallow in our sin, but He showed us a new way. We lived in opposition toward Him, yet He showed us kindness. We deserved judgement because of our sin, yet He who had no sin took our condemnation upon Himself at the cross. Now He's present with us and within us. Now He's strengthening us and leading us. Now He's preparing future blessings for us, and we don't deserve any of it.

People have offended and do offend us, yet if we set our hearts toward getting back at them, all we're really doing is forgetting the ways in which Jesus has chosen to bless us. It isn't our job to retaliate against those who intentionally hurt us. Rather, it's our privilege to bless others just as we have been blessed.

Interestingly, this Scripture tells us that when we bless others, even after they've hurt us, we are fulfilling Christ's calling on our lives and we will experience a God-ordained blessing. In other words, He will intentionally bless us as we model the truth of His gospel by blessing others. Maybe part of that blessing will include giving us a sense of peace in knowing that we've done what was right. Our consciences won't disturb us. Our hearts won't be consumed with rage. When we choose not to repay evil for evil, we're giving this world a powerful glimpse of the very thing Jesus chose to do for us.

November 3

> *"Let every person be subject to the governing authorities. For there is no authority except from God, and those that exist have been instituted by God."*
> **-Romans 13:1**

Naturally speaking, we all tend to have a craving for independence. Children seek independence from their parents. Employees seek to gain independence from their employers, and citizens often express a desire to live independent of their governing authorities. This isn't something new. It seems to be a facet of human nature.

But it's also possible for that desire to stretch too far. By nature, we're sinful. For that reason, the Lord has established governing authorities who have the capacity to encourage order and restrain sin. Ideally, it would be nice if all earthly governments acknowledged the sovereign rule of Jesus Christ, but that isn't the case. Even still, the Lord encourages us to be respectful toward the authorities that govern us.

In addition to showing respect to those who have the responsibility to govern, Scripture also encourages us to lift our leaders up in prayer. When we pray for our leaders, we're seeking the Lord's intervention in their lives. We're asking the Lord to grant them wisdom and character so that they can govern fairly and justly.

What kind of difference do you think it would make where you live if those who professed faith in Jesus also took time to pray for and show respect to the leaders Christ has placed in their lives?

November 4

"who has made us sufficient to be ministers of a new covenant, not of the letter but of the Spirit. For the letter kills, but the Spirit gives life."
-2 Corinthians 3:6

Jesus is doing a work within us that far surpasses what many people realize. At one point, our hearts were set against Him as His enemies. Now He has called us unto Himself, forgiven our sin, granted His righteousness to us as a gift, and He makes us sufficient to serve as ministers of His new covenant.

Some people think of ministers as being a small group of select, super-saints, with years of formalized training and multiple initials after their names. But that's not how the Scriptures describe those whom Christ has called to be ministers. In His grace, He has equipped every genuine believer to minister to others in His name. He enables us to communicate the truth of His gospel. He makes us able to model what it looks like to genuinely follow Him. He is making His appeal to this world through simple, regular people like us.

Have you ever told yourself that "you're not good enough" or "you're inadequate?" That's something we all probably wrestle with to one degree or another. But Christ's gospel tells us something vastly different. He tells us that in Him and through Him we have been made sufficient for every task or mission He has called us to complete. That's a truth we should intentionally remind our hearts to embrace today.

November 5

*"For this reason, because I have heard of
your faith in the Lord Jesus and your love
toward all the saints, I do not cease to give
thanks for you, remembering you in my
prayers, "*
-Ephesians 1:15-16

Paul wrote this letter to the church at Ephesus years after the
church had been planted. There were many people who were
now part of the church that he had never met personally, but the
reputation of the church was rather good. In multiple ways, the
people of the church were displaying Christ-likeness in how
they were responding to one another and to outsiders. For this,
Paul was thankful and he would regularly remember them in his
prayers.

The very things that Paul was praying for on behalf of the
Ephesian church are things that we should be praying for in
regard to ourselves and our church family. In essence, Paul was
praying that the church would become more and more Christ-
like as their faith matured. So what does Christ-likeness look
like and how can we begin to practice it?

Growing in Christ-likeness involves genuine faith in Jesus and
genuine love for our Christian family. As our faith matures, we
rely on the Holy Spirit for wisdom. We come to know God in a
deeper way. The eyes of our hearts are enlightened to God's
truth. We grow certain of the hope we have in Christ, and we
recognize that the Lord has an inheritance for us in His
kingdom that is far greater than what this world can offer us.

Are you growing in Christ-likeness? Do you love Jesus, delight
in Him, and desire to reflect His heart and likeness more and
more in your daily life?

November 6

> *"Then rose up the heads of the fathers' houses*
> *of Judah and Benjamin, and the priests and the*
> *Levites, everyone whose spirit God had stirred*
> *to go up to rebuild the house of the Lord that is*
> *in Jerusalem."*
> **-Ezra 1:5**

A mission tends to exist in the idea realm until God raises up people to follow through with it. When a mission is coupled with action, it finds its fulfillment. God spoke to His people through the words of King Cyrus, and we're told that there were people from various stations of life who were stirred up to join God's mission.

Those who did not manually help them rebuild, gave them silver, gold, animals and other costly items. They did this freely and joyfully. And Cyrus gave back the vessels that belonged in the temple that Nebuchadnezzar had carried away when he first took the Jews captive.

The big picture of what was taking place was that God was preserving and protecting the Jewish people, and in these verses particularly the tribe of Judah through whom Jesus was going to come and fulfill the ultimate divine mission for man's redemption. The words recorded in the book of Ezra aren't just isolated historical stories. They give us part of the picture of God's intentional and purposeful plan to rescue and redeem mankind through Jesus Christ.

Jesus, the eternal Son of God, was always clear about His mission. The Lord loves us too much not to stir us up about it. God hasn't called us to be men and women who spend ten or less decades on this earth sitting on our hands or sitting on our recliners. He's stirring us up to fulfill His word, support His work, and partner with Him in His redemptive plan.

November 7

> *"Is anyone among you suffering? Let him pray. Is anyone cheerful? Let him sing praise."*
> *-James 5:13*

Our Lord Jesus Christ understands seasons of suffering. When we look at the experience He had on this earth, suffering was something He became well acquainted with. Maybe you're going through a season of suffering right now. What does God's word recommend to us when those seasons come? We're invited to pray. We're invited to unload our burdens on the Lord. We're invited to trust Him with our spiritual, physical, emotional, and relational needs.

But not every season of life is consumed with suffering. In fact, there are times when we're blessed to go through long stretches when it feels like everything is going great. Ironically, there is a danger that comes with long and cheerful stretches of life. The danger is that we can forget that the Lord is the giver of all good things. So this Scripture also encourages us to pray when we're cheerful. We're reminded to express our thanks and appreciation to the Lord for these seasons of cheer.

The overall point being communicated in this section of Scripture is that we're invited to come before the Lord in prayer in the midst of every circumstance of life. In our high moments and in our low moments. On behalf of those who are suffering or ill and on behalf of our own concerns. The Lord invites us to confidently and regularly enter into His presence and seek His intervention through prayer.

November 8

> *"And if it is evil in your eyes to serve the Lord, choose this day whom you will serve, whether the gods your fathers served in the region beyond the River, or the gods of the Amorites in whose land you dwell. But as for me and my house, we will serve the Lord."*
> *-Joshua 24:15*

We all have the same amount of hours in our day and we can choose to spend those hours in a variety of ways. We can pour out our effort and energy toward the goal of serving ourselves, or we can use our life to serve the Lord. We can worship our own ambitions, or we can worship the God who lovingly formed us in our mothers' wombs.

Every generation is forced to make a choice as to whom they are going to direct their efforts, attention, and worship toward. The people of ancient Israel had to decide whether or not they were going to worship and serve the Lord, or whether they were going to worship and serve the false gods of the neighboring nations. We need to wrestle with that same decision.

When you came to faith in Jesus Christ, you were welcomed into God's family. You were blessed with His strength and a future that it secured by Him. Every day He gives you on this earth is another day you can express your love toward Him, and your thankfulness for Him, by choosing to serve Him with your life. Don't waste the time He's blessed you with by chasing after false gods.

November 9

But the Lord said to me, "Do not say, 'I am only a youth'; for to all to whom I send you, you shall go, and whatever I command you, you shall speak. Do not be afraid of them, for I am with you to deliver you, declares the Lord."
-Jeremiah 1:7-8

It may not be pleasant to admit, but frequently, we can be better at making excuses than we are at getting things accomplished. We like to tell ourselves that someone else would be a better fit for the task God has called us to accomplish, but the truth is, if Jesus Christ lives within us, we are fully equipped for every task the Lord asks us to complete.

What excuses do you like to tell yourself? Are you too young? Too old? Lacking in formal education? Lacking in experience? Not talented enough? Too introverted? Something else?

The truth is, the Lord doesn't call us to a task and then tell us to rely on our own natural strength and wisdom. He calls us to rely on Him and utilize the gifts He so willingly supplies.

When we read through the Scriptures we see scores of the most unlikely people being used to accomplish great things, with God's strength, for His glory. Don't preach a message to your heart that is the opposite of what God's word communicates. If God calls you, He will equip you, empower you, and direct the very steps you take.

November 10

> *"God thunders wondrously with his voice; he does great things that we cannot comprehend."*
> *-Job 37:5*

How often do you try to figure out what God is up to? How regularly do you try to discern His plans and objectives? Have you ever found yourself scratching your head in wonder as you watch God's sovereign will unfold? Have you ever wanted to change something He has decided?

God's moral will is crystal clear from the Scriptures. He desires that we trust in, and walk with His Son, Jesus Christ, through whom we're made holy and graced with divine righteousness. But it usually isn't His moral will that believers spend a lot of time questioning. Usually we're intrigued by the details of His plans and how He is at work in our individual circumstances.

When we encounter an aspect of God's plan that we don't immediately understand, there are two ways we can react to it. We can question Him and doubt the wisdom of what He's decided, or we can trust Him and rest in the security of knowing that He holds our lives securely in His hands.

There will come a day when the things we have questioned will make perfect sense to us. In the meantime, the Lord delights in His children choosing to trust Him even when we don't immediately understand why He's doing what He's doing.

November 11

> *"remember that you were at that time separated from Christ, alienated from the commonwealth of Israel and strangers to the covenants of promise, having no hope and without God in the world. "*
> *-Ephesians 2:12*

As Paul wrote to the church at Ephesus, he invited them to remember their old lives apart from Christ. Many of them had been involved in the worship of false gods. Some of them were caught up in the worship of their own material prosperity. Some had once practiced and embraced various forms of culturally acceptable immorality.

Paul reminds the church that that was a hopeless way to live. At one time, these men and women weren't believers in Christ. They walked according to the counsel of their own minds. Their hearts weren't joyfully submissive to Christ, and they lived without hope and without God in this world.

In that state, they were separated from Christ, and at one time, so were we. We were outlawed from enjoying the kind of blessings God had historically poured out upon Israel. We were distant from, and ignorant of the promises fulfilled in Christ. We too lived without hope and without God in this world.

But that all changed when we met Christ. We went from being distant, self-reliant and alienated, to close, Christ-reliant, family. In Christ, we find a secure, unwavering hope. In Christ we find certainty, fulfilled promises and guarantees.

November 12

> *"Then I proclaimed a fast there, at the river Ahava, that we might humble ourselves before our God, to seek from him a safe journey for ourselves, our children, and all our goods."*
> *-Ezra 8:21*

In life, we all like to make plans. Sometimes our plans are inspired by our own thinking and sometimes God is the one directing the plans we're making. Ezra's plans were clearly being directed by the hand of God, but even knowing that, he invited the group to humble themselves before God and seek His protection for the journey they were about to take.

Ezra technically could have requested armed protection from the king's soldiers, but he chose not to because he had testified before the king that the hand of God was on him and he didn't want to be someone who expressed faith in God verbally without backing that up in how he lived.

Ezra and the group fasted and prayed, and God answered their request. In our context, we frequently pray, but how often do we fast? When we fast, we're temporarily removing things that we might typically take comfort in so we can focus more clearly on God and learn to find satisfaction in Him. Scripture speaks of fasting from food, from alcohol and from sexual intimacy. If the Lord leads you to take a temporary fast so that you can devote that time to Him in prayer, go for it.

The point of all is this is that we come to a place where we realize that there is no substitute for the presence of God Himself. As we humble ourselves before the Lord, admitting our need for redemption through Jesus, we're invited to find ultimate satisfaction for our hearts through Him alone.

November 13

> *"Since therefore Christ suffered in the flesh, arm yourselves with the same way of thinking, for whoever has suffered in the flesh has ceased from sin, so as to live for the rest of the time in the flesh no longer for human passions but for the will of God."*
> ***-1 Peter 4:1-2***

One of the keys to understanding Christ's mission and ministry is to understand His nature. By nature, Jesus is divine. He is God who took on flesh. He never sinned or violated His holy nature. But even though He never sinned, He was treated by the religious leaders and the government of the day as if He had. Yet He was willing to endure that suffering rather than react in a sinful way to the expectations of the people who opposed Him.

We're invited to do the same thing. If your desire is to follow Christ in the midst of this fallen world, you need to recognize that there will be times when you will be tempted or attacked. But you aren't defenseless. We're told in this passage to arm ourselves with something as if we're going off to battle. This Scripture encourages us to arm ourselves with the same manner of thinking Jesus utilized. What is this manner of thinking?

The manner of thinking or attitude that Jesus displayed was the willingness to suffer for doing the right thing. That's the mindset He calls us to adopt as well. God's will seems fuzzy when we're consumed with worldly passions. His will becomes much clearer when we're approaching life with the mindset of Christ. Are you willing to do the right thing even if you suffer for it? Do you recognize that this is part of God's will for you?

November 14

> *"Live as people who are free, not using your freedom as a cover-up for evil, but living as servants of God."*
> *-1 Peter 2:16*

Freedom is a genuine gift that we receive through Jesus Christ. Before knowing Christ, we weren't free, but upon coming to know Him by faith, we were set free from our bondage to sin, Satan, and death.

Freedom is a very misunderstood concept, even among those who have been set free by Jesus. In many cases, the concept of freedom is treated like it's the ability to do whatever we want, whenever we want, regardless of the consequences. But that's not the kind of freedom we've been granted through Christ.

Jesus has set us free from sin, not so we can continue to indulge in it, but so we don't need to be held back by it any longer. Jesus has opened our eyes to begin to see what matters to Him, and to learn how to value what He is concerned with. It is not His will for us to live as if we are still in the spiritual blindness that we once walked in.

The freedom we have been granted by Jesus is the kind of freedom that is lived out in heart-felt service toward God. It's the freedom to live our lives differently than we once did. We have been granted the blessing of being able to use the days we've been granted to glorify and serve our Creator, instead of living as if our primary desire is to serve the selfish desires of the sin nature.

November 15

> *"Trouble and anguish have found me out,*
> *but your commandments are my delight."*
> **-Psalm 119:143**

It's better to be honest with yourself than it is to lie or try to create a facade. The truth is that our lives on this earth aren't always going to be easy. It doesn't do us any good to try to pretend that we're never going to have any problems. Hiding from our difficulties doesn't make them go away. Denying their existence doesn't rob them of their pain.

But the joy we have in Christ isn't dependent on our circumstances. We can have the most difficult day, but still rejoice in Him. No matter what this world throws at us, we can still be grateful that the word of God is true, and He will never fail us.

The Psalmist delighted in the commands of the Lord. We're invited to cultivate that same perspective as well. The same Lord who spoke creation into existence speaks into our lives through the Scriptures He inspired. He reminds us of the hope we have in Him, even in the midst of our lowest seasons. He reveals to us the kind of future He holds in store for all who trust in Him.

If this season feels like a season of trouble or anguish for you, please remember the words of this Psalm. Your hope isn't in your circumstances. Your hope is in Christ. The commands and the teaching of His word will help keep that truth fresh in your mind.

November 16

> *"Let the words of my mouth and the meditation of my heart be acceptable in your sight, O Lord, my rock and my redeemer."*
> *-Psalm 19:14*

Our words operate like a window into our soul. The things we say communicate what's going on in our minds and in our hearts. Our words reveal what our mind has been dwelling on.

Words matter to our Lord. During the course of His earthly ministry, Jesus took time to speak to small groups and great crowds. His goal was to help the people see their need for Him and the gift of salvation He offered them. Likewise, God's word encourages us to be people who intentionally make the message of His gospel known by verbally sharing it with others.

On the other hand, we can also use our words for selfish purposes. We can cut others down in a vain attempt to make ourself feel superior to them. We can withhold encouragement from those who desperately need it. We can hold back on expressing affection toward others even when we know it would be right to share it.

But, as followers of Christ, our prayer should be that the words we speak and the things we allow our minds to dwell on, would be acceptable in our Lord's sight. He desires to be glorified in what we say and how we think. Do we welcome His presence in those areas of our life?

November 17

*"Your word is a lamp to my feet and a light
to my path."*
-Psalm 119:105

Walking in darkness can be dangerous in both the physical
and spiritual sense. When our physical bodies are walking
in darkness, we risk injury and harm. When we're walking
in spiritual darkness, we miss out on understanding God's
will and the safety of living in a daily relationship with
Him.

By the grace of God, we have been granted the Scriptures.
The Holy Spirit carried along different writers who
accurately conveyed the teaching He wanted us to receive.
His word has been passed along to many generations in
both oral and written form.

The word of God continually points us toward trusting in
Jesus. In God's word, we're shown what it looks like to
walk by faith in Him.

When it comes to wisdom, we only have two options in this
world. We can rely exclusively on the limited wisdom of
man, or we can access the inexhaustible wisdom of God.
When we seek God's wisdom through reading His word,
we're granted divine direction that impacts the way we live
and the nature of our relationship with Him.

What source of wisdom does your heart crave? Where are
you looking for advice? Do you trust the counsel found in
the word of God? What kind of impact has the teaching of
His word made on your life?

November 18

> *"And I am no longer in the world, but they are in the world, and I am coming to you. Holy Father, keep them in your name, which you have given me, that they may be one, even as we are one."*
> *-John 17:11*

Jesus made it clear to us that while we are in the world, we are not of the world. Our mindset isn't governed by a worldly perspective. Our primary ambitions aren't set on worldly objectives. The manner in which we relate to one another isn't dictated by selfish standards.

But just the same, Jesus recognized that it would be challenging at times for His followers to remain unified. Personality differences, individual preferences, and differing backgrounds or life experiences can occasionally result in believers treating each other like adversaries.

What should we do when we find ourselves at odds with another believer? How can we foster a sense of unity, even when we're in the midst of conflict or disagreement?

There are several things we can do. We can be intentional about praying for those we're at odds with. We can also ask the Lord to grant us wisdom and the capacity to see things from their perspective. If the Lord leads us to, we can even go so far as to allow ourself to be wronged while entrusting the matter to the Lord's intervention.

Unity isn't something that happens accidentally. It's fostered when God's people choose to rely on Christ's empowerment and the Holy Spirit's wisdom to love one another with Christlike love.

November 19

> *"How precious to me are your thoughts, O*
> *God! How vast is the sum of them!"*
> *-Psalm 139:17*

King David was trying to search out the mind of God in this passage. He valued and loved God's thoughts. Most people appreciate God's thoughts provided that His thoughts don't conflict with their plans and preferences, but David took God's thoughts to heart even when they were piercing or pointed out his blind spots. Poetically, David imagines trying to count or organize what God knows. Later in this Psalm, David describes a picture of falling asleep while trying to accomplish this task, then waking up and realizing he is still with God.

Do we value God's thoughts? Do we care as much as David did about what the Lord thinks? We are privileged to live in an era that has greater access to the thoughts of God than David's era had. Just imagine what David would have done if someone was able to go back in time and hand him a copy of the completed Old Testament and New Testament. He would have been floored. He would have poured over it day and night. He would have wanted to know as much as possible about Jesus, the Son of God, the foretold descendent of David who would reign on his throne forever.

It's valuable to pray for God's grace and seek His help to develop the desire to know Him like this. Growing in our personal knowledge of our Lord glorifies Him and results in encouragement, comfort, wisdom, understanding, reassurance, and protection from being deceived by the allures of this world.

November 20

> *"For Christ also suffered once for sins, the righteous for the unrighteous, that he might bring us to God, being put to death in the flesh but made alive in the spirit,"*
> **-1 Peter 3:18**

During the earthly ministry of Christ, His body was tortured. Jesus suffered and experienced all kinds of malice at the hands of the very people He had lovingly created. But His suffering was only for a season. He isn't suffering now. Jesus suffered once to pay for our sins. He isn't in a state of perpetual suffering.

Sin has consequences. Before mankind rebelled against God, we were warned that if we broke fellowship with the Lord, we would die. We did it anyway and were doomed to suffer the fate of eternal condemnation and separation from God. We were all at fault, and none of us could correct this problem because we were all guilty of the same thing. Into this mess we had created, Jesus inserted Himself to address the problem.

Jesus, God the Son, took on flesh, became a man, and suffered the penalty we deserved. We were guilty, yet He was righteous. The righteous died for the guilty in order to satisfy the wrath of God against our sin and then bless us with the gift of His righteousness, which we lacked. Then Jesus rose from the grave by the power of the Holy Spirit. And now, all who trust in Jesus can look forward to experiencing resurrection as well, as the Holy Spirit indwells all who believe.

Now, we don't need to be mastered by sin, Satan, or the fear of death. Christ has defeated their power in our lives.

November 21

> *"I give thanks to my God always for you because of the grace of God that was given you in Christ Jesus, that in every way you were enriched in him in all speech and all knowledge—"*
> **-1 Corinthians 1:4-5**

Our brothers and sisters in Christ are a true gift to us. We are blessed to know those who share our faith in Jesus, and God's word invites us to be grateful for their presence in our lives.

The Lord uses our Christian family to make genuine investments in our lives. They model what it means to follow Jesus. They give us wise counsel. They serve us in many Christ-empowered ways, and they help us develop a mature faith.

Scripture tells us that everyone who trusts in Jesus is blessed with gifts that are meant to be used for serving others. These special abilities for service are given to us by the Holy Spirit so that the church will be built up, strengthened, and will walk in humility because we will recognize just how much we need one another.

How are you making investments in the spiritual growth of others? Are you using the gifts the Lord has blessed you with to serve your church family? Can you identify someone the Lord has been using to bless you? Is there anything holding you back from using the knowledge, strength, skill, and wisdom that the Lord has blessed you with to serve someone else?

November 22

> *"Remember therefore from where you have fallen; repent, and do the works you did at first. If not, I will come to you and remove your lampstand from its place, unless you repent."*
> *-Revelation 2:5*

Jesus challenged the church at Ephesus to remember from where they had fallen. He wanted them to think back to the early days of their church where, in the midst of a culture known for its pagan beliefs, they loved Him and delighted in Him daily. They loved Christ so much that they made Him known to their friends, family and neighbors. They loved Him so much that they were willing to suffer persecution or opposition because they weren't ashamed of His name.

Now, they had become a very stoic and seasoned group of people. They were hard, but Jesus wants His people to maintain soft hearts that He can continually pour into. He called them to repent. He warned them that He would remove their lampstand, meaning, He would shut them down as a church, if they didn't repent.

Repentance involves a change of heart or change of belief that produces a change in behavior. Jesus was calling them to repent of their unloving hearts. He was calling them to love Him and love others in His name.

If you want to be a continually growing Christian, repentance needs to be a constant feature in your life. All of the Christian life is one of repentance and belief.

November 23

> *"And let the peace of Christ rule in your hearts, to which indeed you were called in one body. And be thankful."*
> *-Colossians 3:15*

Anxiety rules in the hearts of many people. Fear governs the thinking of just as many. But for those who walk with Jesus, we're told to let His peace rule in our hearts.

When the peace of Christ rules in our hearts, we will find ourselves less apt to give in to anxiety and fear. Instead, we'll walk by faith, and rest in the confidence that the Lord has all circumstances under His control. We'll be joyful in the assurance that nothing escapes His sight, and He is leading the direction our lives take.

When the peace of Christ rules in our hearts, we'll forsake our selfish ambitions and pursue unity in the body of Christ. We'll value the needs of our Christian family and delight in mutually blessing one another.

When the peace of Christ rules in our hearts, we'll be thankful. We're thankful for who our Lord Jesus Christ is. We're grateful for everything He has done on our behalf to rescue us from our hopeless condition. We're thankful that our future is held securely in His hand.

Because we've been redeemed by the blood of Jesus, we don't need to worry about the things most people worry about. We've been rescued, and now we're encouraged to make His gospel known to others so they can leave fear behind and enjoy the peace of Christ ruling in their hearts as well.

November 24

"Remember your leaders, those who spoke to you the word of God. Consider the outcome of their way of life, and imitate their faith."
-Hebrews 13:7

In the context of this Scripture, the early church was given some advice regarding examples of faith worth imitating. Specifically, they were told to observe and bring to mind leaders who had made the word of God clear to them. Leaders who lovingly gave up the comforts and false securities of this world to come to them and help them understand who Jesus is and the implications of His gospel.

But let's be honest, there are plenty of people in this world who can be good talkers. We all have interacted with and been taught by many impressive communicators with the gift of teaching, but what happens when you really get to know them? Do their words match up with their manner of living? Do they practice what they proclaim?

The writer of Hebrews encouraged the church to consider the outcome of the way of life of those who had made God's word known to them. The truth is, if a man truly believes in Jesus Christ, his life will confirm the depth of his faith. Behavior follows belief. There are behaviors and blessings that will become visible in the life of a leader who truly believes what he speaks. Look at his household, they'll tell you. Look at how he interacts with people who have nothing material to offer him. Look at how he handles his position of authority. Can you see Christ in that man?

Leaders who actually live what they proclaim provide a powerful example of faith in Jesus that's worth imitating.

November 25

> *"And whatever you do, in word or deed, do everything in the name of the Lord Jesus, giving thanks to God the Father through him."*
> ***-Colossians 3:17***

Through faith in Jesus, we have been granted the ability to access His divine power to aid us in the midst of every task we seek to accomplish. We don't need to rely on our own strength and we don't need to idolize our own abilities. Jesus is sufficient to strengthen us for every task He has called us to complete. Whatever we do, we can therefore do in His name.

Likewise, as we recognize His presence and His divine assistance, we can be thankful. Scripture encourages us to give thanks to God the Father through Jesus Christ. What blessings has the Lord granted to us for which we can express thanks?

We can be thankful for the love of our Heavenly Father. We can be thankful that we were redeemed from sin's curse by the shed blood of Jesus Christ. We can be thankful for the indwelling of the Holy Spirit who comforts and counsels us. We can be thankful for access to the Scriptures because they grant us wisdom and point us toward Jesus.

We can even be thankful for our trials because the Lord uses them to make our faith in Him stronger while also convincing us that He truly is sufficient for all we need in this world.

November 26

> *"Therefore let us be grateful for receiving a kingdom that cannot be shaken, and thus let us offer to God acceptable worship, with reverence and awe,"*
> **-Hebrews 12:28**

When you look through the pages of the history books, what do you see? You see examples of kingdoms and leaders rising and falling. You read stories of great changes that have taken place in world governments. You learn about geological changes as well, cities buried under volcanic ash, and plains flooded with rising water.

But the kingdom of God isn't like the kingdoms of man. His kingdom is eternal in nature. His kingdom isn't built on a foundation that can be moved or damaged. His kingdom cannot be shaken or torn down.

The Lord reminds us of things like this so that our faith in Him will remain strong and our confidence in His power will grow. Through faith in Jesus Christ, we can approach God the Father. As we do so, we're invited to worship Him joyfully and reverently. We are in awe of His great power as well as His willingness to give us a permanent place in His eternal kingdom.

There are many things in life that feel temporary and transient. People and circumstances change regularly, but our Lord remains steadfast. The Rock of our salvation isn't fickle. The kingdom of God remains strong and secure forever.

November 27

"The end of all things is at hand; therefore be self-controlled and sober-minded for the sake of your prayers."
-1 Peter 4:7

Becoming a follower of Christ not only impacts how you will spend your eternity, it also impacts the way you live in the present. The moment you trusted in Jesus, the Holy Spirit indwelled you. The Holy Spirit gives us counsel, grants us understanding of the will of God, clarifies the Scriptures for us, and bears out the fruit of righteousness in our lives. His presence helps us not to rely on a sinful way of reacting to our problems or the stresses that can be caused by other people.

Because of His empowering presence, we can exhibit self-control and a sober-mind. We don't need to be out of control, spiteful, or erratic, because the Holy Spirit is now guiding our temperament. Even when people and circumstances are stressing us out, we don't need to fly off the handle because we have the help we need living within us.

In this passage, Peter encourages the church to remember that the end of all things is at hand. What he means by this is that Jesus could return at any moment. We don't know how much time we have, but compared to the span of eternity, it isn't much. That being the case, we're called to live under the control of the Spirit so that our prayer life will be sincere, regular, and disciplined.

Practically speaking, this means that we'll be praying for the Lord's help and intervention in our lives, the lives of those we love, and the lives of those who have the capacity to test our faith and patience. If our manner of thinking is being led and controlled by the Holy Spirit, these are priorities that He will bring to our minds and bear out in our actions.

November 28

> *"Oh give thanks to the Lord; call upon his name; make known his deeds among the peoples!"*
> *-1 Chronicles 16:8*

Every believer in Jesus Christ has a testimony or a story to tell. We can testify to the fact that the Lord has rescued us. We can also tell the story of the work He has continually been doing throughout the course of our lives.

For many believers, the thought of speaking openly with others about their faith in Jesus seems intimidating. Because of the common fear that our faith in Christ might be perceived negatively by others, it has become far too common among believers to begin treating their faith like a private matter. Our fear of conflict or creating an offense often contributes to the decision to keep quiet.

One solution to this issue, however, is to simply begin telling the story of what's been going on in your life. You don't necessarily need to be confrontational in your conversations. Just let others know about the work the Lord has done to transform your life, your thinking, and your outlook toward the future. Give them a glimpse of the work He's been doing inside of you. Don't keep it to yourself.

In general, we share about the things we appreciate. Do you appreciate what Jesus has done for you?

November 29

> *"Wait for the Lord; be strong, and let your heart take courage; wait for the Lord!"*
> *-Psalm 27:14*

Waiting isn't an easy thing to do. We like most things to happen quickly. When we're looking for answers, we want them right away. When we're seeking results, we want them immediately. If we're honest, some of our biggest complaints to God have been prompted by seasons when He simply wanted us to wait a while, and trust His timing.

Scripture tells us that in the fullness of time, God sent His Son Jesus Christ to be born of a woman. Jesus took on flesh so that He could live the perfect life for us, die death in our place, and rise in victory over the grave. This was all facilitated according to God's perfect timing.

When the Lord asks us to wait, He isn't doing so to annoy or exasperate us. He's showing us that His timing is perfect. He's teaching us to trust Him more and more. He's granting us the privilege of learning to experience true contentment in Him and peace about how He chooses to operate.

What are you currently waiting on the Lord for? What has He been teaching you while you wait? Can you identify some of the ways He's been helping you experience a deeper sense of contentment and peace while you trust His timing?

November 30

> *"But the day of the Lord will come like a thief, and then the heavens will pass away with a roar, and the heavenly bodies will be burned up and dissolved, and the earth and the works that are done on it will be exposed."*
> *-2 Peter 3:10*

When Jesus ascended into Heaven, following His resurrection, His disciples were told that in the same way He ascended, He would also be returning. His return is imminent, meaning, it could be at any moment. Why do you suppose the Lord has allowed us to know this?

This knowledge has an impact on us. It influences us to make the most of our time because we realize that things can change quickly and dramatically for us. If Jesus returned today, how would you feel about the ways in which you've been stewarding the time He has given you?

Knowing that Christ's return is imminent is also a motivation to pursue living in holiness. If we're absolutely convinced that Jesus could come back at any moment, we will conduct our lives in such a way as to expect Him to show up. What do you expect to be doing when Christ returns? What does He want you to invite into your life while you await His arrival? What does He want you to avoid?

Christ's return is a source of motivation for genuine believers. His return will be a glorious event, but as we await that day, let's be mindful to live for Him now.

December 1

> *"though formerly I was a blasphemer, persecutor, and insolent opponent. But I received mercy because I had acted ignorantly in unbelief, and the grace of our Lord overflowed for me with the faith and love that are in Christ Jesus. "*
> *-1 Timothy 1:13-14*

Why did Jesus come into this world? He came to show mercy to people who deserved nothing but judgement. That includes us. Sometimes in life, we're tempted to complain. When we're complaining, what are we really doing? We're buying into the false belief that we deserved something better than what we got. We're telling ourselves that we didn't deserve to be treated a particular way, overlooked, hurt, insulted or inconvenienced. When we reinforce that false belief, our hearts can easily become bitter and resentful.

But let's be honest. What do we really deserve? We only deserve one thing. From birth we have been sinful. During the course of our lives, we have rebelled against God's laws in every way imaginable. So what do we deserve for sinning against a holy God? We deserve judgement. We deserve condemnation. We deserve to live apart from Him for all eternity because we're sinful.

But God loves us too much not to do something about that. So Jesus, God the Son, came to this earth to show us kindness. He came to take our condemnation upon Himself, offer forgiveness for our sin, and bless us with mercy instead of judgement.

December 2

> *"The saying is trustworthy and deserving of full acceptance, that Christ Jesus came into the world to save sinners, of whom I am the foremost."*
> **-1 Timothy 1:15**

The sad reality is that there is an impression in this world that Jesus is only for the people who look perfect on the outside, had the perfect upbringing, haven't made big mistakes in life, and do the best they can to craft the perfect image. But that's not the case at all. Jesus didn't come to this earth to save those who didn't need saving. He came to save humanity because we're all in the same boat. We're all sinners who are often doing our best not to be seen that way.

Have you ever examined the way Jesus treated those who were struggling with various sins and contrasted it with how He spoke with or about those who liked to pretend they were perfect? Jesus opposed the proud, but showed grace to the humble.

The Apostle Paul used to think of himself as a pretty good guy. Maybe that's how you once thought of yourself too, or maybe you still do. But Jesus didn't come to save good people (because there weren't any other than Him). He's the only one who is without sin, yet He came to this earth to save sinners. Let's be glad that He did. Let's be glad He's willing to look at people like us, welcome us into His family, give us His name, make us someone new, and remind us that we don't need to go back to the kind of life we were living before, because in Him, we're finally free.

December 3

> *"But I received mercy for this reason, that in me, as the foremost, Jesus Christ might display his perfect patience as an example to those who were to believe in him for eternal life. To the King of the ages, immortal, invisible, the only God, be honor and glory forever and ever. Amen."*
> **-1 Timothy 1:16-17**

In Jesus, our hearts find rest. We can rest in the fact that Jesus grants eternal life. We can rest in the fact that we don't have to work for that gift. We don't have to earn that gift. We don't have to spend our lives crushed under the mental burden of trying to obtain that gift. This passage reminds us that Jesus gives us the gift of His mercy and patience, by faith.

That means that if we trust in Him, we're forgiven of our sin and we're freely granted salvation. We don't have to work for it because Jesus already did the work for us. He lived the perfect life that we didn't have the capability to live. He died on the cross to pay for the debt of our sin that we couldn't pay for. He rose from the grave and defeated the power of sin, Satan and death. Now He looks at us and says, "Do you believe in me? Will you entrust your life and your future to me? Will you welcome me to be your God and Lord of your life?" And if our answer to Him is a sincere, "YES," we will be granted the gift of forgiveness and life everlasting.

Jesus gives us new life. He grants us hope, and He blesses us with a church family to experience it all with. What are we celebrating this month? What are we grateful for this season? We're grateful for Jesus who has shown His mercy to sinners. We're grateful for Jesus who graciously shares the gift of eternal life with all who will believe in Him.

December 4

> *Again Jesus spoke to them, saying, "I am the light of the world. Whoever follows me will not walk in darkness, but will have the light of life."*
> *-John 8:12*

In this era of human history, there are all kinds of leaders, influencers, and celebrities attempting to gain our attention. One of the highest priorities of the famous is to build a "following." It's considered social proof of their marketability. The direction that many popular voices are leading others to embrace is, sadly, a road that leads to further darkness and despair.

The same was true during the years when Jesus was in the midst of His earthly ministry. It grieved His heart to observe so many people walking in darkness. They were lost in their sin and were valuing the false promises of leaders who lacked wisdom, and influencers who contributed to the darkness they were stumbling through.

But Jesus isn't like those who seek the vanities of fame and selfish control. Jesus is God in the flesh. He came to this earth to set us free from the shackles of sin. He walked among us to give us light so we wouldn't need to stumble in the darkness that comes when our minds are blinded to the truth. And He invites us to trust in Him so we can enjoy the privilege of becoming truly alive in Christ instead of remaining dead in our sin.

December 5

> *"But we have this treasure in jars of clay, to show that the surpassing power belongs to God and not to us. We are afflicted in every way, but not crushed; perplexed, but not driven to despair;"*
> *-2 Corinthians 4:7-8*

Paul speaks of himself and others who have received the good news of salvation through Jesus as being like, "jars of clay." A clay jar is fragile. It's breakable. It can be very useful, but typically, what it contains is where the real value is found. What he's saying here is that we're fragile people that the Lord has entrusted His invaluable gospel to. We're like jars of clay that carry within us the truth of eternal life. And God's purpose in making this the case is to show that it is His power, not our power, that matters most and makes the most difference.

With that in mind, look at how Paul described the work Christ had called him to. Afflicted, but not crushed. Perplexed, but not driven to despair. Persecuted, but not forsaken. Struck down, but not destroyed. Suffering in a way that resembled Christ's earthly experience for the greater joy of displaying the life of Christ in the midst of that suffering. That's certainly a purposeful existence, but it was far from the cushy life in this world that our hearts probably crave and maybe even idolize.

But Paul stressed that there was a point to it all. In the face of death, there is life. Do you believe there is a point to the adversity Christ has called you to face? What good could possibly come from your pain? What if in addition to strengthening your faith in Christ, the Lord has also intended your struggles to be for the benefit of others, that in the midst of your adversity, pain and discomfort, the life of Christ can be shown to those who desperately need to see a visible example of how real and how powerful He truly is?

December 6

And the king said to me, "Why is your face
sad, seeing you are not sick? This is nothing
but sadness of the heart." Then I was very
much afraid.
-Nehemiah 2:2

In this moment, the most powerful man on earth asked Nehemiah to share from his heart. He wanted to know what was troubling him. We're told that this experience prompted fear in Nehemiah's heart, but he answered the king anyway, and he explained to the king that the city of his forefathers was in ruins, with gates that had been destroyed by fire.

The book of Nehemiah makes it clear that he had a heart for what mattered to the Lord. It's also clear that Nehemiah was a man of faith, prayer, and action. But we're also given a very "human" or down-to-earth kind of glimpse of Nehemiah. In his own words, he says that he was "very much afraid." What do you think about this? Can a person be both fearful and faithful?

It's clear from Scripture that the Lord is pleased by faith, so what place can fear play in the life of a believer in Jesus Christ? Does it make you less of a believer if you experience fear? Was Nehemiah spiritually weak because he wrestled with fear?

The truth is that in many cases, the presence of fear may be evidence of our faith being put to use. We're stepping into unfamiliar territory, we're fighting our natural instincts, we're placing ourselves in a spot that causes us to be stretched beyond what we've been accustomed to. If you're listening to God's voice, and taking steps of faith as He nudges you, the momentary presence of fear might actually be a form of confirmation that you aren't shrinking from the mission He has given you to complete.

December 7

When he had said this, he showed them his hands and his side. Then the disciples were glad when they saw the Lord. Jesus said to them again, "Peace be with you. As the Father has sent me, even so I am sending you."
-John 20:20-21

The time following the crucifixion of Jesus was a confusing and fearful time for the disciples. They expected Jesus to be recognized as king, and they anticipated reigning with Him as His inner circle. They saw Him perform miracles and heal multitudes, but then they saw Him arrested and killed. For fear that the same thing would happen to them, they hid. In fact, Scripture tells us that the room the disciples were in was locked because of their fear of being found and potentially captured and killed.

At this point, Jesus had risen from the grave and He was appearing to people in His resurrected body. Some day, we too will have a resurrected, glorified body, and it's interesting to observe some of the things Jesus was doing because it gives us a picture of our future reality. One of the things He did was walk through solid walls and appear among them.

Naturally, experiencing something like this would frighten most people, so Jesus attempted to calm them down and reassure them of who He was. He said to them, "Peace be with you." Jesus was encouraging them not to be consumed with an unhealthy fear. Then, to make it clear to them who they were seeing, Jesus showed them the scars in His hands and side. He wasn't there to capture them or harm them. He was there to encourage them and build them up through faith in Him.

December 8

> *Jesus said to him, "I am the way, and the truth, and the life. No one comes to the Father except through me."*
> *-John 14:6*

There is no greater joy than what we obtain and experience through a relationship with Jesus. In Him we find all that our souls once lacked and craved. There is no greater peace or satisfaction than what can be found in Christ.

Still, people keep searching as if there might be a better option out there somewhere. Many people are looking for options that fit with their preconceived preferences instead of accepting the fact that Jesus is who they need.

Jesus was very exclusive in His claims. He taught that He alone was the way to the Father. Meaning, to reject Jesus was to reject any hope of a relationship with God. There is no other path to salvation other than Christ.

Jesus likewise describes Himself as the truth. He is incapable of falsehood because that would violate His divine nature. The good news of His gospel can be fully trusted.

Jesus also made it clear that in Him we find true life. We were dead in our sin, but Christ graciously grants abundant and everlasting life to anyone who trusts in Him. How do you respond to the exclusivity of His claims?

December 9

"Until I come, devote yourself to the public reading of Scripture, to exhortation, to teaching."
-1 Timothy 4:13

Timothy had been called by the Lord to devote himself to making the word of God known. Paul gives three related examples of how Timothy could accomplish that in his context, but if we wanted to summarize what's being taught here, it would be fair to say that Timothy was being challenged to preach and teach messages that clearly communicated and conveyed the message of God's word. He was to read the Scriptures publicly, challenge people to live them out, and clarify or explain any aspects that might be difficult to understand.

This verse should be exciting and reassuring to all Christians, but particularly those in church leadership. Sometimes, pastors and other church leaders experience pressure to be somewhat trendy and clever with the word of God. But God's word doesn't need to be dressed up so that it can be more trendy or palatable. It's sufficient as it is. Our goal shouldn't be to make it modern or clever. Our goal is to read it, learn it, understand it, apply it, avoid overcomplicating it, and recognize that the aim of all Scripture is to point our hearts toward Jesus.

If you proclaim the word of God, you can be confident that it will have it's effect. You don't have to dress it up or make it cooler than it's trying to be. Just make it known openly. Help people understand what they're supposed to do with it, and clarify anything that might seem confusing so that they will be encourage to grow in their walk with Christ.

December 10

> *"And he began to teach them that the Son of Man must suffer many things and be rejected by the elders and the chief priests and the scribes and be killed, and after three days rise again. And he said this plainly."*
> *-Mark 8:31-32a*

Jesus teaches us very deep things in His word, but He intentionally does so in ways that are accessible and understandable. If you find yourself in a position to teach or preach, please take note of His example. Your goal should never be to impress others with your understanding of ancient languages or complex doctrines. Your goal shouldn't be to use the most complicated words you can find in your thesaurus. Your goal should be the same goal as that of Jesus. Namely, that those in your hearing would come to an understanding of truth, particularly the most important truth.

Jesus made that clear to His hearers. He told them that He would suffer during the course of His earthly life, be rejected by those who should have worshipped Him, be killed, and then rise again to life. This was of first importance and this is what He wanted them to set their minds upon.

But the disciples' minds, unfortunately, were still consumed with earthly things. In fact, Peter was critical of Jesus for teaching them this information. He was critical in part because they were more eager for Jesus to rule as a political king than rescue humanity as a sacrificial Savior. They cared more about power than they cared about salvation at this point, and Jesus rebuked Peter his mind was still consumed with worldly priorities that reflect the ambitions of Satan more so than the holy, life-giving mind of God. In time, Peter's faith matured and he saw things differently. What would you say your mind is currently focused on?

December 11

And he said to them, "Follow me, and I
will make you fishers of men."
-Matthew 4:19

Please notice a few things about Christ's call on the disciples. He told them to, "*Follow me, and I will make you fishers of men.*" What was Jesus getting at when He said this? Jesus was telling them that their life was going to be quite different from how it was before they followed Him. He was about to give them a new mission and He was going to make them into new people.

His invitation to follow Him was that they would now follow Him as His disciples. He would be their master, teacher, leader, and Lord, and they would experience a transformation of life as they grew in their relationship with Him.

He also said, "*I will make you fishers of men.*" This is an interesting statement that shows that Jesus was using a concept that would have been familiar to this group of fishermen. They were used to understanding the activity and patterns of fish. Then knew the best time of day to look for them. They utilized the best tools they could use to catch them. Now their mission was going to change. They would be made into new people with new eyes and new priorities, and their mission on this earth was going to change accordingly. In Christ, you've been given this mission as well. Embrace it.

December 12

> *"Keep a close watch on yourself and on the teaching. Persist in this, for by so doing you will save both yourself and your hearers."*
> *-1 Timothy 4:16*

Behavior follows belief. Every behavior in our lives comes out of what we believe. We will pursue whatever we believe will bring us peace and a sense of worth. In fact, we can quickly see what we believe will bring us a sense of peace or a sense of worth by how our time and our resources are invested.

Our hearts crave what we are convinced will ease our pain and bring us joy. This, by the way, is why addictions can be difficult to break. It's hard to give up things that we have relied on to ease our pain or make us feel happy.

But only Jesus can truly satisfy our souls. Only He can bring us lasting peace. Only He can comfort our greatest pains. Only He can forgive our sin. And we don't have to be old to grasp that truth. There are many children in this world that come to faith in Christ long before their parents and grandparents do. And Christ will foster maturity in the heart of anyone who earnestly seeks Him.

In the meantime, the word of God encourages us to keep a close watch on what we believe and how we live. Doing so will help us avoid many pitfalls in life, and it will also serve as a visible witness and example to those who look to us for inspiration in their walk with Christ.

December 13

> *"If you love me, you will keep my commandments. And I will ask the Father, and he will give you another Helper, to be with you forever, even the Spirit of truth, whom the world cannot receive, because it neither sees him nor knows him. You know him, for he dwells with you and will be in you."*
> **-John 14:15-17**

Jesus told His disciples that if they truly loved Him, they would keep His commandments. Love is a great source of motivation. It is a greater motivation than fear, duty or obligation. It is the kind of motivating factor that Jesus desires to see present in the lives of those who bear His name.

Thankfully, we aren't called to love Him or keep His commandments in our own strength. We haven't been left here on our own to try and accomplish that. Though Jesus would soon ascend back to Heaven, He tells His disciples that He would ask the Father and to give them another Helper or Counselor to be with them forever. Jesus is referring to the third person of the Trinity, the Holy Spirit. When He uses the word "another", He's saying that the one that will be sent will be like Him, but sadly, in many respects, the Holy Spirit is often forgotten, minimized or misunderstood by many believers.

In this passage, Jesus refers to the Holy Spirit as the "Spirit of truth." This is one of the ministries of the Holy Spirit. He reveals wisdom, counsel and truth to our minds. Likewise, He fosters love, He counsels, He comforts, and He produces fruit in our lives that helps us reflect the heart of Jesus.

December 14

> *"And he was seeking to see who Jesus was, but on account of the crowd he could not, because he was small in stature. So he ran on ahead and climbed up into a sycamore tree to see him, for he was about to pass that way."*
> *-Luke 19:3-4*

During the course of Jesus' earthly ministry, there were many people who were quite curious about Him. People liked and hated Him for different reasons. Very few people seemed to truly understand who He was and what He was doing, at least initially, but some people, with a curiosity that was prompted by the Holy Spirit, sought to gain a better understanding of Jesus or a better glimpse of who He truly was.

As Jesus was passing through the town of Jericho, a large crowd was gathered around Him. People from all kinds of backgrounds and stations in life were likely there, but the Scripture points our attention to one individual in particular who sincerely wanted a glimpse of Jesus. We're told of a rich tax collector named Zacchaeus who wanted to see who Jesus was. Zacchaeus was wealthy and enjoyed some level of social prominence in his day, but he was small in physical stature.

Zacchaeus was likely the type of person who was adept at looking ahead. Usually people who are skilled with the use and stewardship of money do more than just living in the moment. They think about things from a long-term perspective and Zacchaeus seems to apply that kind of perspective to his situation. Scanning his surroundings, he could see where Jesus was headed so he ran ahead of the group and climbed a tree in the vicinity so he could gain a greater glimpse of Jesus.

As believers in Jesus, we should likewise seek a greater glimpse of Him. He delights to fulfill that desire.

December 15

> *"When Jesus had spoken these words, he lifted up his eyes to heaven, and said, "Father, the hour has come; glorify your Son that the Son may glorify you,"*
> *-John 17:1*

Jesus understood that the time had come for Him to complete His earthly ministry. He was preparing to go to the cross, and as He did so, He intentionally prayed in such a way that His words could be heard and recorded for the ages.

This Scripture begins by stating, *"When Jesus had spoken these words,."* What had Jesus just said to His disciples before engaging in this prayer? He was encouraging them to take heart. He was reminding them, even before they knew they needed this reminder, that His victory was certain even though they were about to be convinced that it was lost.

Up to this point, Jesus had been veiling His divine glory. He had taken on flesh, having become a man, so that He could live the perfect life, die death in our place, and experience a bodily resurrection. Now He was praying that the Father would glorify Him just as He had been glorified before He took on flesh. His desire was to be glorified so that in turn His glorification would result in honor being given back to the Father.

Just as Jesus spoke of glorification, so too are we to live our lives to glorify Him. It's actually the chief goal of the Christian's life. To glorify means to exalt, honor, and magnify Him. That means that your life and my life should be centered around living in such a way that Christ is exalted, honored, and magnified. This world should be able to observe our faith in action, and as a result, testify to the power and magnificence of our Savior.

December 16

> *But Peter and the apostles answered, "We must obey God rather than men. The God of our fathers raised Jesus, whom you killed by hanging him on a tree."*
> *-Acts 5:29-30*

The Apostles had been arrested because they were teaching the people about the necessity of faith in Jesus for the forgiveness of sins. While in jail, they were miraculously freed from prison, and from there, they went to the temple and continued to preach the message of the gospel. God gave these simple men great courage to do the task He had given them, even though in doing so they were risking their lives and freedom.

From the temple, they were escorted by officers to appear before the high priest and the council for questioning. Imagine being the apostles at this point. They spent several years following Jesus, learning from Him, coming to the understanding that He was God in the flesh, watching Him be denied by His people, crucified, resurrecting from the grave, and charging them with the task of making His gospel known throughout the world. Now, a group of know-it-alls whose heads were full of knowledge but their hearts were hard as stone, were telling them to stop teaching in the name of Jesus and to stop reminding the people that it was them who emphatically called for Christ's crucifixion.

What would you do in an instance like that? What do you do when your faith gets tested like this now? Prior to Christ's resurrection, the apostles scattered and ran from persecution. Now they had seen the risen Christ. Death no longer held the same level of fear over them. Jesus had already demonstrated that death was defeated, and these men were sent out on mission to make Christ known where He was unknown. Remember their example the next time your faith is tested.

December 17

> *"And after you have suffered a little while,*
> *the God of all grace, who has called you to*
> *his eternal glory in Christ, will*
> *himself restore, confirm, strengthen, and*
> *establish you. To him be the dominion*
> *forever and ever. Amen."*
> **-1 Peter 5:10-11**

There's a pattern we can see regarding suffering when it's mentioned in Scripture. It's treated as a very seasonal concern when it's spoken of in regard to believers. Those who trust in Jesus Christ are not destined for eternal suffering. Our present suffering is real, and it's painful, but it's only for a moment. It's only for a little while.

The truth is, the Lord is using our suffering in preparatory ways. He's refining our character, teaching us to trust in Him through it, and drawing a stark contrast between our suffering and the eternal glory that awaits us in Christ. After this season of suffering is complete, He Himself promises to restore, confirm, strengthen, and establish us. He will accomplish this all in His power. His dominion over all creation is forever.

God cares about you. Don't let yourself forget that, even if this hasn't been your favorite or most ideal season of life. If He is allowing you to go through a season of suffering right now, please remember that, as odd as it may seem, you will be grateful for it some day. It is for your good and for His glory that this is taking place.

December 18

"And let the peace of Christ rule in your hearts, to which indeed you were called in one body. And be thankful.
-Colossians 3:15

What does it mean when this verse implores us to let the peace of Christ rule in our hearts? **"Let"** seems to imply that this is an option that we may or may not choose to make ample use of. As a result, there are many of us who are currently allowing the worries of this world rather than the peace of Christ to rule in our hearts. **"Rule"** is an athletic term that is being used in the way we would use the terms "Umpire" or "Referee." Christ's peace is supposed to be the final arbiter in our hearts when we're experiencing conflict with others or even conflict within ourselves.

In your own life, where have you been struggling to let the peace of Christ rule in your heart? Are you struggling to forgive someone who has offended you? Are you holding on to an experience from your past that you cannot correct? Did you do something that you regret and you won't forgive yourself for it? Are you experiencing a test, trial, or transition in your life and you're worried about the outcome? Does it feel like you're locked in conflict with someone without much relief?

In Christ we find peace for our weary hearts. In Christ we find rest. In Christ we experience genuine forgiveness that graciously extends into our past, present, and future. Take heart because Christ has overcome whatever has been trying to rob you of His peace.

December 19

> *"For the yoke of his burden, and the staff for his shoulder, the rod of his oppressor, you have broken as on the day of Midian. For every boot of the tramping warrior in battle tumult and every garment rolled in blood will be burned as fuel for the fire."*
> *-Isaiah 9:4-5*

Sometimes in life, we experience seasons that are physically burdensome. Other times, we wrestle with emotional burdens. What do we crave during these seasons? For many of us, we crave rest. We want a break from what weighs us down. We want someone to come along side us and lift our burdens from us. In Christ, we find this kind of rest.

The images that are described in this passage cause us to picture people who are weighed down with heavy yokes on their backs. It gives us an image of being taken captive or living like slaves. We're shown a glimpse of people being treated like animals as their backs are described as being subject to the striking of their oppressor's rod. This happened to the people of Israel in the literal sense when they were taken as captives by Assyria. It also serves as a picture of the reality of what it looks like to be overcome with the burden of sin.

But what has Jesus, the fulfillment of Isaiah's prophesy, done with the oppressor's rod? He has broken it. What does He do with the boots and the garments of the armies that amass against His people? Those objects are used as fuel for warmth instead of tools of destruction. Jesus secures the victory over the oppressing forces of evil and He shares that victory with us so that in Him, we can find the rest we need.

December 20

> *and she exclaimed with a loud cry, "Blessed
> are you among women, and blessed is the fruit
> of your womb! And why is this granted to me
> that the mother of my Lord should come to
> me?"*
> **-Luke 1:42-43**

Scripture tells us that after learning she was pregnant, Mary
went to visit her relative Elizabeth. Elizabeth was also carrying
a child, specifically, John the Baptist. These were both women
that the Lord had selected for very important tasks. When
Mary greeted Elizabeth, the infant John the Baptist jumped in
her womb and she loudly testified her praise to God who was
doing miraculous things in their midst.

Elizabeth said, "*And why is this granted to me that the mother
of my Lord should come to me?*" What a beautiful statement.
Elizabeth was expressing one of the healthiest philosophies we
can live by. She recognized that what she was experiencing
was evidence of the hand of God at work around her, and the
presence of God in her midst. She wondered why she was
allowed to experience something so wonderful?

Imagine for a moment if that was the guiding perspective in our
lives? It's a perspective that notices the evidence of God's
undeserved favor all around us. It's a perspective that causes us
to say, "Why is God so good to me? Why does He show His
grace to me?"

It is natural and common for us to focus on the negative in life.
The more we do that, however, the more stuck we can become
in that line of thinking. There are some people in this world
who exclusively focus on the down side of every situation, but
how would your life be different if instead, you kept asking the
question, "Why is God being so abundantly good to me?"

December 21

And Mary said, "My soul magnifies the Lord, and my spirit rejoices in God my Savior,"
-Luke 1:46-47

We can see the presence of a joyful thankfulness in Mary's words in these verses. Mary expressed a song of thanks that described what she was thankful for, and why she was thankful for it.

Specifically, Mary was thankful for the Lord Himself, and His presence in her life. She says that her *"soul magnifies the Lord."* This means that she exalts or praises the Lord from the depths of her inmost being.

Mary states that her *"spirit rejoices in God my Savior."* She acknowledged that salvation is from God. She wasn't dwelling on the hardship, ridicule, or potential shame of her circumstance as an unwed mother in her culture, but rather she rejoiced in the God who saves.

Not only does our Lord save, but He also lifts up the very people this world holds down. In her context, she was a woman, and women weren't typically esteemed in that era. She was young, she was expecting, she wasn't wealthy, and she wasn't from a prominent place. But God looked at the humble estate of Mary and did something miraculous in her life. Mary was chosen to give birth to Jesus. Through Him, humanity would experience salvation and the restoration of all that had been tarnished by sin.

December 22

> *"though formerly I was a blasphemer, persecutor, and insolent opponent. But I received mercy because I had acted ignorantly in unbelief, and the grace of our Lord overflowed for me with the faith and love that are in Christ Jesus."*
> **-1 Timothy 1:13-14**

Why did Jesus come into this world? He came to show mercy to people who deserved nothing but judgement. That includes us. Sometimes in life, we're tempted to complain. When we're complaining, what am we really doing? We're buying into the false belief that we deserve something better than what we got. We're telling ourselves that we didn't deserve to be treated a particular way, overlooked, hurt, insulted, or inconvenienced. We're reinforcing the belief that we deserved better, and when we do that, our hearts can easily become bitter and resentful.

But let's be honest. What do we really deserve? We only deserve one thing. From birth we have been sinners. During the course of our lives, we have rebelled against God's laws in every way imaginable. This is true of every single person on this earth. So what do we deserve for sinning against a holy God? Scripture tells us that we deserve judgement. We deserve condemnation. We deserve to live apart from a holy God for all eternity because we're sinful.

But God loves us too much not to do something about the mess we've made. So Jesus, God the Son, came to this earth to show us mercy. He came to take our condemnation upon Himself, offer forgiveness for our sin, and bless us with mercy instead of judgement.

December 23

> *"And the angel said to her, "Do not be afraid, Mary, for you have found favor with God. And behold, you will conceive in your womb and bear a son, and you shall call his name Jesus."*
> *-Luke 1:30-31*

Scholars believe that Mary was very young, probably around 13 to 15-years-old, when the angel appeared to her. God was about to show His favor in a very special way to Mary, who from our perspective, was still a child. In her culture, even at that young age, she was considered old enough to marry and we're told that she was betrothed to Joseph, which was a legally binding form of engagement.

The angel Gabriel, the same angel that appeared to the prophet Daniel 500 years earlier, came bearing a message. He was about to share God's plan of salvation with Mary, and he was going to tell her how God intended to include her in His plan. But before those details were given, Gabriel encouraged her not to be afraid.

The message God was sending to Mary isn't any different from what He's telling us as well. He's telling us not to be afraid of what we don't know and can't control, because He knows all things, has it all planned out for His glory and our good, and He's got our lives and the lives of those we love under His control.

Great evidence of that can be seen in the angel's message to Mary. He was able to tell Mary exactly what was about to happen and the eternal ramifications as well. She would miraculously conceive a son. He would be called Jesus, which means "Yahweh saves." His true identity would be the Son of God, and His kingdom would have no end.

December 24

And Mary said to the angel, "How will this be, since I am a virgin?"
-Luke 1:34

It's fair to assume that at this point, Mary probably didn't understand the significance of why the Son of God was going to take on flesh, but yet had to be born of a virgin. Maybe that's something that we would benefit from thinking about for a minute as well.

When God created mankind, He created us perfect. He made Adam, and then from Adam, He made Eve. All humans trace their physical ancestry to Adam. When Adam sinned against God, he wasn't the only one affected by that decision. He came under the curse of sin, and from then on had a sinful nature which is passed on to his offspring. It is believed by many theologians that the sin nature is passed along to children through the father.

And if that is indeed the case, we can see why Christ was born of a virgin and without a human father. He was born among us to live a sinless life and then die to pay for our sin. But how could He take our place on the cross if He also had sin of His own to atone for? Just as Adam was born without a sin nature, so too was Jesus born without a sin nature to atone for the sin of Adam's race.

Likewise, Christ was born of a virgin to serve as a sign from God to us. God was using this miraculous event to confirm to the world that He had not forgotten us. He was interjecting Himself into the human race like only God can, to display that He is Immanuel - God with us.

December 25

> *"For to us a child is born, to us a son is given; and the government shall be upon his shoulder, and his name shall be called Wonderful Counselor, Mighty God, Everlasting Father, Prince of Peace."*
> *-Isaiah 9:6*

Isaiah gives very specific details regarding the birth of Christ, the ministry of Christ, and the nature of Christ in this passage. He tells us that a child would be born among the people of Israel. He would be a Son who was given as a gift of grace. In time, the government would be upon His shoulder. He would be one who would rule with peace and benevolence, which would stand in stark contrast to the foreign nations that invaded and oppressed Israel at different times in their history.

The Scripture speaks both of Christ's humanity and His divinity. In addition to being born as a child, we're also told that He would be called Wonderful Counselor. The idea here is that He would be an advocate or one who pleads our case who also inspires awe among us. He's also called Mighty God. Jesus is God incarnate. He is likewise referred to as Everlasting Father. This is a way of telling us that He is the source or the "father" of life everlasting. Christ is also described as the Prince of Peace. Through Him our souls and this world find the peace we can't find anywhere else.

Just as Jesus has promised to literally and visibly reign on this earth at some future point, He desires to reign with justice and righteousness in our lives right at this very moment. Someone is calling the shots in your life. Someone sits on the throne of your heart. Wouldn't you rather it be Jesus, the Prince of Peace, than someone else?

December 26

> *"For nothing will be impossible with God."*
> *And Mary said, "Behold, I am the servant*
> *of the Lord; let it be to me according to*
> *your word." And the angel departed from*
> *her.*
> *-Luke 1:37-38*

We live in a skeptical era, and in some ways, that's no different than the eras that have come before us. It's fair to say that the majority of the world does not believe that Jesus was born of a virgin. Most people would place this teaching on par with fables or fairy tales because they strongly prefer to only believe what they can see.

This is why we need God's intervention in our lives for this kind of spiritual blindness to be corrected. The angel proclaims a truth that would do our hearts good to meditate on when it comes to the miraculous. He says that *"nothing will be impossible with God."* From the world's standpoint, and from the standpoint of our observable experience, we're talking about impossible things. But from the standpoint of the Creator who can speak the universe into existence and breathe life into what He has made, nothing is impossible.

And how can we not love Mary's response to this explanation. With simple faith she humbly replies, *"Behold, I am the servant of the Lord; let it be to me according to your word."* She looks at all of this and acknowledges that she's not the boss, God is. She submitted to God's decisions for her life. She had complete peace about God's will being done. Do you?

December 27

"Humble yourselves, therefore, under the mighty hand of God so that at the proper time he may exalt you,"
-1 Peter 5:6

Some people mistakenly believe that humility is thinking or speaking poorly of yourself, but that's not the case at all. Humility involves seeing yourself as you actually are in light who God is. We may not always realize it, but it can be very easy for us in our sin nature to attempt to place ourselves or our opinions on a higher pedestal than we place God and His word.

For this reason, Peter encouraged the church to practice humility. He encouraged them to humble themselves. They were being admonished to set aside pride, arrogance, and self-righteousness, and in their place, humbly entrust their lives to the caring hands of God.

As those who trust in the Lord Jesus Christ, there's a process that God is bringing us through that we would be wise to notice, particularly in light of this Scripture. At some point, He convinced you that you were dead in your trespasses and sins and that you needed to be forgiven and made alive in Christ. The moment you trusted in Christ, you were justified, which means you were declared righteous by God because the righteousness of Christ was imputed to you. Now you're going through a process called sanctification where the Lord is refining your character and teaching you how to walk in holiness. Someday yet future, you will be given a new, sinless body and you'll live in that glorified state forever.

As followers of Christ, we have a lot to look forward to, but in the meantime, the Lord is using our suffering to teach us humility, while at the same time reminding us that at a future date, He will exalt and glorify us.

December 28

> *"I wrote to you in my letter not to associate with sexually immoral people—not at all meaning the sexually immoral of this world, or the greedy and swindlers, or idolaters, since then you would need to go out of the world.*
> *-1 Corinthians 5:9-10*

In an earlier letter that has not been preserved, Paul encouraged the church not to associate with sexually immoral people. When you think about it, that can be very difficult to implement, especially when you consider that all people have engaged in sexual immorality in their hearts to some degree, and a large percentage of people in this world engage in sexual immorality in the physical sense as well. So Paul clarifies his earlier comments and makes sure that the church understands that he's not speaking about avoiding unbelievers who may have an immoral lifestyle. To do so, he states, would require us to leave this world completely.

The truth is that God's people are highly encouraged to interact with those who do not yet know Him. It is the mission of our lives to be intentional about it. Scripture refers to us as Christ's "ambassadors" and the "fragrance of Christ" to the people of this world.

Unfortunately, we might at times start thinking of life in this world as a battle that pits the good people vs. bad people, but that's not accurate. There are no inherently good people. There are sinners who have been rescued and sinners who haven't been rescued yet. And if we've been blessed to experience Christ's rescue, we should live humbly and gratefully as people who have been blessed with the greatest gift in the universe, even though we didn't deserve it.

December 29

"Every athlete exercises self-control in all things. They do it to receive a perishable wreath, but we an imperishable."
-1 Corinthians 9:25

Self-control is very difficult to maintain in life because there are always things that entice us. Often, we allow our hearts to believe that we can find more peace, joy, or satisfaction in something else other than Jesus. So we submit to our areas of temptation and we prove to our hearts in those moments that our idols still hold a lot of sway in our lives.

Paul was trying to give the church a pep-talk regarding our need to submit our hearts to Christ's lordship. He uses the analogy of a race to describe our lives. Just like earthly life, races are rather brief. They're over before you know it. Runners may train for months or even years ahead of time, and they need to run in such a way that their efforts aren't aimless and unfocused.

We're in the midst of a race against the clock right now. Our lives are meant to count for Christ. He has called us unto Himself, equipped us, and sent us out. He wants us to live a life that typifies submission to His lordship. A self-controlled life for a believer is ultimately a life that continually yields to the Holy Spirit.

That's why we need to continually rely on Christ who supplies what we need for the mission He has given us. It's only through Him that we'll have the desire and ability to live a life that bears the fruit of discipline and control. As that fruit ripens in our lives, by His grace, the hope is that we'll be used by Him to lead many more lives into His kingdom and family forever. This work begins with mirroring the servant heart of Jesus.

December 30

> *"casting all your anxieties on him,*
> *because he cares for you."*
> **-1 Peter 5:7**

The antidote to worry is trust. We're called to trust the Lord with our fears. We're called to cast our anxieties on Him because He cares for us.

So, what keeps you up at night? During this season of your life, what seems to be causing you to worry? Are you holding on to your fears? How does that appear to be working out for you? Or are you handing your cares, worries, sources of anxiety and fear over to the One who can actually do something about them.

Ironically, when we begin to view our seasons of suffering through the lens of God's overarching redemptive plan, we can begin to see that our low or anxious seasons are actually opportunities for us to learn that God can be trusted to handle our anxiety. He's teaching us that He can be counted on to bear the burden of our worries. We crumble under that burden when we worry about things we can't control. In order to be able to shoulder that kind of burden, you truly need to be sovereign. With that in mind, our Lord who is sovereign, who is in complete control, invites us to cast on Him all the things that we were not designed to carry in the first place. Our seasons of suffering offer useful lessons that help us learn to start doing that.

Our loving Lord watches over our lives carefully. He loves us with the fiercest and most protective kind of Fatherly love you can imagine. He can be trusted to carry the burden of what robs us of experiencing the kind of peace we've been called to experience in Christ.

December 31

> *"This is what I mean, brothers: the appointed time has grown very short...For the present form of this world is passing away."*
> **-1 Corinthians 7:29a, 31b**

Our time on this earth usually doesn't feel brief until it has passed. And since even the longest lives on earth are brief compared to eternity, we should live as though the time is short. We should live as if Jesus might return today.

Living as though the time is short is a concept that confuses many people, including Christians. People interpret that thought in several ways. Some think it's about pleasing ourselves before we run out of time. Some give in and call it quits because they don't think their life really matters. But living as though the time is short actually means we're to use the brief time we've been allotted to please and glorify Jesus.

A passage like this provides a good opportunity for us to ask the question, *"Lord, what would you like me to do with the time that I have left?"* Even if you live to be 120-years-old, that's still just a drop in a bucket compared to eternity. Right now, we're in the midst of a brief season where Jesus wants us to live in such a way that we're aware of the fact that we will be face-to-face with Him soon. He wants us to be prepared to have a conversation about how we used the time He granted us.

This year is coming to an end and a new year is about to begin. How will you make use of the next twelve months? What has Jesus been imploring you to remain focused on? How is He trying to refine your character? Who does He want you to invest your time in? What habits or addictions is He seeking to give you victory over? Which burdens does He want you to lay down at His feet? Time is a temporary stewardship. Use every moment you've been blessed with to glorify Jesus.

Would you be willing to do me a favor?

If this book has been helpful to you in your walk with Christ, would you be willing to take two minutes to share a review on Amazon.com? Your review will help us as we seek to help others grow in their relationship with Jesus.

Thank you in advance for your help!

Sincerely,
John Stange
Author of *"Desire Jesus"*

———

To contact the author, view a listing of his other books, read his blog, or listen to his podcasts, please visit...

DesireJesus.com

or

JohnStange.com

CPSIA information can be obtained
at www.ICGtesting.com
Printed in the USA
FSHW04n2038030418
46533FS